SWIMMING IN

DEEP WATER

SWIMMING IN

DEEP

Lawyers,
Judges,
and Our
Troubled
Legal
Profession

WATER

WILLIAM DOMNARSKI

Cover design by Monica Alejo/ABA Publishing.

Printed in the United States of America.

18 17 16 15 14   5 4 3 2 1

Library of Congress Cataloging-in-Publication data on file.

Discounts are available for books ordered in bulk. Special consideration is given to state bars, CLE programs, and other bar-related organizations. Inquire at Book Publishing, ABA Publishing, American Bar Association, 321 N. Clark Street, Chicago, Illinois 60654-7598.

www.ShopABA.org

For Kathleen, Colleen, and Erin, my three shades of K-ness.

Contents

PREFACE

My conceit is that it is with the essay, sometimes general and sometimes familiar, that we can get closest to understanding the practice of law and, by extension, the legal profession. Autobiography, biography, memoir, social science studies, legal academic writing, and journalism have all contributed to a rich literature that presents the practice of law and the legal profession, but invariably individual texts are limited because they respectively explore only parts of the larger whole. This is best seen in the vast literature of what can be called the lawyer's life. Essays that draw on the individual studies in the different disciplines and genres, on the other hand, can cover vastly more territory and can provide, perhaps, the only chance at understanding the issues and even adventures that sketch the lawyer's life, with the further byproduct from this that the reader better understands the broader legal profession.

I draw from a variety of sources to acquaint the reader with some of the leading books and articles on my various topics. The essays are extensively researched but reported with a light touch. I draw in particular on novels written by and about lawyers, what I call legal novels, to go beyond my own experiences in the law to provide the reader with the experiences and insights of others. It is either a paradox or true reflection of the nature of lawyers that in what they write about themselves they seem reluctant to speak the truth. Lawyers might have good reason to be reluctant to tell the truth about judges, for example, but in fiction they can do it. In fiction, lawyers turned novelists can break free and give us inside information about both the practice of law and the nature of the profession.

My approach is more eclectic than idiosyncratic. There are fifty essays in total. I cover in forty-one essays perhaps not all the waterfront of practicing law and the legal profession but quite a bit of it, though not comprehensively or systematically. I then add nine essays on judicial opinions. To be immodest for a moment, the book sets out what might grandly be described as life in the law. Lawyers live a life in the law, and it is in judicial opinions that we find the life of the law itself. I view the two lives as related because the engaged lawyer both derives from reading judicial opinions the various pleasures of reading and secures his place in the profession by that act of reading. The problem with talking about lives in the law is that it suggests an element of comprehensiveness, when the actual struggle is to just define or even describe what a lives in the law might be. We can only make stabs at definitions and descriptions when it comes to something as varied as practicing law or the law itself in action. At best we can describe aspects of it. I have settled on the idea of multiple ways of looking at the profession and the practice of law because it fits the varying degrees to which lawyers have encountered and experienced the many different activities, events, moments, and ideas that separately or in a jumble refer to my chosen subjects of lawyers, judges, and the practice of law. The big idea that is "life in the law" itself is too protean, too elusive, for capture. The best we can do is capture shadings of it.

The book, more to the point and enough to be described in its title, also sets out an ambitious argument that we as lawyers are living in perilous professional times. The profession has been under siege from forces (both actual and threatened) which can have the effect of altering the relationships that lawyers can and should have with what we call the practice of law. Threatened is the core idea that lawyers are autonomous professionals responsible for determining for themselves what the profession and the practice of law mean. Lawyers have not done well in responding to these forces or even in recognizing the perils which we and the profession face. Whether lawyers recognize the forces and the perils is a test of this book.

Of the nine essays on judicial opinions, "Federal Reporter, Third Series" is on the volumes of the *Federal Reporter*, Third Series as books of the law and "Judicial Writing" is on issues relating to the writing of the opinions that we find in the *Federal Reporter* volumes. I report in the remaining seven essays on what I found in both browsing and reading (mostly browsing) through about two hundred volumes of the *Federal Reporter* over a five-year period. Some essays are organized around themes.

"So How Did I Do?" looks at judicial commentary on the work of lawyers that was so bad the courts felt compelled to discuss it and in the process alert a perhaps unsuspecting public as to what to look out for in their lawyers. "Laugh Out Loud" reports on the amusing bits that can be found in judicial opinions, perhaps to the surprise of readers of the genre. I also report in "Movies and Television in Judicial Opinions" on a recent trend in federal circuit opinion to invoke references to popular culture. I look at the both effective and not so effective uses to which literature generally has been put in opinions in "Literary Allusions," while in "Shakespeare" I consider allusions to just the source nonpareil. "You Don't Say?" explores the recent phenomenon of judges feeling compelled to add bits of information in their opinions that do not qualify as footnote material, asides, or even digressions. If it weren't usually amusing, the information would qualify as irritating as well as unnecessary. And, lastly, in the opinion group there is "Introduction to Justice," which follows a well-established practice of distilling the subject, meaning, and sometimes sensibility of a case into an opening paragraph.

Though I have listed the fifty essays alphabetically by title, the forty-one essays about lawyers, which include three about the effect of certain judges on lawyers, can be arranged into ten groups for the reader looking to pursue a particular theme or subject: (1) the profession as organized, (2) lawyerly tasks, (3) lawyer civility, (4) legal fees, (5) lawyer clothes and offices, (6) reading and writing, (7) thinking like a lawyer, (8) lawyer arrogance, (9) the nature of lawyering, and (10) lawyers and judicial unpleasantness.

When it comes to the way that the profession itself is organized, "Dissection of the Profession" provides something of an overview of the profession by drawing attention to the essential connections between lawyers, their clients, and their practice settings. In "Don't Pooh Pooh the Profession" I take the assault of *Winnie the Pooh* author A.A. Milne on barristers and the legal profession to pose uncomfortable questions about the lawyer's proper role in the fair administration of justice. I look at large firms, usually referred to as Big Law, in three essays. "Associates Used and Abused" looks at young associates and their overworked and underappreciated lives "Big Law and Poetic Justice" reports further on the pyramid model for which associates act as the base and points to the ironic development that the urge to exploit which partners have used against associates is now being used by partners against partners and threatening the business model that has made so many partners wealthy. And "Professional Cynicism" tries to uncover the real meaning of the argument that the ways of Big Law are here to stay and should be embraced. If Big Law is the future of the profession, it will not be a happy future, I conclude. But since there is more to the profession than Big Law, other essays consider other parts of the professional landscape. As something of a counterbalance to Big Law, I look at how the other half lives in "Alone But Connected" to see how the solo practice of law compares and contrasts to a Big Law practice. Two essays on specialists round out the group. "Criminal Defense Lawyers and Their Tough Job" looks at how hard that type of practice is, while "Prosecutors" considers the particular pressures and mind set of the prosecutor.

Lawyerly tasks are found in five essays. "Can We Talk?" looks at the dynamics of oral argument, "Clients and Their Lawyers" discusses the joys and frustrations of having clients, "Glib and Oily Art" looks at advocacy from the viewpoint of how lawyers present themselves to judges and juries, "Taking Instruction from Others" considers the different professional model that we see in barristers from England and Australia to find both the good and bad in those models, and "Typographical Errors" looks whimsically, on a part of writing that, for me at least, just won't go away.

Three lawyer civility essays on the way lawyers get along with each other as seen in the discovery process complement the essays on what lawyers do. "Food Fights Masquerading as Depositions" describes lawyers in depositions as adolescents fighting without adult supervision for the client's benefit, "Discovery Wars" examines the pettiness, disingenuousness, and ugliness of lawyers supposedly exchanging information, and "Nihilists Among Us" describes, distressingly for me, what the so-called hardball litigation tactics really mean for the profession—that for the nihilists it is not a profession at all.

Those interested in money, otherwise known as legal fees, will be rewarded, I hope, by my three essays on the subject. "What Am I Worth?" gives a broad view of how lawyers and the public measure the lawyer's worth in the marketplace. "Being Paid to Shower" considers what happens when excessive billing collides with the nature of being a professional and presents a play on Descartes' "I think, therefore I am." "Big Law Fees and

Big Trouble" provides information on what really happens behind the billing scenes at large firms.

Three essays consider ways in which lawyers present themselves to the world. "Dressing for Success" is about the way lawyers dress and what signals they are sending with their sartorial choices. "Personality and Office Space" illustrates that lawyers display aspects of their personalities in the way they allocate and furnish office spaces. "The Saddest Place No More" turns a critical eye to the way that lawyers first present themselves to clients by looking at the reception areas of law firms.

There are five essays on reading and writing. Three essays take on the subject of legal writing. "Lawyers Writing" explains that the term "legal writing" has its problems and in some ways is part of the problem of bad writing by lawyers. Ways in which law schools and the profession itself can get the word out about the actual nature of lawyer writing and provide some useful instruction toward the goal of better writing is covered in "Legal Writing Instruction Misunderstood." In "Modestly Put" I describe what I write in my practice, detail what I try to emphasize and avoid by way of style and structure, and explain that, for me, less is more. "Hope and Dread and the Nature of Legal Research" and "Serendipitous Research" are essays on legal research that seek to improve its reputation among practitioners as something to avoid and argues that much can be gained by just reading law for its own sake.

I look in three essays at "thinking like a lawyer" and the intellectual component of lawyering. I look at the Socratic method as used in law schools in "What Would Socrates Think?" In "Thinking Like a Lawyer" I ask whether there is, in fact, any such thing as thinking like a lawyer. And because lawyers are so fond of talking about brilliant legal minds, I consider just what intelligence for this crowd means in "Brainy Lawyers."

Then there is lawyer arrogance. I handle this in a couple of ways. I first consider the arguments of some commentators that the use of the Socratic method in law school breeds arrogance in essays about legal education. I then return to the arrogance theme in "Arrogance" to draw connections between lawyers, what they do, and this particular personality trait. I consider arrogance yet again in "Why Are We (Lawyers) So Disliked?" because arrogance is one of the main reasons the public has given for not liking lawyers. Arrogance is more illustrated than discussed in "Seeing Yourself and Others," which continues the theme of how lawyers see themselves and how others see them by way of descriptions of particular lawyer personality types. The types make for amusing and perhaps sometimes painful reading.

Five essays explore the nature of lawyering and what the practice of law can do to lawyers. "Are We Happy Yet" looks at our contemporary phenomenon of lawyer unhappiness in light especially of the way the profession is organized. "Nature of Lawyers and Lawyering" looks at the ways that the practice of law can transform the practitioner by insisting he assume a role. "Zeal or No Zeal?" considers zeal as a transforming force and looks at the profession's struggle to determine whether it is a good or bad thing. "Contemptuous" looks at instances in which a lawyer's enthusiasm—or something worse—in court gets the better of him and gets him into trouble with the judge as part of the ongoing tension between the lawyer's duty to his client and his duty to the court. "Lawyers Gone Bad" looks at lawyers at the margins and the forces acting on them that led to the lawyers getting sanctioned by the profession. The good news here is that the profession, for all its transforming capacity, cannot be blamed for lawyers going bad.

Lastly, three essays look at judges and their role in the judicial process and in their relationships with lawyers. "I Am Right Because I Say I Am" discusses black robe-itis, that disease that dare not speak its name, at least in the presence of a judge. "Betrayal in Plain View" presents an ugly side of judges and judging and takes the position that judges should not beat up on lawyers in their courtrooms. "Practice Before an Unhappy Judge" takes the position that we should not have to put up with judges who have lost their sense of mission and inflict their unhappiness onto the lawyers appearing before them.

The following essays in whole or in part appeared originally in the *Los Angeles Daily Law Journal*, often with different titles: "Being Paid to Shower," "Can We Talk?," "Judicial Writing," "Laugh Out Loud," "Movies and Television in Judicial Opinions," "Personality and Office Space," "So, How Did I Do,"and "Typographical Errors."

ALONE BUT CONNECTED

The million odd lawyers nationally in private practice break almost evenly into two groups, those who practice alone and those who practice with others in a firm. Solo practitioners made up some forty-nine percent of private practitioners in 2005 according to the ABA, a percentage roughly equal to what it has been for solo practitioners over the last several decades. In contrast, the number of lawyers in firms with more than one hundred lawyers—a group scarcely recognizable twenty-five years ago—nearly equals, at fourteen percent, the number of lawyers working in two- to five-lawyer firms. That the percentage of solo practitioners has hardly changed tells us something about what lawyers want to do with their professional lives. They want to practice by themselves. Nearly a majority, they do this despite a profession—increasingly dominated by large firms—which marginalizes them. This is the story of our day.

Solo practitioners get a fair amount of coverage in the professional literature, though primarily in a nuts-and-bolts sense. *Flying Solo: A Survival Guide for Solo Practitioners*, a 1994 publication of the American Bar Association, leads this category of writing, delivering exactly what it promises in the title. *Solo By Choice* by Carolyn Elefant celebrates the benefits of solo practice a bit more, but it too is a start-up guide. Bar journal articles take aim at particular problems special to solo practitioners, such as how to wind up a practice, how to share space in an office with others, how to take advantage of the technology and information revolutions, how best to advertise and otherwise market yourself, how to handle an illness and the need to service their clients or get to court, how to manage cash flow, and how to manage an office. There are also websites devoted to solo practitioners covering many of the same topics and blogs tightening the solo practitioner community through the sharing of similar but always unique practice experiences.

It is a tough job, being a solo practitioner. It is hard getting started, and once going income nonetheless ebbs and flows, as does the need for office help. Solo practitioners who litigate have their own particular problems. They have ongoing logistical battles to cover court appearances, often made even more difficult by unsympathetic judges, and they are limited by their resources, making it difficult if not impossible to take on protracted litigation and other forms of practice that call for help from associates. On the personal side, solo practitioners at a higher rate than the general lawyer population struggle with ethical lapses and the debilitating substance abuse demons of the profession. Solo practitioners battle loneliness and isolation— almost by definition—and struggle with motivational issues, so much so that there are web-based support groups for solo practitioners. And finally, there is the problem of what happens to a practice when the practitioner dies. Firms have continuity. Solo practices do not.

It is not hard to argue that each lawyer has his or her own special relationship with the law and, by extension, the profession. Lawyers come into the profession alone and in their first act swear an oath to abide by certain professional principles. One issue that consideration of solo practitioners raises is the extent to which lawyers maintain their personal, individual, and professionally indivisible obligations when they form partnerships. The same problem, though in a different form, applies to lawyers working as associates in law firms. Clients test lawyers on the issue of divided loyalties. One the one hand, the lawyer owes the client his undivided loyalty, but at the same time partners in law firms owe a loyalty to each other to advance the health and prosperity of the firm. It seems to be the definition of a conflict when the loyalty owed to the client runs up against the loyalty owed to the firm. This might explain why barristers by definition are solo practitioners. They may club together in chambers to share costs, but each is a solo practitioner, able to make decisions based solely on the ethics of practice. On the other hand, the ethics of practice might well collide with the profit motive of large firms. Money corrupts, and the more that money is the currency of a law firm, the greater the possibility of corruption. All of this leads to seeing clients only for what they represent—billable hours.

Solo practitioners have tended to be heroes in the popular culture. In television and film, we have Perry Mason, to be sure, as well as the iconic Atticus Finch of *To Kill a Mockingbird* fame. Lawyers cannot be cut from finer cloth. Solo practitioners dominate the genre of legal novels as well, with Paul Biegler of *Anatomy of a Murder* being the best known, a man who penetrates into the heart of our system of law and the true nature of lawyering. The contrast is often between corrupt large firms—the site of skullduggery—and the solo practitioner whose loyalty is to the client and to justice, not to profits. If we believe the messages of popular culture, beating hearts are found not in big firms but in solo practitioners.

Hero to the public, solo practitioners struggle for respect within the profession itself. This is perhaps puzzling. Given the choice, the bigger stage is not for everyone, even for those who once appeared on the largest. Lee Rankin (1907–96), Solicitor General in the Eisenhower administration, left Washington for a solo practice. He rejected numerous offers from large firms and opened a one-man office in New York City. Richard Olney (1835–1917), who had been Attorney General in Grover Cleveland's administration returned, according to *The Yale Biographical Dictionary of American Law* "to Boston in 1897 to a flourishing practice (from which he retired in 1908) [and] was little changed. His office remained uncarpeted and sparsely furnished. He had no partners or associates, not even a telephone until the B&M, by stealth, had one installed. Olney was not pleased. Somehow, 'a perfect stranger from Worcester' had obtained his unlisted number and presumed to call him."

The judiciary seems to be of two minds on the subject of solo practitioners. On the one hand, appellate judges show recognition that a solo practitioner in a nonmetropolitan area is not as inclined as his city cousin to keep up with federal law developments. Inexperience for a solo practitioner, we find, might be grounds for excusable neglect for missing something in substantial litigation that a large firm would have caught, though excusable neglect does not stretch to include a solo practitioner's busy practice as the cause for missing deadlines. A nonmetropolitan solo practitioner is not at fault when he takes on federal matters outside his diet, but he does need to associate with a knowledgeable lawyer to supplement his knowledge and experience. On the other hand, courts have not been willing to accept the argument of large firms in fee-shifting cases that a solo practitioner representing a prevailing party is entitled to a lower rate of compensation based on that fact alone. Courts can consider overhead, but they reject the idea that lawyers from large firms are entitled to be paid more on the theory that somehow they are better lawyers because of the size of their firms. Just because some tasks that a solo practitioner might do would be performed in a large firm by a non-lawyer does not mean that what the solo practitioner does becomes clerical work by default for which the fee is much less. As the court in *Bailey v. District of Columbia* wrote, "attorneys like plaintiffs' counsel, operating either as solo practitioners or in small firms, often lack the resources to retain a large staff of junior lawyers who could handle such tasks more economically. To deny plaintiffs compensation for these tasks would unfairly punish plaintiffs and their counsel for not staffing this case as if they had the manpower of a major law firm." The best statement comes from an appellate court obviously irritated with a large firm trying to keep a solo practitioner down. The court in *Porzig v. Dresdner, Kleinwort, Benson, North America LLC* said it found troubling a defendant's "repeated insinuations to the Panel, as well as this Court, that [plaintiff's counsel's] hourly fee rate should be reduced because he is a solo practitioner. While it is true that courts and arbitral panels deciding reasonable fees can and should take into consideration many aspects of an attorney's practice to ensure a reasonable hourly rate, it is long established that 'courts should not automatically reduce the reasonable hourly rate based solely on an attorney's status as a solo practitioner.'"

The large law firms that have become the dominant force in the profession dismiss solo practitioners as failures who could not meet their discriminating, if not narcissistic, standards. Success in the profession for these practitioners is defined by success in the firm. This, at least, is the message of legal novels and of films such as *The Verdict*. Paul Newman's alcoholic, broken-down lawyer character perhaps too sharply emphasizes the failings of solo practitioners, since he has fallen so far from grace, but his big firm counterpart, the James Mason character, accurately represents what his team and the legal establishment think of solo practitioners. He represents those who have more money, and the firm's lawyers have what they consider to be better credentials. The firm has more of everything—more staff, better offices, better clients, and a greater cause—the preservation of the status quo. Theirs is the swagger of dominance.

While numbers have not changed, the technology revolution has transformed the world of solo practice. Solo practitioners are still limited to being in one place at one time, but the revolution in information technology has made the solo practitioner the equal of any lawyer in any firm, regardless of size. With all the available forms and practice material, solo practitioners can become vastly more productive and sophisticated. Partners in big firms once had an advantage because they could send a platoon of associates to a well-stocked library to research. Now the solo practitioner is himself a platoon and his online research a vast, all-inclusive library. Today, the solo practitioner with a good suit, a sturdy prose style, and online research can go anywhere and do anything.

The argument is not that solo practitioners are pure. It is just that their decisions on how to practice are not subject to the tugs of others and their interests. There is, I think, a certain irony in all of this. In England, for example, barristers are the most esteemed members of the legal profession, far outpacing their solicitor counterparts in prestige. They are esteemed and considered the purer version of the advocate precisely because of their autonomy. Solicitors can form firms together, barristers cannot. Their relationship is to the law and their obligation is to advocacy, not to partners in a firm. Solo practitioners in our system come closest to the barristers in their relationship to the law and in their obligations, yet rather than being esteemed they are often derided from within the profession. Luckily, though, the public gets what the profession does not.

ARE WE HAPPY YET?

Are lawyers happy in their work? This wasn't even a question that was asked in 1954 when Albert Blaustein and Charles Porter published *The American Lawyer* with the University of Chicago Press and brought together pretty much all that was known about lawyers and the legal profession. There were no general questions of whether lawyers were happy or whether they wished they had gone into a different line of work—though some lawyers perhaps implied unhappiness of a sort when they answered in response to questions about income that they did not think they were making enough money. Today, not only would there be all sorts of questions about income, there would surely be as many or even more questions about happiness. We think too much of ourselves not to ask about happiness

The subject has gotten much attention for nearly a generation now. Reporters, journalists, lawyers, and scholars have given us articles and even books on why lawyers are not happy. There have been dozens of articles and books that have either *happy* or *happiness* in the title. Even the Law and Economics scholars, a group not usually associated with happiness, have gotten involved by exploring happiness and, of course, ideas about economic efficiency. For those who consider the more straight-forward, hedonic aspects of happiness, the question for them is generally framed as *why* lawyers are not happy, not *whether* lawyers are happy.

The *happy* and *happiness* that at least the scholars of late use in their analyses refer (most likely) not to Bobby McFerrin's famous song "Don't Worry, Be Happy" but to Martin Seligman's 2002 *Authentic Happiness: Using the New Positive Psychology to Realize Your Potential for Lasting Fulfillment*, which comes from identifying and exercising one's strengths. As Deborah Rhode, a leading scholar on happiness has restated it in a *Syracuse Law Review* article "Personal Satisfaction in Professional Practice," "[u]nlike momentary pleasure, which may not be a frequently occurring state, full engagement of one's talents in some valued activity produces a more lasting sense of fulfillment." Perhaps the reference to a "frequently occurring state" is to what Bobby McFerrin was describing.

All the numbers from the various surveys suggest that lawyers are in trouble. As one measure, attrition rates for associates in large firms are high, as is the percentage of lawyers who just give up on the profession and go elsewhere. Moreover, as a group, lawyers have greater incidences of alcohol and drug abuse. They also far exceed the national average in divorce rates and, most troubling of all, lawyers suffer from depression at a far greater rate than the general population.

Lawyers in fact have been studied extensively over the last few decades, a fact which by itself suggests that we are a troubled bunch. Nearly all of the research has been reported on by Susan Swaim Daicoff in her 2004 *Lawyer, Know Thyself: A Psychological Analysis of Personality Strengths and Weaknesses*, though the book's analyses go far beyond examination of the psychological and personality traits that distinguish lawyers from the general population. There are also studies of lawyers when they were law students and even before then to help understand the effect law school has on students as they transition into the profession. This sets the stage for the key chapter on the relationship between, as she puts it, lawyer personality and lawyer distress. Here all the workplace and non-workplace factors affecting stress and unhappiness are sorted out and patterns created.

There have been nearly as many articles suggesting remedies for the profession's ills as there have been articles diagnosing those ills. There is even the 2010 Oxford University Press book *The Happy Lawyer* by Nancy Levit and Douglas O. Linder to indicate the importance of the problem and the need for solutions. The call has gone out to large firms, for example, to give associates more say in case strategy and more time with the client. Billable hours have been shown to be the principal reason for associate burnout, and remedial articles of course suggest that partners should be less demanding of associates—as if that will happen. The general theme of the proposed fixes turns on reducing the extent to which associates are exploited as cheap labor (relatively speaking) to be leveraged and on increasing the associate's role in what would fall generally under the heading of the autonomous practice of law. Young lawyers can be made happier by treating them like lawyers, is one way to read the solutions.

Not all lawyers are unhappy, of course, especially if we judge from novels written by and about lawyers. There are certainly many unhappy lawyers on display in the novels, but the protagonist lawyers, while not necessarily a happy lot, tend to be thoughtful people who find satisfaction in their work, at least in part because they have taken control of it. A well-worn plot device has a lawyer walk—or be pushed—away from his Big Law job and set up his own practice. The contrasts we find described between the office spaces and clients they are leaving and those they are going to make for good reading, but it is the change in the lawyers themselves that pulls us in the most. Frequently, the lawyers are battling their own demons or at least trying to keep the demons from returning, but almost always the battles end successfully for the protagonists, especially if they are narrating. A recurring theme is that our now solo practitioners are for the first time fully engaged in the law with their cases and their clients. Often and perhaps surprisingly, the plot-propelling devices of fights between our protagonists and evil corporations, Big Law, or prosecutors are just window dressing. I suspect most lawyers read these novels as I do, that is, for the lawyers and their encounters with the life of the law—though I also suspect that some lawyers read the action filled novels of writers such as John Grisham imagining themselves as the main characters, perhaps to give some action to an otherwise sedentary, low-keyed job. But even lawyers seeking action in their imagination have probably struggled with what it means to be a lawyer. The lawyers doubling as smart novelists are writing about the lives their readers on some level are living.

That, at least, is my reaction to novels written by and about lawyers, though it is hard to know whether my reactions spring from being a lawyer or from writing as a critic. What I know is that, despite often delivering my fair share of complaints, I like being a lawyer and lawyering itself. I am always, in fact, trying to sort out the connection between my life as a lawyer and my life—at least a part-time life—as writer. It can be argued—as lawyers are so prone to phrase it—that being a writer makes me an observer, at least in part. I certainly feel that part of me is such an observer, yet I've often wondered if it is my writing that produces the observer feeling. I'm sure that has something to do with it, but only a part. My deeper suspicion is that my happiness—to use that inadequate word—comes in no small measure from the observer perspective and that this observer perspective comes primarily from being a reader. There, I've said it. Sharp, analytical lawyers reading this know what is coming next: the position that lawyers would be happier if they hedged their practice lives in the law with more reading, reading of pretty much any sort, so long as it is not related to work.

It is worth noting that the 1954 study of lawyers that did not look into the happiness question did, on the other hand, include questionnaire results about lawyers and their readings habits, both books and magazines. To a sampling of one percent of lawyers, questions were sent about periodicals such as state or city bar journals or the ABA Journal and about nonfiction and a fiction list of twelve books that included Churchill's *The Gathering Storm* and Norman Mailer's *The Naked and the Dead*, both published in 1948. Sixty-five percent had read Churchill's book in full or partly, for example, and twenty-two percent did the same for Mailer's best-selling novel. Forty-three percent of those responding regularly read state or city bar journals thoroughly and another thirty-one percent read them regularly but not thoroughly. The respective percentages for the ABA Journal were twenty-two and thirty-nine. Reading habits for lawyers today, I modestly suggest, are different—and not in a good way.

While nearly every aspect of lawyer happiness has been studied, we don't have anything resembling a study of the relationship between the reading habits of lawyers and the happiness of lawyers. Critics might suggest that such a study would be futile since, with the extraordinarily long hours that so many lawyers work, there's no time for lawyers to read anything not work-related. That, my dear Watson, is the point.

ARROGANCE

A public not fond of lawyers has identified arrogance as a trait that does not play well. But there's more. One national survey of the 1990s described the public's perception of lawyers as greedy, unethical, and arrogant. A 2004 local survey conducted by the Indianapolis Bar Association found that typical negative terms used to describe lawyers included greedy, unethical, arrogant, thieves, cold-hearted, expensive, and not trustworthy. When business owners in another survey were questioned, the response was that lawyers were perceived as authoritative, conservative, intimidating, and arrogant. Nor do lawyers do better when questionnaire respondents are lawyers themselves. A 1994 study conducted by the Florida Bar found that Florida lawyers thought their colleagues were too money conscious, arrogant, patronizing, manipulative, pompous, self-centered, egotistical, and obnoxious, giving a different meaning to The Big Eight. When 2,500 lawyers in the Milwaukee and Chicago markets were questioned in a survey about family law lawyers as negotiators, the lawyers who fit the category of adversarial, as contrasted with problem-solving lawyers, were described as stubborn, headstrong, arrogant, assertive, irritating, argumentative, and egotistical. Moreover, arrogant lawyers are everywhere in television and film. The Harrison Ford character in *Regarding Henry*, the James Mason character in *The Verdict*, the Keanu Reeves character in *The Devil's Advocate* (to say nothing of the Al Pacino managing partner character, the devil himself), the Richard Gere character in *Primal Fear*, and the James Spader character on *The Practice* are but a few examples. Gregory Peck's Atticus Finch in *To Kill a Mockingbird* and Raymond Burr's Perry Mason are two notable exceptions. Even Gerry Spence concedes in *Gunning for Justice* that lawyers are "arrogant, greed-driven, ethically suspect, and interpersonally offensive." Putting the affect of arrogance on the public to one side, what does arrogance tell us about the profession and the practice of law? Perhaps even putting the question this way sounds arrogant, or at least self-centered.

Certainly legal education has played a role in creating the arrogance monster. Law schools, in using the Socratic method to mentally toughen students, create their version of an attitude rooted in New York City, so that if you can make it in law school you can make it anywhere. After all, newly minted lawyers, having supposedly been trained to think like lawyers, can apply their method everywhere to analyze everything. The result is arrogance. At least that is the conclusion of a recent important study of the teaching of "thinking like a lawyer," which argues that the parsing and mastery of texts that is at the core of the Socratic method (or any of its variants) case analysis can lead those schooled in the approach to think that it can be applied beyond case analysis to the world at large. It can lead, according to Elizabeth Mertz and the anthropological linguistic analysis in her book *The Language of Law School: Learning to "Think Like a Lawyer,"* to a kind of methodological arrogance in which lawyers come "to feel themselves able to master any material with which they are presented by running it through a legal reading." Her study was based on actual instructor–student interactions in first year classes at eight law schools. The Socratic method as she saw it practiced can lead, she says, to an unchecked type of arrogance, since the checks and balances that help define other fields, such as physicists conducting experiments, do not apply to law. Lawyers think it, so it must be true. There's really no surprise here. The master of the Socratic method, Professor Kingsfield in *The Paper Chase* (movie or novel), had said that he was going to give the students "the ability to analyze that vast complex of facts that constitute the relationships of members within a given society." Arrogance naturally follows.

But other factors help explain lawyer arrogance. First, lawyers within law firms enjoy privileged positions. Their status as lawyers is greater than the status of others, such as secretaries or paralegals. This unequal status relationship would provide or reinforce the sense of superiority essential to arrogance. Second, lawyers get their superiority reinforced in the dynamic with clients. The lawyer is the problem solver, the advice giver, the decision maker. He is the one who knows the rules and can manipulate them. The lawyer is the dispenser of wisdom, who has this reinforced because he is, of course, being sought out for his wisdom by the client. And third, in litigation lawyers exercise control over others, feeding their beliefs of dominance.

They get to impose themselves on witnesses during depositions and at trials, always in control with their questions and a set of rules designed to make the lawyer assertive with questions and the witness responsive with answers. Trials allow lawyers to impose themselves fully on juries. They can assume whatever role or voice they want in their opportunity to sway, as an actor, the passive jury. The entire process puts the lawyer in an unquestioned position of control.

And while it does not qualify as a defense of lawyer arrogance, there is something to the idea that knowing rules well enough to manipulate them can lead to arrogance. Acting for others, which frees lawyers from personality restraints—as in the explanation that lawyers act as they do just to advance the client's interests and that their actions have no connection to them personally—can also lead to arrogance, or at least to the appearance of arrogance. Lawyers, and perhaps even some clients, would say that arrogance and its related traits are useful to trial lawyers and should be considered tools for making lawyers better and stronger practitioners. We can come back to the idea that aggressiveness and arrogance can be useful to lawyers and note only that these traits—when coupled with self-entitlement, grandiosity, and related traits—are all indicators of narcissism.

In some ways, it would be surprising if lawyers—successful lawyers, at least—were not arrogant. After all, they have succeeded in a profession distinguished by its obsessions with status, prestige, and hierarchy. Arrogance explains much about lawyers. For example, it explains how lawyers, believing that they can solve every problem—to control everything really—can claim to solve the so-called mystery of who wrote Shakespeare's plays with the tools of lawyers. The spectacle of mock trials on the authorship issue, while ostensibly done as light entertainment, reveals lawyer hubris at its worst. For them, everything can be reduced to its susceptibility to proof through persuasion, even though this approach confuses persuasion with truth. It is of no moment that no reputable scholar believes in the nonsense that anyone other than Shakespeare wrote the plays. Nothing lies beyond the power of lawyers.

It also explains the arrogance that is at the core of the genre of celebrity lawyer autobiography. The genre started with Louis Nizer in *My Life in Court*, whose greatest boast, in a corporate stock voting case, was that he could make two plus two not equal four. The genre then continued with Melvin Belli, Alan Dershowitz, Gerry Spence, and F. Lee Bailey, to name just a few. All wrote of identifying with their clients so much so that their role of simple advocate—as one player in the trial drama—gives way to egotism that has them responsible for truth and justice. Nizer views his role as the fashioner of truth, which, for him, is a function of case preparation and forensic skill, not reality. Dershowitz in *The Best Defense* sees himself as the champion of civil liberties and the obstacle to totalitarian government. As a defense lawyer, he is nothing less than the "last bastion of liberty—the final barrier between an overreaching government and its citizens." Similarly, the only chance the system has of working, Bailey tells us in *The Defense Never Rests*, is when clients are represented by skilled lawyers such as himself. Gerry Spence makes clear in *Gunning for Justice* that he is "no cause lawyer." "I don't flit from one crusade to the next searching for some meaning," he writes. "I help the people in the desolate windblown towns in these parts, grizzled men and plain women who have been chewed up and spit out, usually as the 'cost of labor' in the course of America doing business." Belli tells us in *My Life on Trial*, "I set a sub-conscious pattern for myself early in my career. What I really wanted to do in the law was force the system to make good on its promises and bring due process of law to all the elements in our society, not just the rich and powerful. Unfortunately, the forces of government did not always understand the Bill of Rights. Sometimes it would take all my forensic skills to neutralize them."

These celebrity lawyers enjoyed spectacular success, at least for a time, and their egotism and arrogance are likely related to that success. But given that the forces pushing lawyers to arrogance are not confined to the highly successful, but are instead the near inevitable result of becoming a lawyer, it seems fair to suggest that lawyers see themselves as more important than they really are. Certainly popular culture helps this delusion along by giving lawyers the power to change defeats into victories, chiefly through the lawyer's personality (read arrogance). This might flow from a truth that cuts against the anger and bitterness that drive society's distaste of lawyers and its delight in lawyer jokes—no matter how much you hate lawyers, when you need one you want the nastiest, most ruthless one you can find.

This seems to be the bargain society has struck with lawyers. We hate you generally, but we love you specifically.

It comes at a cost to the lawyer, though. The distorted sense of self-importance becomes part of the lawyer's personality and leads to the interpersonal offensiveness described by Spence, quoted in my opening paragraph. But lawyers who think themselves superior lose or have diminished the ability to be influenced by the world. To learn is to come to an issue with modesty, with the belief that answers can lie elsewhere. Arrogance smothers inquiry and the receptivity to the greater world. Arrogance creates its own bubble. The arrogance of large law firm lawyers comes only in part from the bubble of their law firms. It comes more—as it does for lawyers generally—from the bubble of believing that they are special.

ASSOCIATES USED AND ABUSED

The easy, first response to the whine of Big Law junior associates about employment conditions is to fault the whiner, at least in part, for complaining about that which the complainer actively sought and willingly accepted. It turns out, though, that not only is there something to the complaints, but that the complaints lead to important questions about the legal profession. Not quite canaries in the mines—though associates might well identify with working in a mine—associates nonetheless help us recognize the warning signs of a business model—if not an entire profession—in trouble.

Associates are our reporters from the field. We've gotten memoir, nonfiction, and fiction about the associate's life and life in the law firm. Blogs on the subject have gotten the most attention, perhaps because there are so many of them and perhaps because some are funny while others in raw terms describe these young associates in crisis. Blogs cover the waterfront of labor issues, but usually with a gossipy, aggrieved angle. Personalities, not surprisingly, figure prominently in the entries, hidden, the bloggers hope, from the eyes of their employers. An example would be Andrew Lu's November 12, 2012, entry on "Greedy Associates," (http://blogs.findlaw .com/greedy_associates/) a leading blog, on five law firm partner types and how to deal with them. The advice is mostly statements of the obvious, but it's in the descriptions that we chuckle and the associates likely bond as they read about the English Professor, who takes a red pen to memoranda as though they were freshman composition essays, and the Alpha Male Screamer who "will scream, berate, and verbally assault you because you need to be reminded constantly that he is more of a man than you."

Associates can easily find useful advice on the Internet regarding the difficult workplace problems they confront with management. This is a world in which nothing, aside from the promise of working hard, is what was described or shown to them as part of the hiring process. It is an odd process. Law firms hire their new associates usually on faith, so to speak, because the students are not hired for skills but for their profile. Prized law school candidates are feted for the summer following the second year and then, when hired following graduation, are hit with the reality of politics in the workplace and their respective firm's unquenchable need for billable hours. Candidates correctly left their interviews believing that their law firms wanted their new associates, most of all, to fit in. They did not realize at the time, though, that their idea of "fitting in" was very different from what the law firms thought "fitting in" meant. For them it meant *submit*. Putting aside that the law firms, to their discredit, did not make clear what was required of new associates, we realize upon only brief inquiry that there is reason to look kindly upon these associates. Who can fault them for responding to more of the same stimuli that got them into good colleges and even better law schools? Who wouldn't be excited about the promise of playing with the so-called "big boys"? There might be something to what one memoirist calls being a "prestige-whore" in taking the Big Law associate position, but that, like everything else, had been part of the sales process. To their credit, associates know from the start that it is not going to be easy money, but of course it is not known until experienced how awful it is to lead a slave's life—even if well paid

It is in fiction and memoir that the associate's life and the life of the firm are fleshed out. Here we learn about associate toadying and, as one associate character puts it in Michael Hogan's *Man Out of Time*, his "pecking-order smile . . . signifying a sense of place and diplomacy." As the never-ending highway of work and billable hours unfolds ahead of them, we learn especially of the career second-guessing that goes on among so many of the associates. This points to a deeper social issue of college graduates going to law school as a default choice and without much commitment. As Cameron Stracher puts it in his memoir *Double Billing: A Young Lawyer's Tale of Greed, Sex, Lies, and the Pursuit of a Swivel Chair*, "for most [law students], the decision to go to law school must be viewed as a combination of fear, coercion, curiosity, self-interest, and entropy." Not surprisingly, given this, we learn from him that "[t]oday, law students have nothing but doubts; about the nobility of their chosen profession, about their interest in it, and about its interest in them." The tension between who they might want to be and who the firms are pressing them to become produces coming-of-age anguish and helps explain why so many young associates not only leave their firms but leave the law altogether. It would perhaps be different if the associates got to practice law, but all they do are variations of law school assignments—that plus work on document production discovery requests. The struggling narrator of Hogan's *Man Out of Time* learns from a more experienced colleague that the work "is a piece of cake once you learn the rules, which have nothing to do with practicing law and have everything to do with the way you look and the way you impress and all of that." Our narrator has a problem because he acts at the firm the same way as he does outside the firm. He is not giving what is required—the willingness to sacrifice. A colleague tells him, "[the firm bureaucracy] sees someone who's a little different, and what happens? It begins the long, hard grind, and you either conform or you leave." The fiction tells us what happens when marginally committed young lawyers work in an environment of non-practice and office intrigue.

Associates are on the production line. The nature of what they do for their firms is set out in Kermit Roosevelt's delightful *In the Shadow of the Law*, which describes the lives of various associates in a large Washington D.C. law firm. "For the young associates," he writes, "law was industrialized. They were assembly-line workers, and what they made was time. Torts, contracts, anti-trust cases came through the doors of the firm, and associates took these raw materials and turned them into hours." The associates help us understand about the billable hours that could well be labeled the scourge of the profession because of what they do to lawyers, firms, and clients. Associates are told how many hours they need to work, usually an unfathomable 2,200 hours per year or more, and then they are driven on with promises of bonuses for exceeding expectations. Associates effectively give up any personal life to meet their quotas, struggling with physical, emotional, and psychological stress, all of which are exacerbated because it is generally understood that reaching the rank of partner is unattainable. But associates have been chosen for their willingness to work long and hard and don't disappoint. One study has shown that employers covet law review members because they are used to doing two jobs in law school. Though for different reasons, the associates we meet end up as dispirited as Melville's famously soul-suffering scrivener, Bartleby.

In a rather ironic way, learning about associates in Big Law firms advances the inquiry into what lawyering is. The associates do not work with clients, have no real responsibilities aside from meeting deadlines, and have little or nothing to say about strategy or execution. Work is given to them, lots of it to be sure, but in the way of law school assignments. Yet there is more to being a lawyer than having been a law student. In part, it is figuring out what needs to be done in a case, and then how to get it done. It is about asking the questions that give direction to the representation. And, of course, it is about working with clients, opposing lawyers, and the courts. A lawyer's life is not a cubicle life.

Perhaps it is a surprise to recognize that young associates are caught up in sociological, economic, and professional experiments in laboratories known as Big Law firms throughout the country. It turns out that the life of the young associate has been the object lesson in the unsustainability of the Big Law business model, at least from the point of view of the profession. It might continue to work for the partners at the top of the pyramid, but only for them. It is the structure that is to blame. Solicitor firms in Australia and England use the same pyramid structure, and based at least in part on what solicitors-turned-novelists from those countries tell us—Nick Laird in England with *Utterly Monkey* and Richard Beasley in Australia with *Hell Has Harbor Views*—the structure has also stunted, manipulated, and exploited those at the bottoms of those pyramids. It is simply the nature of the organizational model that it exploits the many for the benefit of the few. For a profession such as ours in which all lawyers are minted as equals before the bar, it cannot be healthy to have a subculture starved of what makes law worth practicing.

BEING PAID TO SHOWER

What would Rudyard Kipling—he of filling the "unforgiving minute/ with sixty seconds' worth of distance run" fame—think of the way that lawyers can fill—in theory, of course—the sixty minutes of a billable hour in ten six-minute bits in which a minute is actually worked for each tenth of an hour, turning six minutes into sixty?

Hourly billing for many lawyers presents challenges, not limitations. Insight into the billable hour comes from legal novels set in large corporate law firms, in which the overriding idea is that law firms exist to survive and that the billable hour is the means to survival. The model for getting the most out of the billable hour, from the partners' perspective that is, is with the multi-level law firm, with its junior, middle, and senior associates and with its junior and senior partners. In this model, leverage matters. *Leverage* here is a term of art that refers to the ratio of associates to partners. The higher the number of associates billing at the highest possible rate divided by the fewest possible partners (owners) equals the highest possible profit. Associates are billed out to the client at an hourly rate well above what the law firm pays the associates, and once the overhead costs of the associates are deducted, the rest is profit for the firm. With each associate representing a profit margin—assuming there is work to be done—the more associates a partner can keep busy, the more money the firm makes. The partner gets his reward when the percentage of the firm's revenue attributable to him is determined. The easiest description of the business model is a pyramid. Scott Turow in *Pleading Guilty* provides a more colorful spin. "A large law firm," he writes, "is basically organized on the same principles as a Ponzi scheme. The only sure ingredients of growth are new clients, bigger bills, and—especially—more people at the bottom, each a little profit center, toiling into the wee hours and earning more for the partnership than they take home."

The issue with what a lawyer's time is worth might not turn on how much the client is willing to pay for that hour. The issue might be what the lawyer puts into that hour. But if the argument is that an hour of a lawyer's time is worth whatever a client is willing to pay for it, that still leaves the question of what the lawyer charges for in that billable hour. Obviously, padding the billable hour with the kind of nonsense described in the legal novels cannot be justified. The lawyer's not really working when he or she bills for bathroom breaks and the like. "Hold on," the lawyers would say, "what if the lawyer is thinking about a case he or she is working on during that bathroom break?" In fact, a scene in Kermit Roosevelt's *In the Shadow of the Law* has the senior partner telling the junior partner to bill his bathroom time when the associate says, to remain in good standing, that he is thinking about a case while he is at the urinal. Not to be outdone, John Grisham has one of the senior lawyers in *The Firm* advise the young associate at the center of the novel that he should bill clients for "every minute you spend even thinking about a case."

William Ross, the leading commentator on hourly billing abuse, takes the charitable view and argues that lawyers slide into abuse without larceny in their hearts. He politely and understatingly writes in his *Rutgers Law Review* article "The Ethics of Hourly Billing by Attorneys" that "[w]ith ever-increasing compensation and billing pressures, attorneys are finding ways to generate more hours in a way that is not always ethical." Reports are that it starts with charging for unnecessary work, such as unneeded phone calls and follow-up memos, and then escalates into charging more time than is actually spent on various tasks. From there, it is a short step to complete fabrication. All falls under the heading of Padding the Bill.

If bill padding is not the villain of the piece, it is as least one of the usual suspects. It takes many forms and all are made difficult to identify if the billing firm uses block billing which does not detail time spent on particular tasks. A popular bill padding technique is to use vague descriptions such as "file review" or "research." This would typically be the work of an associate, but partners can get in the mix by over-reviewing the work of associates. Putting more lawyers than necessary on a file produces its own type of padding. There's usually no need for that extra associate at the deposition or motion hearing. And getting back to the sixty minutes run in an hour, a recurring problem that has not been adequately dealt with by the profession is what to do when a lawyer checks his e-mail and reads, to use an example, e-mails from ten different clients in one six-minute period. Perhaps reading the e-mails takes even less time. Can the lawyer bill each of the ten clients one tenth of an hour for reading that client's e-mail? This would be a windfall to the lawyer, but it comes at no cost to the client, the argument runs, because the lawyer's time for each client was legitimately spent. The easier question is how the lawyer bills for the ten e-mails if they were all for the same client, at least if they were read in one six-minute segment. But what if the ten e-mails are spread out throughout the day and read so that the time reading one does not fit with any six-minute period in which another was read? The factual variations, when set against only vague precepts on such billing, indicate the ripe room for mischief.

Bigger examples of double billing highlight the problem. Firms routinely charge for travel time—as well they should. It is obvious that when a lawyer travels for a client he incurs an opportunity cost, as those in Law and Economics would say, that is equal to the fee he would have charged that or another client if he had not been traveling. But what if a lawyer, on a six-hour flight from New York to Los Angles for one client, feels inspired and works six hours on another client's file? For most lawyers, it is opportunity doubled. It's not a question of whether he filled the six hours legitimately. It's just that he is going to bill two clients for the same six hours, with descriptions that without question pass muster with the client, unless the client knows, of course, about the other client for whom the lawyer was working for during those six hours.

What should be done with bathroom time and shower time, to use just two examples, in which the lawyer is in fact thinking about a case? How lawyers think of themselves and their work might come down to this question. The novels tell us that lawyers feel that they can justly bill for this time, and even if we didn't have the novels, reported cases show that lawyers bill for such time. The cases uniformly reject the claims, and, in at least one case, a lawyer was sanctioned for billing for idea-generating time. This makes it something of a surprise that William Ross—the leader of the honest billable hour movement, remember—argues that lawyers should in fact be able to bill for this time. He echoes many lawyers when he writes that, in billing, the issue is whether the lawyer is thinking about the case, not where he does the thinking. Such thinking about a case can take place while the lawyer mows the lawn or talks about the case with a colleague at a baseball game. "If such time is actually productive," he writes in "Kicking the Unethical Billing Habit," also from the *Rutgers Law Review*, "then it should be billed. I do some of my most creative thinking while I'm bathing or taking walks—surely this thinking is no less 'work' merely because I am not sitting at my desk."

Lincoln famously observed that all a lawyer can sell is his time. If we put contingency fees, flat fees, and multiplier fees at the margins and accept them for the particular benefits they provide to clients, we come back to the question of what a lawyer's time is worth, or, to put it differently, what part of a lawyer's time should be paid for by the client? To hear William Ross explain it, the client should pay whenever—and wherever—the lawyer is thinking about his or her case. Descartes's famous dictum can be transformed to read, "I think, therefore I bill." But this can't be right.

Law is a profession, a learned one at that, if we apply the traditional categorization. People become lawyers—or at least this should be true—because it is a profession. As a profession, it rewards its practitioners constantly. It has brought them into an intellectual world of sorts that provides its own rewards through understanding. If Ross were right, lawyers could bill for nearly all time they are awake. And knowing lawyers, they would bill for time asleep because they might dream about a case and remember something of it in the morning. The client surely benefits when the lawyer thinks about his case while showering or going to a baseball game, but that does not mean that the lawyer should bill for it. The lawyer thinks about the case he is working on in the shower or at the baseball game because he lives the life of the law. By not charging the client, he is merely paying the profession for the privilege of being a part of it. Fees are the bonus of working in the law. To make it the objective is to take the professional out of the lawyer. The problem—the paradox—is that the lawyer might get more money that way, but almost by definition he or she becomes less of a professional.

BETRAYAL IN PLAIN VIEW

What's to be done about abusive federal judges—the judges who are rude, imperious, and ill-tempered—who are prone to tirades, and who enjoy knocking lawyers around for the sport of it? We hear about them and sometimes get stung by one, forced to stand there and be humiliated, to take it.

The question of why some judges act this way has two obvious answers. One is that they can get away with it. Federal judges face little effective accountability. Impeachment is not the right response, since its sense of good behavior is rooted in the high crimes and misdemeanor mode. For discipline short of impeachment, in 1980 Congress passed the Judicial Conduct and Disability Act as 28 USC 372 *et seq*. In fact, its claim to constitutionality rests on the distinction between discipline—such as not having cases assigned to a judge, for example—with an encroachment on what must be the unfettered exercise of Article III judicial discretion. The operative phrase in the latest version of the Act concerns whether a covered judge "has engaged in conduct prejudicial to the effective administration of the business of the courts." When it comes to ill temperedness, misconduct includes "treating litigants or attorneys in an egregiously and demonstrably hostile manner."

It is true that lawyers can be difficult to deal with, and it is of course true that to maintain order in the court judges sometimes need to be stern. This explains principles that allow for judges to be something more than robots but still maintain their fundamental obligation to impartiality. We find in the cases the principle that even a stern and short-tempered judge's ordinary efforts at courtroom administration do not establish bias or impartiality. More to the point, we find that expressions of impatience, dissatisfaction, annoyance, and even anger do not establish judicial bias or partiality. Nothing wrong with sharp words or a modicum of anger, the cases hold, given sufficient justification. Judges are human like everyone else, is the reasoning.

Reading through the cases raising the judicial misconduct issue reveals all sorts of sanctioned conduct that can often give us pause. Appellate courts find no particular problem with judges scolding lawyers for speaking too quickly, warning lawyers to move along, admonishing them to stick to the facts, ridiculing them before the jury, interrupting their presentations of evidence, belittling their ability, criticizing the questions they asked of witnesses, threatening to hold them in contempt, referring to their methods as nonsense, taking over their questioning of witnesses, and rebuking them for persisting in pursuing lines of questioning to which the judge has already sustained an objection. The descriptions are mine. The verbs—*admonishing, scolding, criticizing, threatening, ridiculing*, and *warning*, for example— come from the cases.

The concern in these cases is with a litigant's right to a fair trial. Whether the jury was present is usually the key factual issue in the analyses. If it was not present, it is almost impossible for the judge's conduct to have infected the fairness of the trial. A judge would have to be a serial offender and even then would have to couple in-court misbehavior with out-of-court abuse to qualify for a disciplinary inquiry. This is what happened in the case of Northern District of Texas judge John McBryde in his tangle with the Judicial Conduct and Disability Act. Nine days of hearings produced hair-raising accounts that centered on McBryde's tendency to question the integrity of anyone who disagreed with him, to humiliate lawyers, and to hold them in contempt for no legitimate reason. The hearings produced a 159-page report and recommended sanctions of reprimanding him, not assigning him new cases for one year, and disqualifying him for three years from participating in any cases involving certain attorneys—the ones he had humiliated. He was, in short, a nightmare to appear before and so terrified lawyers that their advocacy was chilled. In one memorable incident, a lawyer breached McBryde's standing order and failed to appear in person at a settlement conference. McBryde ordered that the lawyer attend fifteen hours of a remedial reading course and submit an affidavit attesting to her compliance with the mandate. The humiliated lawyer complied but had her affidavit rejected because it was not sufficiently detailed for McBryde, furthering her humiliation.

McBride's case is at the margins. There is, as any lawyer or court watcher will report, the judge who practices abuse in the far more common setting of arguments to the court or status conferences. No jury to worry about in these settings. These abusive (and often angry) judges have their pet irritants and preferred methods of abuse and humiliation. It happened to me once, but once was enough. It was a trial setting conference, and I was stuck in unusually bad traffic and arrived ten minutes late. When the court got to me I began to apologize, but the judge was having none of it. In his world there can be no excuse for being late. He chewed me out for ten minutes, with me getting redder by the minute, as he attacked what he considered my casual attitude. This was done in front of the ten other lawyers in the case and, of course, the clients. I wanted to point out in response that not only had I never been late before in my career, but that nothing in that career suggests that I have a casual attitude toward my court obligations, but, of course, this was a dressing down, not an exchange. It took a minute, but I figured out why I was so troubled by what was being done to me. My first thought—spurred by my turbo-charged sins of vanity and pride—was that this man had no right to speak to me this way. After all, I thought, I've written books. I have a Ph.D. I am a learned man and should be respected as such. None of this mattered to the judge. He saw only a tardy lawyer. He felt free to humiliate me, instead, because he had no respect for lawyers—this even though the law as practiced is a process that requires collaboration between judges and lawyers. In humiliating me, the judge was declaring that he was the only player in the drama who counted. He had forgotten the limits of his role and the dimensions of mine.

The second answer as to why judges mistreat lawyers is the well-known phenomenon of black robe-itis—the belief that they are entitled to. Judges should, however, know that what they are doing when abusing a lawyer is wrong. For one thing, it is too easy. It is the worst kind of unfair fight. The lawyer can't fight back and is just pummelled. Asking themselves what sense of fairness would allow for such a fight would ordinarily be enough for judges to recognize why such abuse is wrong. But, of course, judges with black robe-itis do not ask such questions. Their sense of virtue and entitlement is coursing through their veins as they beat up on the lawyer. And, to be fair, it can be described in no other way.

In a remarkable article reflecting on black robe-itis and its corruption of the fair administration of justice, Senior United States District Judge John L. Kane describes in his *Litigation* article "Judicial Diagnosis: Robe-itis" watching and trying to learn from judges about the judicial craft while a lawyer because he knew that he wanted to be a judge. He saw both good and bad. On the bad side, for example, he saw that "for some judges, whipping lawyers into shape was not simply a prerogative, but a mission." Lecturing defendants as part of pronouncing a sentence was also something that he saw, but he did not understand until later that a judge has no business doing it. In the article's penultimate paragraph, we learn why the abusive conduct I have been describing here is so wrong. It is a betrayal of the judge's oath of office. Powerful stuff. Judge Kane puts it better than I can: "When a judge is fulfilling the oath of office, the thought that must be foremost in mind is that authority is easily abused. It is most often abused when it is exercised without restraint. It is not the job of a judge to shame litigants into being better persons, nor to scold litigators into being better lawyers, nor to make either grateful for small mercies extended to them. We judges acquire our office as a result of circumstance, fortune, and training. We do not serve by divine right."

So what's to be done with the abusive federal judge, the one afflicted with black robe-itis—or with any judge similarly afflicted who abuses lawyers? Enforcement mechanisms almost never apply. All we really have is the right and obligation to look to the judges, explain that they are just lawyers with robes (replete, of course, with the dignity of the office), and insist that they treat their fellow lawyers with respect and courtesy. Nothing less should be tolerated from judges.

BIG LAW FEES AND BIG TROUBLE

For decades, Big Law was sitting pretty in its catbird seat. Big Law leaders, as masters-of-the-universe, determined what their corporate clients needed and never expected to have their judgments challenged. The unquenchable thirst that their firms had for cash had been matched only by what was thought to be a deep reservoir waiting to be tapped and no one caring how open the spigot was. Then everything changed.

Hourly billing, which had been at the core of the relationship between Big Law and their corporate clients, was reexamined beginning in the new millennium and found wanting. Financial pressures in the form of recessions and the like (and a general financial squeeze and urge to reduce costs) got corporations to think about their Big Law costs, especially when a new type of general counsel—themselves either refugees or escaping heroes from Big Law— took a stand against it to benefit their new corporate masters. These general counsel knew the score—knew that Big Law had a regrettable, if not unethical, tendency to see their corporate clients as currency printing presses. Corporate clients also began to hear from stockholders who no longer wanted to spend so blithely on legal fees. It was stockholder money that was being spent, not money in the abstract. In a dramatic change from past practices, the general counsel of various corporations began to share billing information with each other in the Alliance Counsel Engagement System. This changed the business model from both ends and turned everything upside down. There was even the heretical notion raised and sometimes used as leverage against Big Law that long-standing, special relationships between the law firm and the corporation no longer seemed necessary for the work to be done successfully. Work that had always gone to one Big Law firm could now, with a new cost-conscious general counsel looking for leverage, be spread around with firms looking to offer better rates. This meant that the stability that went with a long-term client was now in doubt. In a twist, clients would need to be persuaded by way of comparison and contrast that it was still in the corporation's interests to maintain that long-term relationship with its particular Big Law firm. This was a world away from when a corporation's law firm would send an un-itemized bill when a project concluded for services rendered, as they so often had. Both the corporation and the law firm had been comfortable with such a bill. Those days were now gone forever.

Billing practices that had not dared speak their name came into full view recently and confirmed what had long been suspected. It was all too fitting that, in a suit brought by the huge firm DLA Piper for $625,000 in legal fees from a client for whom the firm had done bankruptcy work, DLA Piper's client counter-claimed for excessive billing and in discovery uncovered internal e-mails in which DLA Piper's lawyers joked about running up the client's bill through random and unnecessary research and through other well-known padding techniques. The e-mails can be summed up with the directive in one to "churn that bill, baby." Apparently both sides were surprised—DLA Piper by being sued by the client and the client by what it found out its former lawyers had been up to. The parties resolved their dispute soon after the e-mails became public.

An op-ed in *The Wall Street Journal* in the aftermath of the DLA Piper debacle by the managing partner of a competing thousand-lawyer firm became perhaps the inevitable next development in the fight for fees. On full display was Big Law turning on itself and acknowledging the idea that law firms had an inherent conflict of interest in the hourly billing model. The DLA Piper revelation made it difficult to deny what had at least been obvious in theory—that the need for law firms to meet their own bottom lines could and often did conflict with the firm's obligation to meet the needs of the client. To have a Big Law managing partner acknowledge that problem and then to suggest that law firms and corporations move away from the hourly billing model and consider alternative fee arrangements stood as proof that change was afoot.

Nonfiction and especially fiction by and about lawyers provide bracing examples of how Big Law could abuse the hourly billing model. DLA Piper as fact did not follow fiction but instead illustrated a sensibility that had been fleshed out in novels and in nonfiction years before. In part, we can thank for this the complaints of associates to produce billable hours—thousands of them each, to keep their masters happy and well-leveraged. In the wonderfully splenetic *Anonymous Lawyer* by Jeremy Blachman, for example, the narrating partner, intolerant of anything but complete commitment and full time sheets, hits the mark squarely. He explains, "[w]e're a law firm. Time is billable. The client doesn't pay for small talk. Every minute you spend away from your desk is a minute the firm isn't making money off your presence, even though you're still using the office supplies, eating the muffins, drinking the coffee, consuming the oxygen, and adding to the wear and tear on the carpets. You're overhead. And if you're not earning your keep, you shouldn't be here."

There is a certain beauty to the rapacious sensibility that drives the billing of even something as small as a telephone call. Lisa Scottoline describes a senior partner at work piling up nickels when she writes in *Everywhere That Mary Went*, "Martin hangs up the telephone and immediately puts a finger to his lips, a tacit *whoooo!* He makes a note in his red day journal to bill his time and another in his blue telephone log to bill the call. Later, Martin will bill for the time it takes him to write a file memo about the call, and he'll bill for the cost of duplicating the memo. Martin makes $265 every hour and 15 cents every page. In the name of the Father, of the Son, and of the Holy Ghost." But at least it all seems legitimate. Billing that does not fall into that column can take our breath away. Blachman in *Anonymous Lawyer* dishes on the cut corners, sharp trading, and fraud that can go into the prized billable hours, counted out in six-minute chunks. Wonderfully candid and incriminating, our anonymous narrating partner details what many have suspected. We find that he bills for everything. For example, he even bills for the time he spends trying to find ways to derail the ascent of his nearest rival in the firm. "I call it 'research,'" he tells us. "The clients never question it." And then he goes on to divulge the secrets of the counting house. "'Research' is code for surfing the Internet, 'drafting' is code for eating in your office, 'misc. legal forms' is code for ordering gifts online, and 'preparing for meeting' is code for taking a crap. Everyone knows. It's no big deal."

How, then, does a lawyer bill for two thousand two hundred hours in a year? Our dyspeptic narrator in *Anonymous Lawyer* tells us.

My secretary takes care of the billing for me. There's an online system I haven't bothered to figure out how to use. An hour on matter #43651, two hours writing a memo for #71273. All day you keep a running tally. Apparently some people don't like doing this. I don't see what the big deal is. People cheat, of course. They don't cheat maliciously, at least not in most cases. The consequences are too high if you're caught, either by a colleague or by the client. But half an hour becomes an hour, and that break to read some movie reviews for a movie you'll never get the chance to see suddenly ends up absorbed in the hour you spent doing work. The hour at two in the morning becomes two hours, just to penalize the client, the hour on vacation becomes three hours, and the hour spent on making a paper clip chain with the client's file open on your desk—well, you were thinking about the client, so that counts. And the hour you spent on the flight to client #43651, doing work for client #43652, gets billed to both of them. Because why shouldn't it? You have to take the hours where you can get them.

Alternative fee arrangements have not become the rage of the marketplace, but have clearly affected it. There has been a rise each year in the number of clients opting for project-based fees and for other arrangements that tie fees to productivity. But as many commentators have pointed out, the hourly billing model for Big Law and its corporate clients still dominates by far and will likely continue to do so. It provides a level of assurance for both firms and corporations. Firms get a measure of productivity and information necessary for planning the firm's future, while clients can monitor work as it is detailed in billing and achieve certainty and stability. They can also negotiate the billing rate itself. Assuming that the bills are honest, there are no surprises.

Even if clients stay with the hourly billing model, they no longer look at their law firms in the same way. Trust has been lost in Big Law that will prompt all clients to look more closely at what they are paying for. The hourly billing system was based on trust. Big Law was thought to be the preeminent example of the ethical law firm, but now that has all changed. Clients have also changed as well. The cozy relationship between CEOs and Big Law leaders has changed not just because the CEOs need to be more responsive to shareholders, but also because general counsel overseeing legal expenses now exists and is intent on reducing costs. Clubby days of the status quo are gone, much to Big Law's dismay and to its shame for wanting to hold on to them.

BIG LAW AND POETIC JUSTICE

Before the sea change in the corporate practice of law, Wall Street lawyers had so much in common that they radiated clubbishness. There were deep similarities in their elite college and law school educations, in their race, and in their class—they even dressed alike: dark suits, white shirts, and club ties. They were clubby at their firms and even clubbier at their clubs. Their firms, which were to grow and become what is now known as Big Law had, to state the obvious, all their own deep similarities. To read Louis Auchincloss—pretty much any Louis Auchincloss novel or short story about lawyers in the 1960s and 1970s—is to understand what these elite lawyer class and their law firms were like. And then it all changed. Blame Steven Brill and those like him writing in his magazine *The American Lawyer* and elsewhere on what was really going on money-wise behind the reception areas of dark woods and oriental carpets. Once word got out about salaries and profits a new era was born.

Whether Big Law is dead, as some say, or whether it can regroup, the Big Law phenomenon on the legal profession landscape began when what used to be known as large law firms—though their numbers make them seem so quaintly small today—began to grow significantly in the 1970s and 1980s. Moreover, the number of firms that qualified as large also increased, changing the landscape of firms catering to corporate clients. The question of why firms began to grow during this time and then continued to grow is less important—unless you are an economist or sociologist—than the question of what growth has done to lawyers and the practice of law.

Life in the firms themselves changed with increased size. Big Law thought it had figured out the nature of its growth and indeed its essence in the 1980s in what shrewd observers dubbed the "tournament to partnership." Setting senior associates against each other as the partnership prize drew near produced not just Darwinian winners, but an expanded client base that required firms to hire more associates, which in turn increased the profits of the partners. But the tournament was not sustainable without change in the firm structure. The tournament model had too few winners outside the partnership level, which led to a restructuring of what had been the classic model of associates leaving the firm if they did not make partner. In the new order, there were now different off-track positions in the firm for the losers. It was no longer necessarily "up-or-out." They had titles such as Senior Counsel, Senior Attorney, Special Counsel, Counsel Consultant, and Associate Counsel. These lawyers could stay with the firm, make a nice wage, but not expect to advance.

What emerged most of all, perhaps ironically, was the cult of the rain-maker. Lock-step compensation schemes surely could not cabin these new superstars, nor could primitive, "eat what you kill" profit distributions. The superstars could now take the valuable possession—the large clients whose loyalties had shifted from the firm to individual lawyers—and go wherever the deal was best. And if a better deal emerged elsewhere again, they would then bring themselves and the client to that new deal.

The changes in firm structure helped get the work done. The problem for firms was that the work was getting more and more linked to particular rain-making partners. These partners became the superstars of the profession and could make or break firms depending on whether they stayed or left. There had already been a tradition-shattering change in the compensation structure for partners, but that was nothing compared to the change that the superstar lawyers brought to the world of Big Law. The days of lock-step compensation, in which partners continued to make more as they ascended in seniority and without regard for the billings attributable to them, had slid from sight with the trend in the 1980s and 1990s of firms hiring office managers and trying to retain partners by rewarding the producers with more compensation The increasing number of under-contributing senior partners earned less and were encouraged to rethink their place in the firm. Now, with firms living and dying on their ability to keep big clients through their superstar performers, some laggers were simply pushed out. The new reality was that no one was safe anymore. Partners, rather than working less and enjoying firm life more, were working harder and longer—mimicking associates, you could say. The billable hour that helped determine their fates was now helping to determine the fates of the partners as well. This brave new world may have had its start in the press. New journalists such as Steven Brill and what can almost be called a new type of journalism caught the change in the air and reported on what was driving it—money—spilling how much firms and individual partners were making and how much associates started at and what their incremental increases were.

In the halcyon days, everything had seemed so orderly. A white shoe law firm apologist such as one in Louis Auchincloss's fiction would be a mainstay character who believed in maintaining the status quo based on rank, privilege, and honor. For example, Auchincloss has one lawyer character say in *Tales of Manhattan*, "I lunged into the pool of law like a hot boy on a July day. The orderly, hierarchical atmosphere of the firm, where one knew precisely at all times what was expected of one and where one rose from tier to tier pretty much in proportion to one's efforts, seemed to be a tiny civilization in the midst of chaos, a Greek city state on a plain surrounded by barbarians. I loved the law from the beginning and loved the practice of it. I never believed in the sincerity of those who profess to find it difficult to live within a code." Now no firm seemed to be immune. The oddly named white shoe firm was as susceptible to the forces of change as any other firm. This story is nicely told by journalist Ellen Pollock in *Turks and Brahmins*, which describes the changing of the guard at the gentleman's firm of Milbank, Tweed. Restraint, caution, and probity, formerly the virtues of firms such as Milbank, Tweed, gave way to a rapacity for profit. The desire for money was so great, to paraphrase Shakespeare, it was if an increase in appetite fed upon itself. There was greed on Wall Street—and not in a good way—and there was also criminality in furtherance of that greed.

Large and extremely sophisticated and complex economic and social institutions such as Big Law firms defy simple analysis, one view would have it. Maybe so, but on one level, the analysis seems simple, though an analysis rooted in irony might not qualify as an analysis. What had bonded partners before Big Law—shared backgrounds, goals, and ethics—was not strong enough to hold off the future. The aristocratic master-of the-universe, it turns out, subscribed to naive ideas that could not withstand market forces.

Statistics linking lawyer happiness with where they work should worry those running large law firms. It is no surprise, at least to those in the profession, that being a law firm associate has been determined by a survey to be the worst job in America; nor is it surprising to learn from a different study that lawyers in large firms are the least satisfied lawyers in the profession. Public service lawyers are the most satisfied, with small practitioners and small firm lawyers rating in between. And in a statistic that links low job satisfaction to large firm employment, top tier law school graduates are the least pleased with having become lawyers. Fourth tier school graduates, on the other hand, reported being extremely satisfied with their career choice.

Students of Big Law have been considering the forces at work as well as the numbers from the field and have come to different conclusions. One school of thought, led by the late Larry Ribstein, has argued that the splintering of partnerships at the top because of the superstar rainmaker factor and the rise of the role of corporate general counsel spells the doom of Big Law. On the other side, Law and Economics scholars such as Daniel Currell and M. Todd Henderson have argued that, while Big Law has continued to thrive despite the various internal and external forces, such as the recent recession, its long-term future does not look good unless it can change its role to something akin to being a general contractor. Legal process outsourcing for projects such as discovery review will lead to the atomization of representation, so that five to ten different firms could be involved, they argue. Unless Big Law wants to go the way of architects, who ceded the general coordinating function to contractors and lost their place atop the pyramid, Big Law will find itself in a world of specialists to whom clients can separately turn to complete their projects. Once the one-stop-shopping model of Big Law falls away, so too might Big Law.

Big Law is in for a tough time. The greater the split becomes between the production of information on the one hand and the legal services that interpret that information on the other, the more vulnerable Big Law becomes as the provider, as it is now, of both. My interest is elsewhere, though. It is with what might be called poetic justice. The money that has driven the rise of Big Law is now driving its difficulties. More to the point, the unhappiness that partners have visited on associates in the name of billable hours to feed partnership profits has, in a "hoisted by his own petard" way, brought its own unhappiness to those very partners. The house of Big Law has been remodeled, but discontent is shaking the foundation.

BRAINY LAWYERS

Lawyers, when they assert that they have sway over the world, are not asserting superiority at a particular physical skill—the way, for instance, that surgeons might point to their facility with a knife to distinguish themselves from others. For lawyers, it is their brains and what they do with them that make them superior. Intelligence for them is wrapped up with what is described as "thinking like a lawyer" and presents its own questions about intelligence and how it is used by those living in the law.

For something so talked about by lawyers, it is surprisingly difficult to get good answers about their take on the nature of intelligence. Performance on the LSAT or in law school can distinguish one lawyer from the next, but it can only suggest a connection to intelligence. Descriptions of intelligence that look to standard markers do not help much. We need the help of people who have been around the intellectually gifted and have seen how intelligence operates. But even then we struggle. Consider the example of Henry Friendly, a figure of staggering intellect by all accounts. He had earned the highest grades at the Harvard Law School since Louis Brandeis and was considered by all who worked with him to be brilliant, if not a genius. We find in David M. Dorsen's fine judicial biography of Friendly, *Henry Friendly, Greatest Judge of His Era*, a useful description of Friendly's intelligence as a lawyer by an associate in his law firm, who writes "I cannot overemphasize Henry Friendly's ability to marshal, exhaustively, complex facts, to isolate legal issues, to fix sensible priorities, and to sum up his conclusions or arguments in his ever-increasingly clear, pungent, literate style." This is another way of saying that Friendly had the ability to identify, memorize, discern, and articulate.

We find the best and most detailed descriptions of intelligence in novels by and about lawyers. These descriptions reveal just what lawyers think intelligence is and how it is used. They describe intelligence in various lawyers that has awed them. It is something of an irony that some writers describe fictional worlds in which intelligence is prized above all but nonetheless have difficulty describing what intelligence actually is, raising doubts about the whole enterprise. Louis Auchincloss writing about the white shoe law firm world he spent a long career working in is a good example of this. His upper crust lawyers, who are invariably educated at elite prep schools, ivy league colleges, and law school at Harvard, Yale, or Columbia, live in a world in which everyone is brilliant (How else can their elite law firm success be explained?), but in which some are more brilliant than others. Here's Auchincloss's senior partner character Lloyd Degener in *Tales of Manhattan* on Eric Temple and his father, who had been a figure of legendary brilliance and industry in the firm his son would later join. "Let me say at once that he [Eric Temple] was as brilliant as his father. Even one as grudging as myself had to concede this after a single day of working with him. What I had thought was merely facile turned out to be lucid; what I had taken for detachment was in truth philosophy. If Eric did not 'grind' the way the rest of us did, it was because he had an uncanny sense of mental direction that sent him at once to the pertinent paragraph, to the relevant case. He looked before he leaped, and it was a long, cool look." This is as close as Auchincloss gets to defining intelligence. It helps some in answering the question, but not much. We need to look elsewhere.

National Book Award winner and former British barrister Joseph O'Neill wrote about barristers in his novel *This Is the Life*, and gives us the top-of-the-line English version of a lawyer, Michael Donovan, QC. The description is so evocative of memory, speed, and analytical power that we wonder if we'd rather have the barrister's brain power or the author's brain power in fashioning the description. "That mind of his," we learn from our narrating solicitor who both admires and detests Donovan, "it was naturally and freakishly powerful, like a once-in-a-blue-moon tidal wave, or a tree-plucking wind in England. Perhaps this is a pedestrian or fanciful metaphor, but I most easily visualize it as one of those fat Swiss army penknives, deceptively stocked with cutthroats and instruments of severance, disassembly and dissection: razors, scissors, corkscrews, bottle-openers, screwdrivers, magnifying lenses, the lot. In a flash, before you could mobilize a brain cell, he would have dismantled an issue, anatomized its components and analyzed its implications." Ten pages later, our narrating solicitor continues, pointing out that "Donovan had a brain housing a huge repository of legal authorities which he could instantly cite; it brimmed like a grain-bin with sweet precedents and nuggets of jurisprudence. He had a party trick where, if you quoted a case to him, he would rattle off the ratio of the decision, the year, the judges and barristers involved and even, if the case was remotely near his field, the page where it appeared in the reports."

We get glimpses in other novels by and about lawyers of examples of intelligence admired and even envied by lawyers. Speed impresses, we learn. From Scott Turow in *Pleading Guilty* we get this description of managing partner Martin Gold from our narrating protagonist, Mack Malloy. "Martin is one of those men who abound in the legal profession whose brains seem to make them a quarter larger than life. His mind is always zipping along at the speed of an electron. You sit down with him and feel surrounded on all sides. Jesus Christ, you wonder, what is this fellow thinking? I know he's turned over every word I've said three times before I get another one out of my mouth." In Turow's novel *Innocent*, the sequel to *Presumed Innocent*, we get an emphasis on yet a different set of qualities. Brilliance here is contrasted with intellectualism. Rusty Sabich, now a judge but once again charged with murder, tells us that Anna, one of his former law clerks and now his lover, "is like many people I knew in law school, not intellectual but brilliant, so agile with the lawyer's tasks of mating fact and law that it is as thrilling as watching a great athlete on the playing field."

For most intelligence aficionados, though, it is the ability quickly to understand the new that lies at the core of intelligence. Steve Martini in *The Arraignment* has lawyer Paul Madriani describe colleague Nick Rush, who has the prized gift of great intelligence. His is marked by speed and discernment. "[He] doesn't waste energy on details that aren't essential to the grand picture, the task at hand at any given moment. He has an intellect like a vacuum. He can suck up details of a trial in three minutes, organize them in the order of importance, and march them out like an army to do battle in court while his opponent is still trying to get his briefcase open."

If we hit the lottery at birth, we might get one of the brilliant minds so far described. That there are not many of them means there is a lot of room to use whatever gifts we have, though, ironically, recognizing that we do not have the greatest gifts might be a predicate to getting the most out of what we do have. We find in "Testimony and Demeanor," an early short story by National Book Award winner and Harvard Law School graduate John Casey, a description of a mind more hard-working than talented that should give comfort to the rest of us striving to do our best. Our young associate narrator has been asked by one of the partners in his Big Law firm how he had gotten along in law school. He tells the inquiring partner that,

> whatever advantage I'd had—since I was clearly no Frankfurter—was a capacity for work and for organizing other people's ideas. Right away I saw there were some minds which were quick and subtle. Some of them could grind too, and they went on to be *Law Review*. But some of them had no organizing power. They were happy to break up a problem in class. Suggest all the difficulties. Sometimes I wasn't even sure I understood all of them. But having done all that work out loud—scored a few points for wit and elocution—they'd be tired of it. Maybe bored. That was *their* problem. I picked up the pieces. Not all the little cute ones. Early on I figured out that if you put too fine a point on an argument it's likely to arouse suspicion. Ingenious but unsound, as the saying goes. Which means baloney no matter how thin you slice it.

While intelligence is and should be prized, the good news is that to see to the core of a case turns not on a lawyer having great intelligence, but on an openness to see what the case is really about. It takes a version of garden-variety common sense. In his 1915 presidential address, American Bar Association President Peter Meldrim described that "the most important thing for a lawyer to possess, in order to discharge his simple, every-day duty to his client, is common sense, the ability to see things as they are, not as he would like to see them. To have a just appreciation of the true relation which one fact or one principle bears to every other fact and every other principle involved in the case. To have a sense of legal perspective, and the skill to present effectively the strong points in his case and the art to conceal the weak ones. To have that common honesty which prevents one not only from trying to fool another, but from fooling himself."

It requires effort to see things as they are. Discipline is effort, something we have to work at. Intelligence is just a fact, not a process, while seeing things as they are is. The truth, perhaps one rarely described, is that having great intelligence is an asset only if the intelligence is combined with an intellectual process that centers on what is there, not on what we want to be there. The profession is strewn with lawyers who have great intelligence but who have never used it as they should, or who used it for a while but then gave in to narcissism. When we are in the presence of great intelligence, the response should not be awe but the question of whether it is being used properly.

CAN WE TALK?

The judges in the federal district in which I practice insist on a podium rule—though, technically, it should be called the lectern rule. The rule is that, whether it is argument to the court, examination of witness, or arguments to the jury, the lawyers from both sides have to restrict themselves to standing behind the lectern which is placed front and center in the courtroom. Not all courts, even federal district courts, insist on the rule. But for the judges in my Central District of California it is the rule. No closing in on the witness Perry Mason style, no roaming around the court when addressing the court, Alan Shore style.

Some might say that for the judges it is a control issue, an issue of dominance, of power. Maybe yes, maybe no. What matters for the lawyers is how to form the relationship with the lectern that meets the rules of the court and gives them the comfortable feeling they need to do their best work. We are not used to being cabined, so the struggle is ongoing.

How to relate to the lectern becomes more complicated because the lawyer is engaged in a variety of activities at the lectern. There's the presentation to the court, but after argument, or even during the argument, the court asks questions or in any number of ways challenges what the lawyer is arguing. How to relate to the lectern when fielding questions? How to relate to the lectern when, while still at the lectern, the court engages opposing counsel at his counsel table? And for those occasions such as a change of plea or sentencing when the client is with the lawyer at the lectern, how then does the lawyer relate to the lectern now that he is sharing space, so to speak? And what about those times in which the court, such as part of a sentencing, has to read from a set script, such as in stating the terms of supervised release that follows incarceration? There's a lot that has to go on the record. The lawyer listens and perhaps makes notes as the judge goes along. Not seen by anyone, he is also trying to sort out his relationship to the lectern.

45

The lawyers I see practice a variety of classic lectern moves and poses. The most amusing are the ones who bring hundreds of pages of documents and notes to the lectern, spread them out, and then proceed to sprawl. They take a half step back and throw their arms out on the side of the lectern, as they are attempting some sort of reach around. They then hang their bodies down and look up to the judge, creating an arch effect. Another version of this pose has the lawyers placing their palms against the front edges of the lectern sides and pushing off from there. Others have their version of the thoughtful pose whereby they rest one elbow on the side of the lectern and balance themselves against that, searching for a certain insouciance. Rare are the lawyers who stand behind the lectern and only on occasion rest their hands on its side. Also rare are the lawyers, who, having abandoned their poses, argue with great gesticulation, sawing at the air, as Shakespeare once put it. That they usually come to the lectern with their jackets unbuttoned and ties loosened somehow completes the scene. If they were plumbers, their pants would not cover their assets.

I do my best not to even touch the lectern. I'll bring some papers to the lectern, in case I get stuck, but since I try always not to use notes and to address the court as if in a conversation, putting the papers on the lectern is the closest I hope to come to touching it. I make into a kind of game, to see if I can get through an entire appearance without falling prey to touching the lectern, believing that doing so signals weakness, a kind of crutch. When it is just me engaged in argument, I do my best to just stand there, sometimes putting my hands behind my back, sometimes with my hands in my pockets. It's just too hard to keep your arms at your sides the whole time. When I'm not engaged and standing with my client listening to the opposing counsel or listening to the court recite from a script, I move to the left of the lectern and find minor diversions, moving a step to the left and right, front and back, usually with my hands behind my back.

I've only lately taken to at times putting my hands in my pockets. It is not particularly visible to an observer that I have my hands in my pockets because my suit jacket covers that part of my trousers, but it is clear from the stance that comes from keeping my hands in my pockets what is happening. I used to wonder if this was too casual a stance, that it might be sending the wrong message to the judge. It was a comfortable and natural position to take. And since I tended to do it when I was more an observer to the scene than an active participant as when, for example, I was arguing a point, I thought that whatever message it was sending was minimized. But given that I would sometimes keep my hands in my pockets when I was engaging directly with the court, I had to determine if I was crossing some etiquette boundary. It didn't feel wrong, but, as we know, that is not the best test of whether some activity is acceptable.

I scouted around for some authority on hands-in-pockets, but didn't have much success. I discovered that it is bad form for visitors, such as in Hong Kong or in Denmark, to converse with strangers with hands in pockets, but there isn't much on the American rule generally and on court etiquette in particular. And of those sources I did find, they were of the "don't wear white after Labor Day" sort. Certainly nothing I found turned me away from what I suspect had been my influence in all of this, Thomas Eakins's famous full-length portrait of Louis Kenton called *The Thinker*. Eakins, considered by some to be our greatest 19th-century painter, portrays Kenton in his handsome three-piece suit, head down and ruminating, with his jacket open and hands in pockets. If the jacket were buttoned it could be me—or at least it could be my image of myself.

Truth be told, it was from an English manners book of the 18th century that I found described what I guess I had been thinking about all the while. The directive found there is that a person is not to stand before a superior with hands in pockets. That's it. I don't think of the judge as my superior. We have our different roles, but we are all there trying to get some work done. As a participant, I have at least some sort of right to seek a comfortable place, a place facilitating the work at hand. Sometimes, like Eakins's *The Thinker*, that place for me is with my hands in my pockets. After all, it's not as though I'm standing there, arms akimbo, sending some sort of odd message. Nor am I standing there with my arms crossed, sending the passive aggressive message of having closed off my engagement in the process. I'm just there thinking and engaging, sometimes with hands in pockets.

Tales of Supreme Court advocacy have limited use because of the nature of High Court arguments, though stories of advocates asserting themselves help on the general issue of oral argument. With Erwin Griswold in one case in which he had filed a friend of the court brief, it was a physical insistence of his role. According to the entry on Griswold in *The Yale Biographical Dictionary of American Law* he "placed his chair squarely in the middle of the courtroom in order, he told the Court, to make it apparent that he was there as a true friend of the court rather than one of the parties." The ideal for any advocate was pulled off by Henry Clay in what we are told was his first argument in the Supreme Court. The story, as laid out in a 19th-century book of sketches of famous lawyers, tells us that when he rose to argue Clay was agitated but soon regained his composure. Then "Judge Washington, who was in the habit of taking an occasional pinch of snuff, took out his snuff-box, and Mr. Clay, on observing it, instantly stopped, and advancing gracefully to the bench, participated with the judge in the refreshment of his nasal organs, remarking, 'I observe that your honor sticks to the Scotch,' and immediately resumed his argument. Judge S.[Story], who related the incident, said he did not believe there was a man in the United States who could have done that but Henry Clay."

The goal of an oral advocate is to establish the argument as a conversation with the court, and the advocate as one asserting the equality of a conversation partner. The reason for this lies in the dynamic of conversation. William Hazlitt in his essay "On the Conversation of Authors" has the insight here. He distinguishes between conversation and argument (in its general, not oral advocacy term of art sense but in the sense of just a more heated and edged exchange) and explains that the reason anyone wanting to persuade would prefer conversation is that "[argument] is the death of conversation, if carried on in a spirit of hostility: but discussion is a pleasant and profitable thing, where you advance and defend your opinions as far as you can, and admit the truth of what is objected against them with equal impartiality: in short, where you do not pretend to set up for an oracle, but freely declare what you really know about any question, or suggest what has struck you as throwing a new light upon it, and let it pass for what it is worth."

For us, Hazlitt's insight is not just about persuadability through conversation, it is that conversation requires an honesty that argument ignores. This insight for the advocate should spur him to concede when conversation requires concession. Most advocates believe that any concession smells of submission, but this just misses the bigger picture. The point of oral advocacy is that the advocate is trying to enhance his bona fides, to get to be considered a participant in what has been established as a conversation. Our American system has always stressed the written aspects of argument, unlike other systems such as the British or Australian that have a tradition of orality. We do this for a reason. An oral advocate is not going to reshape the court's deliberative process and rely on oral argument and dispense with the briefs. The briefs are the core of argument. The most the advocate can do is put in the judge's head the idea as he reads the briefs that the advocate is worth listening to.

CLIENTS AND THEIR LAWYERS

Clients, there is so much to love. They come with an unrealistic set of demands. They want us to see everything from their point of view and to agree that they are justified in their cause. They want us to adopt and even enhance whatever emotion that drives them—anger, revenge, vindication, and the like. They want theirs to be the most important case we have in our offices. They want us to always be available to listen and respond to them. They want us to do it all for nothing, and if not for nothing then at a discounted rate. And then they want to not pay us once they receive our bill. After all, all we did was follow their directions. We can blame our culture of narcissism for how clients can interpret a professional relationship this way, or we can blame ourselves for selling clients some version of their narcissistic fantasy when we are courting them to be our clients. After all, that's what we do with advertising these days. What's worse than all of this, though, is that in this dance with the client we have been giving up willingly or inattentively the role of counselor that most defines what we do. After all, what are we if we can't say no to the client? A lawyer without a client, most would say. A cynical lawyer would say that the idealized counselor's role does not matter and that what the lawyer offers and does is just for show anyway. The art of lawyering, some would say, is getting the client's money. Smile, smile, and be a villain to the client is the directive.

The less jaded, the less cynical, would modestly suggest that we should be more charitable to clients and see matters from their point of view. There is something to that. But first we need to acknowledge two truths. One is that clients are necessary for a lawyer to be a lawyer. A lawyer without clients is just sitting in an office. This is what happened to Charles Francis Adams, the great grandson of our sixth president and the great-great grandson of our second president. He reported in his autobiography (he had some time to spare) that after entering the bar he sat for years in an office in a building in Boston, owned by his father, without a single bona fide client because potential clients thought him too rich to need the business. Everyone knew that there was money in the family and assumed he did not need clients. A second truth is that it naturally follows, since lawyers need to have clients to be lawyers, that a lawyer's life is bound up in some measure with his or her relationship to clients. Looking at lawyers and their clients tells us something about lawyers and the profession. It also necessarily tells us something about clients —a group for whom there are no easily identifiable traits beyond the obvious.

Few clients come to lawyers because they want to be there. There are occasions, such as a closing in a real estate transaction, in which, unless it is a sinking market, everyone in the lawyer's office will leave happy. More typically, people become clients only when they are in crisis. Even having a will drafted can be difficult for the client, forcing a summing up of a life, and especially if the decisions dictated to the lawyer will cause grief and dissension among family members. The great Learned Hand gave some insight into how clients might respond when caught up in the law when he famously noted that, "as a litigant, I should dread a lawsuit beyond almost anything short of sickness and death."

Clients want lawyers who will respond to their crises with all of the client's emotion, whether it is fury, anger, resentment, or outrage. Clients want lawyers who can give them the emotional satisfaction they seek either to go after someone if aggrieved or to fight back if sued. A dazzling passage from Janet Malcolm, the fine *New Yorker* writer, helps us understand this. She found herself in a much publicized defamation lawsuit in which the plaintiff alleged that Malcolm had distorted the meaning of what the plaintiff had said to her. She was immediately relieved, she described in her book *The Journalist and the Murderer*, when her grievance got a sympathetic hearing from her lawyer. She then says that conventional psychotherapy would start an unpleasurable inquiry into the plaintiff/patient herself while "the law cure never ceases to be gratifying." Then, in a remarkable passage, she writes that "what the lawyer says and writes on his client's behalf is gratifying beyond the latter's wildest expectation. The rhetoric of advocacy law is the rhetoric of the late-night vengeful brooding which in life barely survives the skeptical light of morning but in a lawsuit becomes inscribed, as if in stone, in the bellicose documents that accrue while the lawsuit takes its course, and proclaims with every sentence, 'I am right. I am right. I am right.'" She goes on to say that "of pleasurable reading experiences there may be none greater than afforded by a legal document written on one's behalf. A lawyer will argue for you as you could never argue for yourself, and, with his lawyer's rhetoric, give you a feeling of certitude that you could never obtain for yourself from the language of every day discourse. People who have never sued anyone or been sued have missed a narcissistic pleasure that is not like any other."

For many there is a completely legitimate reason to litigate. But at the same time many clients come looking to litigate to express whatever anger or outrage they are feeling toward someone who has wronged them—the neighbor with a shed one foot over the line into the client's property, for example. Some use litigation as a business strategy to deplete the resources of competitors. Others use it as part of a negotiation strategy. These last clients use lawyers as weapons. Whether lawyers want to be used or should be used this way are important questions for the profession in light of the precept best articulated by Lincoln that it is a lawyer's obligation always to discourage litigation. One answer is that the lawyer does not have much of an option when the client looking to litigate for strategic business decisions shows up at the lawyer's office, war chest in tow, and says that a good chunk of the war chest has been earmarked for the lawyer. It is one sort of problem if the lawyer is a solo practitioner or a member of a small firm. These lawyers can more easily say no if they want to. It is a different problem if the lawyer works for a large firm with enormous overhead costs and the constant need for new clients and more billable hours. That lawyer needs thousands of billable hours, and the client offers just that, all allocated for in the business strategy. Who's to say no?

At the most manipulative level, a client might know that he is in the wrong but wants to press ahead for a variety of psychological and financial reasons. This is true even for a king. The remarkable opening scene in *Henry V* makes this point. Henry does not need his counselors to tell him that he has a right to go to war with France, but he wants to use the bishops, standing in as his lawyers, to put on the record, so to speak, the justification for war based on an intricately parsed analysis of the law Salic. The bishops do not start with an analysis of the law's dubiousness (annotators to the play, such as A.R. Humphreys for the Penguin Classic edition, describe the law Salic as "the supposed law by which the crown of France could descend only through males") but instead present an orderly account of its application to justify the decision to go to war. No fools they, the bishops. As has been the case with so many lawyers over the centuries, they recognize what the client wants and deliver it. Their church in return will receive large financial rewards. King Henry bought and the bishops sold. These bishops were not of the sort to discourage litigation at all costs, as Lincoln has told us is the lawyer's charge.

Following Lincoln's directive is the most difficult challenge lawyers face if they want to do their jobs properly. The lawyer's obligation is to try and persuade the client not to litigate. What does the lawyer do, though, if he does all he can to dissuade but the client nonetheless wants to litigate? Lawyers do not have to turn the work away, so long as the case has sufficient merit and is not a nuisance or frivolous suit. The problem tends to be that lawyers just follow the client wherever he wants to go because they are following the money. Clients can apply forms of heavy pressure to get a lawyer to say yes, to be the friend in need. Saying no is not just the tricky part, it is the fundamental challenge of lawyering. Some would say that following through on the directive to discourage litigation in our litigious times with demanding clients creates a negating paradox for the lawyer if he needs the client to practice law. Put differently, how can a lawyer who tells people not to sue remain a lawyer for long? It's a fair point, even if it is presented so starkly. The answer is that there is no point in being a lawyer unless the lawyer can practice on his own terms. Sorting through this problem might be the challenge of the profession.

CONTEMPTUOUS

There is an impulse, I've been told, for some lawyers in situations of perceived miscarriages of justice to drop into an Al Pacino impression and declare, for an ever-diminishing group that has seen . . . *And Justice for All*, "you're out of order, the whole trial's out of order." These lawyers are indifferent to the contempt finding that will naturally follow and proud to wear its badge. I'm more of the sort to keep things to myself and instead to see in my cinematic imagination the offending judge or opposing lawyer caught in quicksand or walking into an uncovered sewer opening on the street to get their suitable punishments. It is both more amusing and more professionally prudent this way. Some lawyers, though, defy prudence and act out.

Criminal contempt in the federal system—far more interesting an animal than civil contempt—is governed by 18 U.S.C. §401, which gives the court the power to punish by fine or imprisonment misbehavior of any person in its presence or so near thereto as to obstruct the administration of justice. State statutory versions are generally similar to the federal statute. Civil contempt need not be in the judge's presence, such as disclosing information to the press that the court has ordered the lawyers to keep secret. It's conduct in the judge's presence that directs us to the essential dynamic between lawyers and judges that is at the heart of the adversarial system. We can find fireworks, or at least a deadly weapon, there.

Filing a contemptuous pleading can be enough to invoke the statute, even though the "presence or so near thereto" requirement seems unnaturally stretched to reach this result. At least, this is what one defense lawyer found when in defiance of an order he filed a motion to withdraw as counsel on the basis of not getting paid. Most contemptuous conduct as reflected in the reported cases, though, takes place during trial. Repeatedly interrupting the court, persisting in a line of cross-examination, or even repeating an aimless cross-examination can get a lawyer in trouble. A lawyer's stating an objection at the top of his voice and angrily slamming hand on counsel table and refusing to sit down can be enough, as can dancing, prancing, grimacing, and gesturing before the jury while the court announces a ruling. The criminal defense lawyer's trick of putting someone other than the client in the defendant's seat to wreak havoc with an in-court identification goes too far. So too for not sitting down and shutting up when ordered to. Using vulgar language toward the court or toward opposing counsel, such as telling your opponent to kiss your ass, can lead to criminal contempt. Displaying a sardonic sense of humor, on the other hand, in one case at least, was not enough. Another 19th-century case held that a member of the bar who appears in court armed with a deadly weapon was guilty of contempt of court.

Reported state court cases feature hard-to-fathom outrageousness. It was criminal contempt for a defense lawyer at a plea bargain inquiry in Texas to make a simulated masturbatory gesture with his hand after the prosecutor objected to the defense lawyer's interference with the inquiry. A defense lawyer in Florida was charged but not convicted of criminal contempt for pounding his fist and yelling "Yessss" when the verdict was read and his client acquitted. It was criminally contemptuous for a lawyer to describe proceedings in a Florida courtroom as a kangaroo court and to allege that the judge had been bought. Defense counsel's slapping the table after an objection had been overruled and shouting, "How come everything he does is right and everything I do is wrong?" was contemptuous in an Illinois court. Also in Illinois, a lawyer who, on the ninth day of a hotly contested trial, said, when interrupted by opposing counsel, "May I complete my God damned statement?" was found not guilty of contempt. In Pennsylvania, the disruption element of contempt, which included the awareness that the lawyer was engaging in wrongful conduct, was met, not surprisingly, when a lawyer after receiving an unfavorable ruling remarked that the judge was "such a fucking asshole." In contrast, in Florida a lawyer's out-of-court statement to a judicial assistant calling her "little mother fucker" and the judge a "motherfucker son of a bitch" could not be punished as direct contempt because the statements did not constitute a clear and present danger to the orderly administration of justice, even if the assistant was so upset she had to go home for the day. The good news from Colorado—albeit in 1884—is that if a judge and a lawyer get into a brawl outside the courtroom on an unrelated matter, it is not contempt.

The presence requirement is what has saved many lawyers from criminal contempt when tardy to court or not appearing at all. Not surprisingly, tardiness or non-appearance appear frequently in the reports, especially in the federal reports. Civil contempt is far more likely to stand than criminal contempt. The courts point to the intent element to put tardiness, or even missed appearances, into the "stuff that happens" category. Cells phones going off in court would fall under this category also.

It's hard not to conclude that some judges have been overly sensitive to perceived slights and have reacted disproportionately. In one case, a federal judge issued a summary criminal contempt order to a lawyer arriving five minutes late for a hearing. The appellate court reversed. There have been cases in which lawyers have been cited for contempt for not standing when the judge enters the courtroom, for not following a judge into chambers at a recess when beckoned, and for calling the judge "sir" rather than "your honor."

The appellate courts reviewing criminal contempt convictions are put in a difficult spot. On the one hand, they want the trial judges to know that the appellate bench won't micro-manage how they handle disruptions of their courts, but on the other hand, the number of reversals and even some language in cases affirming the trial court suggest that the appellate judges recognize that some judges are thin-skinned and have hair-trigger responses to issues such as tardiness that go to a controlling nature and a failure to accept the legal process as a collaborative enterprise.

An essential tension exists between proper decorum and orderly courtroom management on one side and the lawyer's belief in zealous advocacy on the other. As one court nicely put it, the adversarial system encourages vigorous advocacy to the point where lawyers sometimes forget themselves in the heat of combat. Trial judges are not allowed to use, however, contempt power to ensure an atmosphere of decorous understatement. Disrespectful conduct, the court concluded, is not contemptuous. For there to be contempt, not only must there be an actual obstruction of justice, it must be material.

The test relating to the obstruction element of criminal contempt, while perhaps never easy to apply, is at least easier to apply than the test for the intent element. The rule is stated easily enough, that a lawyer possesses the requisite intent to be guilty of contempt if he knows, or reasonably should be aware in view of all the circumstances, that he is exceeding the outermost limits of his proper role and hindering rather than facilitating the search for truth. Judges making the intent determination, while having their own ideas about the limits of proper advocacy, do not see the world as the lawyer does who is convinced that his client is not getting a fair trial either because of perceived judicial bias or the belief that the law is wrong. This is what makes judging contemptuous behavior so difficult.

The stakes are high in making the judgment about contemptuous behavior. Nothing less than imposing a chill on advocacy is at stake. For lawyers, though, being as self-centered as we are, the question of contemptuous behavior looks not so much to the broader questions of the fair administration of justice, but to the nature of the experience in trying a case before a judge seemingly keen to drop the contempt hammer. Good lawyers—not the adolescents acting out or the bomb throwers—have an appreciation for tyranny that few others can have when they are before one of the thin-skinned, obsessively controlling judges who believes that the law is all about them. In that dynamic, of the lawyer before the judge making an argument, the judge can—and judges sometimes do—adopt a look that says, "I will put you in the holding cell if you don't cut it out and there is nothing you can do about it." Add angry and unhappy to the mix of anti-judicial traits and you have the dynamic of the tyrannical and the terrorized. The faint-hearted lawyers wither, and only the brave step forward.

CRIMINAL DEFENSE LAWYERS AND THEIR TOUGH JOB

Defense lawyers both in and out of court have always been more colorful, whether we find them in fiction, autobiography, nonfiction, or newspaper headlines, than their prosecutorial counterparts. Defense lawyers are the ones ripping at the fabric of authority, trying to metaphorically gouge out with their diamond-ringed fingers the eyes of perceived wrongs in the fair administration of justice. They are depicted as colorful in and out of court. They drink too hard, chase long-legged women (for some reason they all seem to be long-legged) against their better judgment, and generally battle any number of demons as they try to sort out their lives while at the same time saving the lives of their clients. They are the conflicted lawyers, brought to the breaking point because of irreconcilable tensions. The criminal defense lawyer is badgered by the public and friends alike. "How can you defend those people?" "You're becoming just like your client. " "I'm not the enemy." "Don't cross-examine me." Complaints, always complaints.

Criminal defense lawyers in fiction, television, or movies are almost never depicted as dignified. Sandy Stern, though, who has a starring role in three Scott Turow novels, rates the dignified description, as does Atticus Finch in *To Kill a Mockingbird*. Paul Biegler in Robert Traver's *Anatomy of a Murder* is a remarkably decent man, but he falls short of dignified. Usually the criminal defense lawyer in fiction is a brawler of sorts, perhaps not on the streets but in the courtroom. Add street smarts and an "anything goes" attitude and you have the Al Pacino character in . . . *And Justice for All*, the benchmark of criminal defense lawyers on the screen.

Criminal defense work is, or at least can be, dispiriting. In the federal system, the government wins almost all of the cases that go to trial. The government increases the odds of success at trial by beginning with over-whelming evidence. The others end in guilty pleas. Some might argue that taking such an approach reflects an especial sensitivity to losing, though others would point out that it is not a bad thing that only alleged crimes supported by significant evidence get people indicted. With the sentencing guidelines (even in their diminished state because of *United States v. Booker*, which has given sentencing judges discretion to deviate from the guidelines) the result in a case is known from the beginning based on what is charged. Defense lawyers have some, but little, chance to affect the result and work only at the margins. Not being able to have much affect on the sentence of clients who plead guilty is dispiriting enough. Cases that go to trial get there almost always because the client has been unreasonable and insists on a trial. The lawyer defending at those trials would probably prefer to bury his head in his hands throughout because it almost always starts out bad and then gets worse. Usually there's nothing the defense lawyer can do. Defense lawyers, in playing their only cards, always put on their show of bravado by attacking the credibility of government informants, as if such an attack actually matters. Maybe the attack on the cooperating witness is for the lawyer's benefit. It gives him a moment of satisfaction to go through a witness's usual string of convictions to argue later that the witness should not be believed, but the satisfaction is only momentary. The rest is not silence. It is the sound of the government machine rolling over the defendant and his lawyer. Being a defense lawyer is hard work.

The defense lawyer's clients tend not to make matters easier for the lawyer. They have been known to either lie to the lawyer about what happened or, if not lie, omit large chunks of the truth. Defendants work under the peculiar reasoning that a lawyer deceived or misled can do a better job than an informed lawyer. I've had clients lie to me from our first meeting to the last. Perhaps the client is in denial as to what happened, a handy self-defense mechanism, but I think not. There's too much fun to be had in jerking the lawyer around. This kind of client knows that the result cannot be changed, so why not have a laugh of sorts? More cynical defendants turn on their lawyers and use them as leverage. Defendants with appointed lawyers will make claims that the lawyer is ineffective or worse and seek to get a new lawyer appointed. The goal sometimes is as simple as to string out the process, turning one year into two, as if somehow the extra year in any way benefits them.

But in the same way that experienced criminal clients can cause mischief with the system generally and with the defense lawyer specifically, it is often true that the experienced criminal client can assess his own case in a way that first time criminal clients cannot. Certainly, some people are not good at assessing risk and making decisions, but for some first time criminal clients, the element of imagination leaves them and they cannot envision a conviction following a trial happening. They can't recognize on their own that a guilty plea can be a good result. It brings a certainty to the very thing that they are desperate to avoid. In the end, it will be forced upon them, but they cannot see this. For them hope, even all wildly unreasonable hope, springs eternal.

Beyond all of this, two other factors can make criminal defense work especially difficult. One is the ironic desire to shape what the client tells the lawyer to make it as helpful as possible. This can get the lawyer into ethical trouble. The lawyer wants the client to describe something a certain way to fit a theory that the lawyer thinks he might be able to sell to a jury, but he knows he is not supposed to tell the client what to say when he knows it is not true. That would be suborning perjury if the client took the stand and gave concocted testimony to the lawyer's theory. Lawyers who say that they don't want to know the truth live in an ethically questionable and unrealistic world. The lawyer has to know, but in knowing there is the pull to shape the facts. Prudent lawyers deliver The Lecture to the client, aware that in following through on it danger lies. The Lecture gets its name from *Anatomy of a Murder* and has become a focal point of ethics classes in law school because it precisely identifies the line that the lawyer must not cross. Here's its description from our narrating defense lawyer Paul Biegler. "The Lecture is an ancient device that lawyers use to coach their clients so that the client won't quite know he has been coached and his lawyer can still preserve the face-saving illusion that he hasn't done any coaching. For coaching clients, like robbing them, is not only frowned upon, it is downright unethical and bad, very bad. Hence The Lecture, an artful device as old as the law itself, and one used constantly by some of the nicest and most ethical lawyers in the land. 'Who me? I didn't tell him what to say,' the lawyer can later comfort himself. 'I merely explained the law, see.' It is a good practice to scowl and shrug here and add virtuously: 'That's my duty, isn't it?'"

For the lawyer tired of losing and wanting to help his client as much as he can, The Lecture is a tempting way to increase the chances of a better result. Yet it is the lawyer who pays the price for giving The Lecture or even for thinking about giving it. Life would be easier, as it is for English barristers, if the lawyer never had to sort his way through such ethical mazes.

The second factor springs wholly from the *noir* of lawyering. There is something, sometimes hard to define or describe, that draws some lawyers to criminal defense work. One take is that criminal defense lawyers have, or want to have, something in common with their clients. The phenomenon has made its way into fiction. Novelist Steve Martini has his criminal defense lawyer character Paul Mondriani in *Compelling Evidence* explain that some lawyers have a taste for what he calls "felonious voyeurism," though it is not confined to criminal defense lawyers or even to lawyers. Mondriani explains that "[i]t happens. Lawyers, judges, cops, and jurors all find themselves titillated from time to time by the stories of violence, drugs, and sex. The criminal side of the law provides a window on the dark side of life that exists nowhere else." Scott Turow makes the more direct link between the criminal defense lawyer and the client's life as a criminal. "There are certain defense lawyers," Judge Sonia Klonsky as narrator tells us in the novel *The Laws of Our Fathers* "who become rogues with their clients, enjoying a commando existence, striking from the borderland beyond the rules. It's the one part of their job I knew I could never handle." In my non-fictional world I have never had any interest in felonious voyeurism or in a commando existence, but I know dozens of criminal defense lawyers to whom the phrases would apply. You know these lawyers have a problem because they like to explain over lunch and the like what the client *should* have done not to get caught. They cannot betray that they have spent some time thinking about what they as a criminal could do knowing the law as they do.

Two truths about criminal defense lawyers: The first is that there is not much variance between the way they are portrayed in fiction and on the screen, whether big or small, and the way they are in the wild. This is not a criticism, just the truth, generally speaking, of course. The second is that the swagger and willingness to brawl that criminal defense lawyers project in the courtroom is a function of what the client wants to see. No matter the odds, the client wants to see his lawyer as a fighter. But there is also probably a third truth, which is that the criminal defense lawyer assumes his pose to help him get through it all, partly because he has closed ranks with his clients and partly because such a pose is a hedge against the difficulty of the job and the near constant defeat that the lawyer faces. It's a tough job.

DISCOVERY WARS

It is hard to know when everything in the world of discovery changed and became so contentious; when it became so like a battlefield on which lawyers who thought themselves Rambo warriors fought whenever they could—which was always—to harass and wear down the other side, with that other side doing the same thing back again. We can't point with the precision of Virginia Woolf when she wrote that human character changed on or about December 1910. Though, to be fair to Woolf, she chose the date arbitrarily because the change had not been definite and sudden. We can say the same about the changing attitude toward discovery and note that by the end of the 1980s, organized resistance to the changes was showing up in conferences and court-sponsored studies. Sometimes discovery would be a topic entire, though often it was part of a larger interest in civility, as in the Seventh Circuit 1991 Interim Report of The Committee on Civility study.

Interrogatories, requests for productions, requests for admissions—these are all durable horses rode in discovery. Depositions are sufficiently unique in the discovery stable to demand an essay of their own on their uses and abuses. No matter what the type of discovery, though, in the beginning it was not thought that any of the discovery tools posed a threat to litigants or to the system as a whole when used. So much for that.

Discovery rules, when the Federal Rules of Civil Procedure were adopted in 1938, rested on different premises from today's rules. It was thought then that more was better and that courts would not need to get involved in the discovery process because it would be self-regulating in a fashion. Lawyers, the theory went, would have no reason to ask for too much or to avoid providing information because to do either would take too much time and cost the client too much money. Whatever center there might have been, it could not hold itself against what have been dubbed The Aggressor, for seeking too much, and The Grand Obstructor for, well, obstructing.

Most commentators see the chain of events leading to the discovery wars as beginning with the rise of the corporation in the 1970s. This led to large law firms (relatively speaking) adopting the new billing model of billing hours and to the increase in the size and number of large law firms serving the corporations that had also grown in size and number. With the reason for fighting in place—the billable hour—the wars began in earnest. Then the amendments to the federal rules in 1984 changed the philosophy of discovery and imposed limits. The goal in part was to avoid redundancy, and what was described as disproportionality, as in big discovery did not fit with small cases. Later amendments continued with the streamlining approach. But even with the rules tightening discovery, claims of abuse persisted. Those claiming that discovery abuse was more a myth than a fact pointed to studies indicating that discovery usage had not changed over the decades, so that it was still the case that in half of the federal civil cases there was little or no discovery. Those claiming abuse said that this was the wrong measurement and that the abuse lay not in the number, even including the number of instances in which judges had to settle discovery disputes, but in the tenacious positions each side was taking about pushing the limits on requests and on resistance. It didn't even help much when more information had to be mandatorily disclosed. Despite this requirement, parties (by way of their crafty lawyers) found ways not to yield, at least not completely, keeping tensions high.

Aggressors continued to do what they have always done. Their document production requests seemed to have no limit and no goal but to fish. Those responding to requests continued to act as vandals of what they produced. Acting more like children than adults, some pushed the rules to their outer edge and frequently crossed into sanctionable territory. Producing documents on red, difficult to read paper to limit further reproduction is just one example, while infusing the documents with a noxious odor to truly heighten the reviewing experience is another. Both are from the same case.

There are more classic moves that the Grand Obstructor can use. Popular ones include not responding on time, not responding completely, claiming an inability to understand the very words of the interrogatory, claiming non-existent privileges, providing the vaguest of answers, using boiler-plate responses for everything, and, of course, claiming that the requested information could not lead to discoverable information. On the production side, a favorite is claiming that the documents are not in the party's possession or that it would be unduly burdensome to have to produce them. Each side, putting it differently, would give as good as it got.

The promise that had been held out by e-discovery was quickly dashed. It just meant even more information was fair game. The goal of using the technology that should have brought more efficiency failed and instead more billable hours were needed to sort through it all, especially when the produced digital files could be manipulated to be essentially orderless. The e-discovery dance thus began. Invariably, e-discovery requests were followed by claims that the data was not reasonably accessible, which put the burden back on the requestor to show good cause. Both sides all the while angled to make the other side pick up the tab. As courts do, the response was to set up a multi-factor test to sort out the good cause element. Some judges said that the multi-factor test did not add much, and relied instead on a smell test. Either way, e-discovery drew the court into the process, a result not anticipated at the beginning in 1938.

There have been a variety of proposed fixes. Do away with interrogatories in light of mandatory disclosure, impose heavier sanctions, and get the courts more involved from the beginning are three. The proposal-turned-new-rule about mandatory "meet and confer" meetings before the discovery war starts, either surprisingly or not surprisingly depending on your level of cynicism, did not solve discovery problems as expected.

A cynic might even say that the combatants want to keep on fighting. Why this might be true is found in the operative dynamics of the world of big litigation. One dynamic is that almost no cases go to trial and are instead settled. Another is that big law firms are famous for, even defined by, their over-preparation in litigation. And the third is that all of the over-preparation—the overly zealous seeking and resisting of information—is paid for by large corporations and almost always on an hourly basis. Big firms work against themselves if they do anything but take the over-zealous path.

Tales of abuse as they make their way into the law reports prompt commentary and scholarly investigation. The argument about whether there is discovery abuse has been fought, though, by academics, not litigators.

Litigators themselves may complain about thuggish tactics, but when the statement in question from the Federal Judicial Center to the litigators was whether they thought there was discovery abuse in almost every case, the statement got more disagreement responses than agreement responses. That is at least what the Federal Judicial Center determined in a very recent survey. Why, we have to wonder, do the lawyers not see the same problems with discovery that the academics do? We just need look to the underlying dynamics to find the answer. Both sides, and by sides I mean the sides of lawyers, profit from discovery, making their complaints more token than anything else. The war must go on.

"Discovery is antics with semantics," Mark Herrmann, one observer of the discovery wars, writes in *The Curmudgeon's Guide to Practicing Law*. These antics can be amusing to read about, though they are frequently equally dispiriting. An inquiry into the behavior of lawyers in discovery cannot end with only descriptions of what lawyers in discovery combat do. Why they act as they do must be considered. After all, bad manners, discovery abuse, and unethical conduct are not accidental. We know that much of what goes on happens for strategic purposes, such as delay, or to simply frustrate the other side into giving in. Why lawyers can feel justified in taking these approaches is perhaps the most interesting question. Wanting to win is too simple an explanation. The better answer comes from a sensibility about themselves in relation to the profession that frees them from responsibility and justifies all.

The American Bar Association's 1998 Task Force on *Ethics: Beyond the Rules* went to big firm lawyers and asked them the probing questions of what goes on in discovery and why they do what they do. One general conclusion as set out by Robert Gordon in his 2003 law review article "The Ethical Worlds of Large-Firm Litigators" is that the lawyers give themselves room for mischief through definition. They will define for themselves what constitutes unethical conduct or misconduct. This makes it hard to go wrong if you get to determine what is wrong. No pesky external professional standard to consider. If you think it is acceptable, then it is acceptable. So long as rules are not violated, anything goes. Gone is the area short of a rule that would ordinarily be governed by ethics. "You stay within the rules," one respondent noted. "To the extent that it's within the rules, you have a duty to do everything you can for your client's interest." For this lawyer, when it comes to discovery requests, lying is frowned upon, but anything short of that is just "aggressive" and therefore is acceptable. This leads to the conclusion, we learn from other respondents, that there is nothing wrong with making your opponent work for his discovery, which translated means that it is acceptable to throw up all the roadblocks of the obstructionists.

This sensibility justifying everything has one additional component. It turns out, according to these big firm litigators, that when there is a discovery dispute or conduct that gums up the system, it is always the fault of the other side, especially if the other side is not made up of big firm lawyers. It is hard to see how anything can change with these lawyers as long as they can see a problem only when it involves someone else.

DISSECTING THE PROFESSION

How do we sort through the more than one million lawyers to find some useful organizing principles? We could follow the lead of the young associate in Kermit Roosevelt's *In the Shadow of the Law* who links physical traits to the work the lawyers in his firm do: "the solid litigators, big in the shoulders and the belly; the corporate types, who had only the belly; the tax attorneys, rail thin and burning with intellect." This is an appealing but incomplete option. We could divide the world—not evenly I suspect—into jerks and non-jerks, but that's not nearly enough division when it comes to personality. Joseph Addison, in his *Spectator* essay No. 21, "Divinity, Law, and Physic Overburdened with Practitioners," could look at the legal profession in 18th-century England and divide it into two groups, the litigious and the peaceable. The litigious are those who are carried down to Westminster-hall in coachfuls every morning in term time, where they hire out their words and anger, allowing "their client a quantity of wrath proportional to the fee which they receive from him." Peaceable lawyers, on the other hand, remain at their inns of court and "seem to be the dignitaries of the law endowed with those qualifications of mind that accomplish a man rather for a ruler than a pleader." We could take this lead and divide American lawyers into litigators and office lawyers, noting along the way that Addison's described relationship between a lawyer's wrath and the price paid for it remains true today. But while Addison's division is useful, it is not sufficient for our purposes. We need to look instead to the profession in action.

The American Bar Association comes out with a comprehensive statistical analysis of the profession at five-year increments. Its only problem is that it always lags behind a bit, so that the most recent analysis is pegged to 2005. Of the approximately one million lawyers, three-fourths make up the group we are most interested in, private practitioners. Of this number, not quite fifty percent (49 percent) work as solo practitioners. This number

71

has changed little since 1970, and we need to go to 1960 to see the number not quite reach two-thirds (64 percent). Going beyond solo practitioners, 28 percent work in firms ranging in size from two to five lawyers. Two-lawyer firms are the most popular within this subgroup at 12 percent. We find big changes in the percentage of lawyers working in firms with more than one hundred lawyers. Once we exclude the percentage of solo practitioners in our group of private practitioners, a full one-third work in these large firms, exceeding by five percentage points the numbers working in two-to-five-lawyer firms.

We need to turn to other sources for deeper levels of analyses of the profession. Two in particular are studies of Chicago lawyers. John Heinz and Edward Laumann first studied Chicago lawyers and reported their findings from a 1975 survey in *Chicago Lawyers: The Social Structure of the Bar (1982)*. In 1995 they and additional co-authors Robert L. Nelson and Rebecca L. Sandefur conducted a second survey of Chicago lawyers and published the results in 2005 in *Urban Lawyers: The New Social Structure of the Bar*. For both studies, nearly one thousand Chicago lawyers, ranging from solo practitioners to lawyers from large firms, were given detailed questionnaires and/or interviewed. The surveys produced astonishing amounts of information and provide unique insights into who the lawyers are, where they come from, where they work, and what they do, just as a starter. We get closer to understanding the profession in action from reading these surveys than we do from reading anything else.

There is a relationship between legal education and particular practice settings. The Chicago researchers used the accepted division of law schools into four groups (the labels given them by the Chicago researchers of elite, prestige, regional, and local correspond to the better known labels of first, second, third, and fourth tier schools) and determined which percentage of graduates of each group worked as solo practitioners or for firms ranging in size from 2–9 lawyers, 10–30, 31–99, and more than 100. Anything larger than one hundred lawyers we now call Big Law. For the 1995 study, the categories of firms with 100–299 lawyers and firms with more than 300 lawyers were added. The usual suspects made up the various tiers of law schools, so that the University of Chicago would be an elite school, for example, Northwestern a prestige school. In 1995, 10 percent of solo practitioners were elite law school graduates, 8 percent prestige school graduates, 25 percent regional school graduates, and 58 percent local school graduates. Turned around, for firms with more than 300 lawyers, 30 percent of the lawyers came from elite schools and 24 percent from prestige schools. Local schools accounted for only 17 percent of the lawyers.

In both the 1975 and 1995 surveys, the work done by Big Law firms was considered the most prestigious. Large corporate work led the way in the cluster of fields, with anti-trust work within the cluster coming in as the most prestigious, followed in this cluster by patent work and then by securities, banking, general corporate, business litigation, and commercial work. The next most prestigious cluster, which includes business litigation, business real estate, and insurance defense work, went primarily to large firms. Small firms, perhaps not unexpectedly, worked mostly in the areas of general litigation, criminal defense, plaintiff personal injury, personal real estate, probate, and general family law. Changing the inquiry a bit and looking at the respective intellectual challenge that these various areas presented to their practitioners, the responses to the 1975 and 1995 surveys indicated a near direct correlation between the intellectual challenge rankings of different fields and the prestige rankings of those fields. Securities work comes in first and general family practice comes in last. Criminal defense and personal injury are near the bottom and trademark and copyright, anti-trust, and corporate civil litigation near the top.

The easy translation for these various statistics about type of practice, practice prestige rating, and practice setting is that, on the one hand, the most respected work by survey respondents is done for corporate clients and that corporate clients bring their work to big firms. On the other hand, the least respected work was for individual clients and that these clients went to small firms or solo practitioners. More than anything else, then, the profession's landscape has boundaries marked primarily by types of clients and the practice settings they go to. The statistics correspond to our general perception of how the profession is organized. Researchers since 1975 have used the term "two hemispheres" to describe the profession's composition. In the strict sense of the two hemispheres definition, the profession is divided between lawyers who represent corporations or other large entities and those lawyers representing individuals. The statistical information from the 1975 and 1995 surveys allows us to go a further step and note that client distinctions translate into practice setting distinctions. Put differently, large corporation-type clients are represented by large law firms, while individuals are represented by small firms and solo practitioners. The two hemisphere description means that Big Law lawyers are half-right in saying that what they do is a world away from what solo practitioners or lawyers in small firms do.

The problem for lawyers, if you can call it that, is that they do not get much of a chance to choose their clients. Certainly, there is nothing to keep Microsoft from going to a solo practitioner to handle its anti-trust work, but it is obvious on its face why this doesn't happen. If anything, if lawyers have a choice to make when it comes to clients, it is with their practice setting, whether big firm, small firm, or going solo. But this choice is more theoretical than actual for many lawyers because where they end up in their practice settings has everything to do with where they went to law school or how well they did in law school. Big Law hires primarily from first tier schools, making it much less of an option for a fourth tier graduate. All the statistical information from both the 1975 and the 1995 surveys supports this. The only oddity is that some first tier graduates choose not to work for Big Law but for themselves as solo practitioners. This was true for 12 percent of the elite law school graduates responding to the 1975 survey and 10 percent to the 1995 survey. In contrast, 7 percent of fourth tier graduates responding to the 1975 survey worked for Big Law and 17 percent in 1995.

The question contained within the mass of information about practice setting, types of work, types of clients, and prestige is whether there is one profession or many subparts to the profession such that they qualify as autonomous parts of that profession. To be more direct, the question is whether a solo practitioner or a lawyer working in a small firm can live as greatly in the law as the lawyer working in Big Law handling its "prestigious" kind of work. The answer would, of course, be no if prestige was all that mattered. A solo practitioner's desire to handle Microsoft's anti-trust work would not be enough to make to it happen, keeping him from that kind of work. Luckily, though, all does not turn on prestige and particular kinds of clients and particular kinds of work. The reassuring news is that, within limits, lawyers make of their case, whatever the type, what they want to make of it. Even complexity isn't a useful measure. Big litigation between two large corporations isn't, in theory at least, different from litigation between small businesses or even between individuals. More of something does not make the something more complex, more exotic, or more difficult.

The practice of law, as it is played out every day and with every case, is what the lawyer makes of it. That is the good news for lawyers thinking that some artificial limit relating to clients and professional challenges has been placed on them. If the question, as Karl Llewellyn put it in *The Bramble Bush* in 1930, is what the law can offer you, the first answer is that "it all depends on what you want out of law." Then, shining a light on what is possible, he writes, "[t]hat turns, in turn, on what you want out of life."

DON'T POOH-POOH THE PROFESSION

An essential challenge to the legal profession came not recently but nearly one hundred years ago, and it came not from an American but from an Englishman, A.A. Milne, who is well known not as a commentator on the legal profession but as the author of books about the teddy bear Winnie-the-Pooh. Pooh, though, did not make the case against the profession. Instead, Milne did in his essay "On Learned Friends" from his 1920 collection *Not That It Matters*. A witty and engaging personal essayist, Milne, like others practicing his craft, often looked to slices of life that can cut with sharp edges and irritate us. He asks the question of why barristers (and society) think of law as a profession and argues that, because their interests are with their individual clients alone and come at the expense of the public good, the law does not meet the qualifications of a profession. A century later, Milne's essay prompts us to consider and reject the idea advanced by zealous advocacy proponents that a lawyer serves the public interest by serving the interests of clients one at a time, no holds barred.

Milne does not explain, wittily or otherwise, what prompted his assault on barristers and their profession. He takes it as a given that barristers should be scrutinized about their fidelity to the principles of a profession and jauntily assumes the risk his essay creates of alienating members of a profession he like anyone else might have need of in the future. But it is with an ostensibly light touch and the occasional joke that he poses challenging questions.

Milne asks from two points of view what we can expect from a profession. The professional, he answers, can expect the chance to earn a living and the chance to work at something interesting. Equally important, a noble profession such as law gives its members "the opportunity of working for some other end than [their] own advancement." This is good for both society and the professionals, and society, as the second point of view, is entitled to complain when the opportunity given is not taken. Artists, educators, and

77

doctors can all let the public down if the artist chooses money over truth, the educator "drops all his theories of education and conforms hastily to those of his employers," and the doctor "neglects research and cultivates instead a bedside manner." It is all a matter of choice. "[T]he light is still there for those who look."

Part of essay's power comes from Milne's personal involvement and challenge. He writes that he wants to know what the barrister is after. He challenges barristers to look inward. He writes, "[i]n the quiet hours when we are alone with ourselves and there is nobody to tell us what fine fellows we are, we come sometimes upon a weak moment in which we wonder, not how much money we are earning, nor how famous we are becoming, but what good we are doing." Good comes in the form of advancing the administration of justice. The barrister, Milne writes, "must be able to tell himself that the more expert he becomes as an advocate, the better he will be able to help [in the administration] of justice." On this score he finds that barristers are not engaged in good work. They are instead interested only in themselves. He imagines that "[t]he whole teaching of the Bar is that [the barrister] not bother about justice, but only about his own victory."

The only problem with Milne's analysis is the he was apparently unfamiliar with an advocate's obligations to the court. Milne's essay mistakenly assumes that a barrister fails to fulfill his public obligation through the act of taking on the cause of the client, an act that marks him as being indifferent to any applicable social interest. But this is not so. What Milne in 1920 did not understand and nowhere points to in his essay is that the good lawyer, in addition to his loyalty to his client, owes and acts on a professional loyalty to the court. Barristers in Milne's time (and, of course, today also) adhered to a rigid code of obligations for truthfulness and candor to the court. Their clients' causes aside, barristers were relied upon by the court (as they are today as well) to facilitate the judicial process. If Milne had better understood this, he would not have doomed the barristers of his time to selfishness.

But while Milne's barristers deserved a far better shake from him, Milne nonetheless points us in the right direction in assessing contemporary lawyers. We hear the same complaints today that Milne describes about lawyers putting the interests of their clients above all other interests. One persistent complaint comes in the form of a question: "How can you defend those people?" Other complaints go well beyond Milne's portfolio and are best expressed as accusations by the public that lawyers make too much money, that they care only about themselves, and that they will say and do anything to win cases and make money. This last in particular has helped give the image of lawyers its patina of sleaze.

These complaints, which have their roots in Milne's core complaint, have special significance here because lawyers seem to struggle with their obligations to the court, either not fulfilling them or going further and arguing against their existence with the position that a lawyer's loyalty and other obligations are to the client alone. This by itself, they would argue, contributes to the public good.

These lawyers—these zealots—would point to *Polk County v. Dodson* of 1981, in which the High Court noted that the public's interest in truth and fairness is advanced by defense lawyers advancing the undivided interests of their clients. They would also point to commentators such as Monroe Freedman in his article "In Praise of Overzealous Representation" and former U.S. District Judge Charles Wyzanski from two generations past in *Whereas—A Judge's Premises* who argued that, in the right circumstances, lawyers have license to tell falsehoods to the court or to mislead it. The problem with that argument is that the Supreme Court has never said that loyalty to a client's interests means that anything goes. That is a leap too far.

The fair administration of justice is a collaborative enterprise in which lawyers are almost as important as judges. The lawyer—the good lawyer— properly performing his role pushes an argument as far as the facts and law will take it, but no further. Neither the facts nor the law can be misstated or slanted. The good lawyer cannot be guilty of, to paraphrase Emily Dickinson, telling all the truth but telling it slant. Moreover, the good lawyer will present arguments in their most palatable form. Fair argument is not just for the courtroom; it is for briefs as well. The good lawyer can be trusted. He can be believed. The judge can rely on what the good lawyer writes and argues. And, of course, the good lawyer in his examinations does not mislead the hostile witness, lead the friendly witness, or ever abuse a witness of any stripe. Questions are always supported by the facts. Outside the courtroom, the good lawyer honors the purpose and rules of discovery.

Documents and witnesses do not go missing. Deadlines are met, and, above all, witnesses at depositions are treated civilly and with respect. Rambo, go home. Lastly, the good lawyer gives advice that is in the client's—not the lawyer's—best interests. Discretion is indeed the better part of valor and advice not to litigate does not mark a lawyer as weak.

Lawyers are too often led to believe by peers or by the public that, since lawsuits are contests, all is fair. Lawyers seem to be staggeringly unaware that lawyering comes with limitations. It's in working within those limitations that the legitimate fun can be had, fun that comes from participating in the whole, not just a particular side.

It is too bad that Milne was not more aware of what barristers actually do in their work. He would have been able to see easily how a barrister's collaboration in the administration of justice serves the public good. It is an oddity that his complaints about members of the legal profession have more application today than they did in his own time. Luckily, though, we have his essay.

Milne asks all the right questions about the nature of a profession. He knows as well that, as with the barrister in the quiet of his study asking himself about the good he is doing, what lawyers make of their profession is a personal choice. We can only hope that each lawyer will have one of those conversations with himself and make the right personal choice.

The profession has a steep challenge. It has to push lawyers to recognize and then act on their obligations to the court that are separate from their obligations to clients. But it then has to educate the public to respect lawyers more than it does now for their role in the legal process. We need to stop slipping down the slope we are on to tribalism.

DRESSING FOR SUCCESS

Intended or not, lawyers deliver messages about themselves by the way they dress. That's certainly what the nation thought when Archibald Cox, sporting a bow tie well out of fashion, served as a special prosecutor in the early 1970s. When his brush crewcut and half-glasses were added, the whole look projected the sensibility of the Old Yankee distinguished by his probity. Shakespeare got it right when he wrote that, "apparel oft proclaims the man." Just look at the state court practitioner who sins first with slacks and a sports coat and then sins again with checks and stripes, often fighting each other in the same ensemble.

The costumes that our players wear in our drama called the law are not as important to that drama as they are in England. There they have barrister robes, silly wigs for both judge and barristers, and those robes for the judges that late Chief Justice Rehnquist, known more today for his whimsical decision to add three gold bars to his robe than anything else, would have surely endorsed. Judicial robes in America, even without the gold bars, have particular meaning and strengthen the idea that what we wear matters. As Chief Justice William Howard Taft once put it in a volume of collected speeches, *Modern Day Problems*, "judges should be clothed in robes, not only that those who witness the administration of justice should be properly advised that the function performed is one different from, and higher than that which a man discharges as a citizen in the ordinary walks of life, but also, in order to impress the judge himself with constant consciousness that he is a high-priest in the temple of justice."

There can be an advantage to an even garish sartorial display, as when the boldness of an argument is matched only by the boldness of the lawyer's outfit. We learn in the wonderful *Yale Biographical Dictionary of American Law* that Hayden Covington, known as a flamboyant performer, argued the important Second Flag Salute case before the Supreme Court in 1943 wearing a vibrant green suit and resplendent red plaid tie. We're told that

81

he was truculent and eloquent, with an almost sublime disregard of consequences. Only with such an attitude would he be able to not worry about the fashion police taking him in. Perhaps he needed the jolt he got from a mirror to be able to argue hyperbolically that the case he was asking the Court to reverse, the First Flag Salute case from just two years earlier, was "one of the greatest mistakes that this Court has ever committed," rivaled in magnitude only by the Dred Scott case.

Dressing for success has been the subject of countless bar journal articles. Some articles give advice to new lawyers on law firm dress codes, paying attention to East coast, West coast, and Midwestern style sensibilities. Many address the problems women face both in the office and in the courtroom of being accepted as equals but not dressing as clones of men. How women dress for court has even produced off-the-bench judicial commentary from both male and female judges. To date there have been no easy answers. Sloppily or too casually dressed men have also made impressions on judges in their secondary roles as fashion police, none to the good. Putting aside allowances reflected in clothing choices for weather that is too hot or too cold, the basic rule seems to be, especially on the federal side, that a courtroom is a serious place and that the lawyers, both men and women, should dress accordingly. Purpose rather than personality should dominate.

In dressing to impress, lawyers have options that only begin with the suit. Statements are made by way of watches, shoes, cufflinks, scarves, handkerchiefs, glasses. Briefcases also count, though strictly speaking they are not worn. Tom Wolfe in *Bonfire of the Vanities* can rely just on accessories to capture the élan of a young master-of-the-universe lawyer: "[h]e was wearing a covert-cloth Chesterfield topcoat with a golden brown velvet collar and carrying one of those burgundy leather attache cases that come from Madler or T. Anthony on Park Avenue and have a buttery smoothness that announces: 'It cost $500.'" Five hundred 1986 dollars, that is. Sherman McCoy, Wolfe's master-of-the-universe stockbroker character searching for a criminal lawyer to help him out of his hit-and-run mess, of course knows his clothes. The clothes and location that Sherman must endure signal how far he has fallen from Wall Street and Park Avenue when he finds his man, Tom Killian, in New York's legal profession's underbelly. We read that Killian "wore a double-breasted navy-blue suit with a pale blue overplaid and a striped shirt with a stiff white collar. The collar had an exaggerated spread, very much a sharpie's look, to Sherman's way of thinking." The prosecutor assigned to Sherman's case, to continue the sartorial theme in the novel and in the case, burns with a fire to take some social standing revenge. He's perfectly accoutered for the job, with "his dirty raincoat, his old gray suit, which was too short in the pants, his Nike sneakers, [and] his A&P shopping bag" for the commute to work.

Descriptions of sartorial elegance can go beyond character definition and be worth reading just for their images. Louis Auchincloss, of a white shoe Wall Street legal world that began dying in the 1970s, has a wonderful description of one such lawyer in his short story "Power of Suggestion" in his collection *Powers of Attorney*. He writes that the lawyer, "so smooth and big in the dark blue, almost black suit that fell, creaseless, from his broad shoulders to his thin ankles." That's drapery that the rest of us can only aspire to. Some fashion sensitive lawyer novelists even provide characters with sartorial fetishes in fabrics and design that rival Patrick Bateman's business card fetish in *American Psycho*, giving new meaning to "clothes to die for."

High-end labels are thought to impress the most, so not surprisingly in novels by and about lawyers we find descriptions of Chanel skirts and Armani suits. Novelists certainly use what a lawyer wears to emphasize the larger point of personality. Sheldon Siegel does this in *Special Circumstances* when he describes an unbearably patrician District Attorney, Skipper Gates. "At fifty-eight, his tanned face is chiseled out of solid rock, with a Roman nose, high forehead, and graceful mane of silver hair. His charcoal-gray double breasted Brioni suit, Egyptian-cotton white shirt and striped tie add dignity to his rugged features. He looks like he is ready to assume his rightful place on Mount Rushmore next to George Washington."

Women can similarly impress with their put-together presence. In Sabin Willet's *The Deal* we find a description of a lawyer known as Seven Fifty because of her hourly rate (in 1996) who can really make an entrance into a room to dominate a meeting and close a deal. "Seven fifty, and a knockout, Elizabeth Russell, who had recently made partner at Fletcher, Daye & Symmes, represented the buyer. She was the only person in the room who looked fresh. A striking woman, tall and slim, with thick dark hair pulled back in a ribbon and skin lightly tanned, she usually did. On this particular morning she arrived perfectly coiffed, wearing a blue suit of fine wool. About her throat was an Hermès scarf. Her eyes were a riveting pale blue, wide and penetrating."

The profession has been tough on women and what they can wear. No matter how you cut it—or tailor it—the profession wants women to dress in the style of men. Understandably, this does not suit some women. In Lisa Scottoline's *Everywhere That Mary Went*, her Mary DiNunzio bristles at the thought that she must dress to impress the masculine law. "I'm wearing my navy-blue Man Suit," she writes about one court appearance. "It's perfect for that special occasion when a girl wants to look like a man, like in court or at the auto mechanic's."

In paging through the catalog of lawyers in arms we realize that it is too easy to read too much into the impression created by clothes. I would suggest that it is just a quirk that David Boies wears off-the-rack polyester suits from Sears or Macy's and sneakers in court. He is, after all, the same man who wins and loses big in Las Vegas and who flies in private jets, according to the entry on him in *The Yale Biographical Dictionary of American Law*. But for me, there has been a truth about looking the part. Though I practice by myself, I sometimes end up in court or in conference rooms of very large law firms both checking out and being checked out by my competition. I'll accept the jury's guilty verdict on my shallowness and admit that I feel more comfortable at the table because I have tastes that run to extravagantly expensive suits. Very conservative, but very expensive.

I thought in the beginning of my career, before I could afford what I really wanted, that a good suit and a sturdy prose style would allow me to go anywhere and do anything. I'm sure that other lawyers don't care much about my prose style, but about the suits they care. I draw the line at cuff links and expensive shirts, though. It's the suit that matters. My message? "I'm here. Deal with me."

FEDERAL REPORTER, THIRD SERIES

A single volume of the *Federal Reporter*, Third Series is by itself impressively handsome, with its tan buckram covers and gold-bordered red, black, and tan spine and its phonebook heft size. Hundreds of them neatly arranged on shelves go further and make quite a statement. As perhaps an unintended consequence, the move to the digital version of the series has meant that we do not have many opportunities these days—in libraries or elsewhere—to get the full effect of seeing bookcases covering entire walls filled with the 300 volumes of the first series (1880–1924), the 999 volumes of the second series (1924–1994), and the more than 700 volumes of the ever-increasing third series (1994–present). We feel when we see those shelves the weight of the law, gravitas bound, so to speak. Before the hardbound copies disappear completely, we should take a closer look and describe the *Federal Reporter*, Third Series as the law books—the books of the law—that they are. Looking through a recent few years' worth of the *Federal Reporter*, Third Series (some 200 volumes) can tell us much about the law as it is being decided in the federal courts and how it is being written.

Each volume of the *Federal Reporter*, Third Series runs to not quite 1,400 pages, not including the front matter. The front matter contains the topics and entries in the digest system for that one volume; a listing of all the circuit judges; cross-referencing material for the various statutes mentioned in the opinions; and an index, circuit by circuit, of the opinions found within and their page numbers. Every ten volumes or so, West reproduces a tribute or memoriam to a circuit judge and marks the inclusion with a reference to it on the volume's spine. Each volume on average contains 135 cases from the various circuits. West publishes approximately thirty-five volumes per year, or approximately five thousand cases. This number is but a small fraction of all the cases decided by the circuits around the country. To each opinion West adds its digest apparatus, setting out the digest notes in the beginning and then cross-referencing them numerically within the opinion itself for easy use. Each volume reflects the extraordinary jurisdictional range of the federal appellate courts. The cases invoking the diversity jurisdiction of the federal courts are often the most interesting, especially the surprisingly large number presenting classic types of common law issues.

There are oddities and curiosities to be found. There's the patent case in which Richard Posner, sitting by designation on the Federal Circuit Court of Appeals, writes an opinion on sexual devices. We know we are in for some fun when Posner begins by writing that "both firms produce what the parties call 'sex aids' but are colloquially referred to as 'sex toys.' A more perspicuous term is 'sexual devices,' by analogy to 'medical devices.' The analogy lies in the fact that, like many medical devices (thermometers for example), what we are calling sexual devices are intended to be inserted into bodily orifices, albeit for a different purpose." The devices, for the curious, "are generally in the shape of rods of various curvatures and are made out of rubber, plastic, glass, or some combination of these materials."

We encounter a lawyer by the name of Frankenstein—nicely put together, I'm sure--arguing an appeal. In another case, the esteemed former federal circuit judge and former White House Counsel Abner Mikva is himself arguing an appeal on behalf of a legal aid clinic. And back to a sexual theme, we find an opinion discussing the qualifications of an expert to opine on veins in erect penises based on the physician's experience in examining fifteen thousand penises in his work as a specialist in erectile dysfunction.

Another oddity is running across appeals in criminal cases in which lawyers as defendants are appealing their own convictions. One lawyer-gone-bad case involves a high-profile defense attorney and former federal prosecutor convicted of leading an extensive criminal enterprise. In another, a lawyer has been convicted of obstruction of justice relating to her defense of a client charged in a criminal enterprise with importing large amounts of cocaine into the United States.

And while few, if any, read the *Federal Reporter* for the photographs, there are more to be found than ever, often contributing greatly to the respective opinions in which they appear. In *Bloch v. Frischholz,* a case, for example, about Mezuzah-related issues, it makes sense for the reader to have a photograph of a Mezuzah to examine. The geographically inclined get perhaps the biggest return on their reading investment, with maps and especially

Google Earth images. And in Town of Barnstable, *Massachusetts v. Federal Aviation Administration,* a case involving Cape Wind Associates and its proposal for 130 wind turbines, each 440 feet tall, in a twenty-five-square mile area of Nantucket Sound (an area roughly the size of Manhattan island), the court follows its opening paragraph with an aerial photograph of all of Cape Cod with the area at issue marked, greatly helping the reader understand the scope of the proposed project.

The *Federal Reporter* also serves something of a journalistic function, joining an extensive tradition of journalism reporting on trials, though not so much from the perspective of trial as drama. Instead, we learn about how the lawyers and judges have been performing and behaving. The issues that the circuit courts are ruling on made their way to them from the district courts, and while a fair number of these cases did not make it all the way to trial, such as when the circuit court reviews a district court's ruling on a motion for summary judgment, what happens at trials provides most of what the circuit courts consider. Trials are public events in which, on the criminal side, we see the government in action. In reading the *Federal Reporter* we recognize that Assistant United States Attorneys do not always live up to their obligation to seek justice, not convictions. The judicial branch of government comes under its own scrutiny when the circuit courts review claims of bias or judicial misconduct. For bias claims, we get to be a spectator and see how judges run their courtrooms and conduct their trials. Judicial misconduct off the bench is also reported when the circuit courts publish opinions arising from complaints under 28 U.S.C. §351(b) and investigated by a circuit Judicial Council. The opinions detail the conduct at issue. An example is *In re* Complaint of Judicial Misconduct, 575 F.3d 279 (2009), in which the Ninth Circuit's Alex Kozinski was investigated and admonished for keeping pornography on his work computer.

We are also reminded by the volumes of the state's machinery of death in capital cases—nearly all of them habeas corpus cases from the states. In these death penalty cases we sometimes find opinions in which death itself is discussed and even described. These death penalty cases from state courts raising federal claims on a habeas corpus petition have opinions often describing—in chilling detail—how the murders at issue took place. And in the recent wave of litigation over the method of execution and whether the usual three-drug cocktail used in most states violates the Cruel and Unusual Punishment clause of the constitution, detailed descriptions are often provided as to how, minute by minute, a condemned prisoner is put to death. But more generally, the death penalty opinions are giving us, as we read them, the last words on a prisoner's life. We know, when we get to the end of the opinions and relief is denied, that in effect nothing more will be said or done and that a prisoner will be put to death. While, in theory, the Supreme Court can reverse the decision of the circuit court, it rarely does, making the circuit court the last word. The fact of state-sanctioned killing is put before us, all rather matter-of-factly, judging by the tone and cold dispatch of the opinions. Not an instance, to paraphrase Shakespeare, in which the word is well suited to the action. It is almost reassuring to read at the conclusion of an opinion affirming the denial of habeas relief in a death penalty case, "in so doing, we are mindful of the gravity of our decision."

The *Federal Reporter* carries the news from the front lines on both what is happening to the law and what is going on with the judges. We can see, for example, the consequences of a major United States Supreme Court decision in a case such as *United States v. Booker* by looking, after cases go through the trial courts, at what the circuit courts around the country do to give meaning to what the Supreme Court has decided. With *Booker*, years of pent-up frustration with the severity and rigidity of the USSG (United States Sentencing Guidelines) led to the idea that, with courts finally enjoying sentencing discretion if they decided to use it, major changes could take place in sentencing. Certainly many decisions suggest that many trial judges were keen to exercise discretion and that various courts of appeal affirmed their positions. Some circuit judges, on the other hand, saw what was happening and argued in their opinions against what was termed a "rear-guard assault" on the USSG.

The *Federal Reporter*, on this and all other issues, tells us how a number of circuit judges are making names for themselves. Until the recent appointment of Elena Kagen, it had been true since the appointment of William Rehnquist in 1971 that all of the Justices confirmed thereafter had served as circuit judges. In earlier times in our history, different paths to the High Court had been marked, such as the promotion to the Court from the position of Attorney General or Solicitor General. Now, with the emphasis on nominating judges with a circuit court track record, judges thinking themselves eligible for promotion are busy making those circuit records, both with decisions saying *yea* or *nay* and with the way they express themselves in their opinions. Some conservative judges seem to go out of their way to dissent when the majority takes a perceived liberal position. Some judges produce opinions that seem to be seeking attention because of their style. It is all on display in the *Federal Reporter*.

Opinions do allow judges to express themselves, whether they themselves write the distinguishing bits or entire opinion or whether they direct their clerks to add particular stylistic touches. Judges can use dramatic introductions, a sense of humor, wit, and literary allusions to bring their opinions to life. Dissenters can write with outrage, anger, or even fury to make their opposition clear. It might be a small audience reading the opinions, but they are being read—or will be read—if a judge has ambitions and hits the lottery with interest from an administration for a High Court vacancy.

As to the quality of opinions generally, it could well be that we will grow to see today's crop of high-end circuit judges as representing something of a golden age of judging. Richard Posner of the Seventh Circuit towers above all and is joined in an elite group by Frank Easterbrook, Michael Boudin, and Diane Wood, to name just four. As set out between the covers of the *Federal Reporter*, we can see if we look that there are more gifted circuit judges sitting today than at any time in our history. It is at this circuit court level, ironically, that the law is being written—not at the Supreme Court level.

FOOD FIGHTS MASQUERADING AS DEPOSITIONS

"The transcripts of depositions are often very ugly documents." This is a near throw-away line in a Seventh Circuit opinion about discovery abuses. The observation captures what every lawyer who has participated in a deposition knows to be true, in spades.

Depositions are a popular, if not the most popular, discovery tool—especially if popularity is measured not by number, but by the desire lawyers have to conduct them. Everyone makes money at depositions. It is always argued that depositions allow the examining party to probe the opponent's case by taking the measure of the witnesses expected to testify. The fact-finding effectiveness of depositions can be questioned in light of how grudgingly witnesses give up information and because other discovery tools, such as requests for admissions, are well suited for the task. The biggest problems with depositions is that their application is limited to impeachment, unless you are in California's Superior Court system, which gives depositions extra meaning by allowing lawyers to read from them at any time in the trial as direct evidence when the deposition testimony concerns a party. But California is the exception to the rule, making the effectiveness of depositions a fair question. But these are asides. In big litigation, the kind that almost never goes to trial, deposition work is what trial lawyers do.

The list of improper deposition conduct is well known and fairly short. It just depends on whether the lawyer in question is taking or defending the deposition. In the catalog we find repetitive questions, harassing questions, misleading questions, patronizing and belittling attitudes, insults, and gender specific insults. For those defending, the hot items are constant interruptions, groundless objections, signaling to the client as to how to answer, taking breaks to coach the witness, instructing the witness not to answer, speaking objections, and interpreting the question for the client. One court captured much of what went on in a deposition-gone-bad by pointing to what was phrased as combative and macho posturing of the lawyers. Perceptive and often amusing author Mark Herrmann in *The Curmudgeon's Guide to Practicing Law* writes that in discovery, "it's two-year-olds flinging mashed potatoes at each other. It's you and the sociopath, *mano a mano*."

How deeply ingrained this bad behavior is at depositions was hinted at when one Big Law lawyer, responding in an interview for the ABA's Task Force project *Ethics: Beyond the Rules* more or less freely admits that, while he is otherwise complaining about the other guys, he himself does what they do, but only to a lesser extent, of course. He explains deposition dynamics this way in Robert Gordon's *Fordham Law Review* article "The Ethical World of Large-Firm Litigators": "When you get warm, they throw up roadblocks, attack you personally . . . blow up, throw out some smoke, 'let's go talk to the judge, you're attacking the witnesses,' keep the questioner from getting comfortable. I do this to some extent, but as a matter of personal style I won't raise my voice or [attack] the adversary's integrity. . . Others feel very free to threaten sanctions, [engage in] high-pitched yelling . . . Others do it nicely, but continually go off the record, throw up roadblocks."

But to list specific tactics—and even to gloss them with descriptions such as combative and macho posturing—does not capture the often poisonous atmosphere of depositions. To throw clients who hate each other into the mix is to risk spontaneous combustion. We find mixtures of anger, hatred, and feral defensiveness, all when it should just be about information gathering in the style of trial witness examination. It is a sign of our "hardball litigation" times. We know such litigation tactics when we see them, but a good definition of this type of litigation is nonetheless useful. Judge Helen Wilson Neis, as part of the Federal Circuit's 1992 Tenth Annual Judicial Conference, tells us that "in hardball litigation, every request by the other side is opposed with paper, with briefs, and requests for argument, even a request for a two-day extension of time. Discovery requests are made deliberately ambiguous and sweeping and no matter what reply is made, there's a charge of non-compliance . . . If a minor motion is lost, there's a demand for sanctions for a frivolous pleading." Our subject, depositions, gets particular treatment. Judge Neis explains what is all too familiar, "[d]epositions are scheduled at inconvenient times and mail is sent by slow boat to shorten the other side's time to respond. At depositions, there are senseless objections, bickering and delay, and depositions are endless in numbers, whether there's anything under the next stone or not." "Many stones," she reminds us, "do not have to be turned over."

The reasons depositions become ill mannered and filled with anger are as obvious as the obstructive and improper tactics used by both sides. One is to grandstand for the client, to show what that hourly rate is going for. Another is that very hourly rate and the chance to increase the number of hours, further increasing the disproportionality between hours billed and actual work done and results achieved. The most obvious reason of all, since it accounts for so much of the ill manneredness, is to let the witness know that, as unpleasant as the deposition is, cross examination at trial will be even worse. To instill dread into the deposition witness at the thought of trial testimony is the object of the deposition exercise. It fits neatly into the well-established technique of making the other side want to give in just so that it no longer has to deal with its opposition tormentors. It is primitive, but exceedingly popular.

There are other tactics that tend toward the stylistic. A practice article in one practice publication lists a dozen such tricks, more, I suspect, to promote the author's cleverness as a trickster than to argue for the probity of his helpful hints on how to respond to those very tricks. He goes so far as to acknowledge that as a so-called senior lawyer, the described tricks are part of his repertoire. The examiner can use a long pause as part of his question in his hope that the witness will rush "to fill the silent void," so to speak. Another is to speed up the questioning when the opponent has assumed a bored stance at the plate. Yet another is to use a metaphorical stick to get the witness angry to throw him off stride. The CIA is unlikely to adopt any of these techniques now that waterboarding is officially frowned upon.

How to remedy what is wrong with depositions has brought many suggestions. The naive approach is to think that it always takes two to make an ugly deposition and that holding your tongue will be enough. Lawyers are advised that if they respond calmly to all the bad behavior and nuttiness from the other side that the offending lawyers will be shamed into behaving themselves. The essential problem is that the misbehaving party misbehaves because the other lawyer in this no-man's land is powerless to stop him. There have long been calls for the judiciary to become more involved as umpires. The problem here is that lawyers do not want to be perceived as running off to an adult to solve their problems. The adults get annoyed when forced to intervene. Lawyers know that judges do not like getting involved in such disputes, for a variety of reasons. "No judge wants to spend more time on discovery," one judge is quoted as part of the ABA's Task Force *Ethics: Beyond the Rules.* Another judge noted that, "discovery disputes are a nuisance. If a lawyer seeking to compel seeks sanctions, there's litigation within litigation, cross-motions for sanctions. We judges have different interests; we want to get to the truth. We want to resolve cases on the merits. If we award sanctions, we are saying, let's keep the pettifogging game going."

A cynic might argue that litigators don't push hard for deposition reform because they take advantage and abuse the process as often as they are abused by it. It's all part of the game. If the test were changed from finding an honest man to finding a lawyer who hasn't used some of the blatant or even stylistic tricks at a deposition, Diogenes at a bar association meeting would have a hard time finding a lawyer who qualifies. Few are more sinned against than sinning. There is also that element of performance art to consider—the lawyer inflamed and the lawyer as punisher and all that. It plays well for the client. And those billable hours, especially if more than one lawyer on a side can attend the deposition. It is a veritable feast.

As a phenomenon of its own, the popularity on YouTube of what can be called depositions-gone-bad points to one way to solve the problems with depositions. Depositions transcripts can indeed present as ugly documents. But the effect of a transcript can hardly match the effect of seeing lawyers at their worst in video depositions. The bench and bar need to find a way to make videotaping depositions as affordable—or as inexpensive, depending on how you look at it—as having them transcribed. Ideally, it could be both services for the price of one. Knowing that a judge will see a lawyer in his obstreperous and obstructive glory in the video deposition would dampen any lawyer's enthusiasm or urge to act out.

GLIB AND OILY ART

Talk to ten lawyers about what it takes to be a good trial lawyer or appellate advocate and you'd get not just ten different answers (and likely be charged a fee for those answers) but ten lawyers who understand the question to be a challenge which can be met only by making their answer into something of an object lesson in advocacy. The ability to persuade through speech has always been considered a hallmark of a lawyer's competence, or slipperiness if we listen to the public. Lawyers don't describe themselves to each other as glib or smooth talking, though the public sees them this way. Consider the great opening scene in *King Lear* in which Lear plans to divide his kingdom, as he relieves himself of his affairs of state and crawls toward death, as he puts it, among his three daughters based on their ability to wow him with their expressions of love for him. Lawyers reading the scene would identify with both Regan and Goneril who, not much liking their aged, demanding father, want part of his kingdom and are willing to dissemble on their true feelings for their father to get what they believe is their due. That's the goal, lawyers would say, to persuade and claim the prize. In taking such an approach, Cordelia's cutting observation about her sisters would have equal application to them, that in their speeches they are using a "glib and oily art/ to speak and purpose not," that is, to use fluency, insincerity, and slipperiness in their language without any intention to fulfill what they have promised in their speech.

Glibness has not been an admired trait, though it has usually been considered an aspect of lawyering and treated with some gentle mocking humor. One 19th-century journal article "Lawyers and their Traits" collected in *The Green Bag* (1889) notes that there is no doubt or dispute that lawyers need to talk a good deal before it quotes a British sergeant, the forerunner of the barrister, to the effect that one way to be a good lawyer is to read all morning and talk all afternoon. The sergeant, we learn, "thought so highly of gab in law, that he defined the latter by the former, calling it, in the dog-Latin of his craft, '*Ars Bablativa*'—the art babblative." One notable 19th-century voice not ordinarily associated with law or lawyers happened to consider glibness in lawyers. Ralph Waldo Emerson wrote in his essay "Society and Solitude" that "there is a petty lawyer's fluency, which is sufficiently impressive to him who is devoid of that talent; though it be, in so many cases, nothing more than a facility of expressing with accuracy and speed what everybody thinks and says more slowly, without new information, or precision of thought, but the same thing, neither less nor more." Glib speech, the suggestion is, waste's everyone's time by adding nothing. *The Lawyer* magazine in 1906 reprinted a Harvard Law School address by Professor Wilson Gaynor that, as part of its general advice on oratory, notes that, "lawyers who are glib are a bore. They talk as though they had been to a feast of language and stolen the scraps, but they say nothing and do no good."

We can find relevance in routine long arguments of the 19th century even though our modern practice places severe time restrictions on advocacy. It was a different world for the advocate. We are told in a biographical sketch of Chief Justice Marshall in Irving Browne's 1878 *Short Studies of Great Lawyers* that while this was not a common occurrence it was not unusual for a case to take up three or four days in argument. "One lasted five days at the term when Story first took his seat, and in this case he says a printed *brief* of two hundred and thirty pages, was put into his hands in addition." [Emphasis in original]. John Quincy Adams as a single advocate spoke for eight hours in his closing argument for the defense in the *Amistad* case. This 19th-century penchant for extraordinarily long oral arguments certainly raises the question of volubility and loquaciousness, cousins to glibness. Perhaps sensitive to this, some describing the oratory of the long-winded seemed aware that glibness or long-windedness could be charged and in their descriptions tried to preempt the suggestions. Even though Rufus Choate (1799-1859) sometimes wrote and spoke in extraordinarily long sentences, we learn that in spite of their length the sentences were rarely involved and seldom contained a superfluous or misplaced word. Daniel Webster we are told had laid down a rule for himself "to use no word which does not suggest an idea, or modify some idea already suggested."

In looking through compilation books and biographical dictionaries profiling or thumbnailing a lawyer's life, we find descriptions of how famous and almost always well-regarded trial lawyers related to juries. These too have relevance, even great relevance to the lawyer looking to understand what advocacy is all about on his way to finding his own style. These are the descriptions of our most successful lawyers as they faced the challenge of persuading an audience that has not changed since lawyers first came on the scene. Rufus Choate, for example, threw himself into persuading a jury. We read in William Mathews's 1878 *Oratory and Orators* that when addressing a jury "his whole frame was charged with electricity, and literally quivered with emotion. The perspiration stood in drops even upon the hairs of his head; and he reminded one of the pythoness upon her tripod." For emphasis, as if such an idea was possible with his over-the-top performance, he took what was usually a "rich, grand, and melodious" voice and pushed it up to its highest key. From the *Albany Law Journal* of 1876–77 we read that "he shrieked; he raved; he tore a passion to tatters; he swung his fists; he ran his trembling fingers through his longcurling locks, dripping with perspiration; he shook his head like a lion's mane; he raised his body on his toes, and brought his weight down on his heels, with a force that shook the court-room." When he finished he would stagger to his carriage.

Theophilius Parsons (1750–1813), often known as Chief Justice Parsons, was, when contrasted with Choate, a minimalist in his lawyer days who stressed a direct appeal to the jury. None other than Daniel Webster in *The Writings and Speeches of Daniel Webster* noted that Parsons's manner was steady, forcible, and perfectly perspicuous. "He does not address the jury as a mechanical body to be put into motion by mechanical means. He appeals to them, as having minds capable of receiving the ideas in his own. Of course he never harangued. He is never stinted to say just so much on point, and no more. He knows by the juror's countenance when he is convinced." He would, as someone else described, talk about the case to the jury as a man might talk to a neighbor. Joseph Ball (1902–2000) took a similar approach. Anthony Murray, in his entry in Roger K. Newman's *The Yale Biographical Dictionary of American Law* on Ball, writes that "before a jury, Ball had a friendly, conversational manner. He seemed to be confiding in each juror. He did not preach, rant, or shout. He was not flamboyant. He quietly reasoned with jurors, using plain, simple words, like a chat with a neighbor over the back fence. He liked people and they liked him." The infamous Aaron Burr (1756–1836) went the other way as a courtroom lawyer. The great Chancellor James Kent in his *Memoirs and Letters* described Burr as "acute, quick, terse, polished, sententious, and sometimes sarcastic."

In our time, David Boies takes a different approach. Richard Cohen in *The Yale Biographical Dictionary of American Law* writes that Boies, "the lawyer everyone wants," is known for "meticulous preparation, a love of taking risks, a flair for publicity and for complex pre-trial tactics, and a brilliant courtroom style, at once predatory and ruthless, but mixed with the ability to charm juries, influence judges, and lure witnesses into saying too much." Donald Vinson's *The Yale Biographical Dictionary of American Law* entry on Stephen Susman tells us that when juxtaposed with his keen intellect Susman's "earthy charm and dynamic personality has made him enormously effective with juries. Businesslike, low-key with no theatrics, and no flowery wordsmith, he gets directly to the heart of a case and does not object to small points. He has an extraordinary ability to communicate abstract and even complicated legal and factual issues in ways that are understandable and persuasive. He is respectful to all except when examining expert witnesses on the other side. Then he becomes a wolf after red meat. He can become passionate when arguing to the jury."

We get as well descriptions of oratorical styles and the effects that the oratory had on the lawyer's audience. *The Yale Biographical Dictionary of American Law* entry on Gerhard Gesell (1910–93) by Seth Waxman tells us that Gessell as a trial lawyer before going onto the federal district court bench "liked to establish a key point and pound it home with staccato statements and planned repetitions, all to create a dramatic effect. He could also be calm and deferential if necessary, or become theatrical. Gesell's commonsense style was exemplified in his winning 1956 Supreme Court argument in the government's 'Cellophane' monopoly case against DuPont when, eschewing lofty debate, he distributed to each justice samples of competing packaging materials so that they could examine the products' interchangeability." Thomas Addis Emmet (1764–1827) spoke with a strong voice and bold gesticulations, Roger Newman tells us in his entry on Emmet in *The Yale Biographical Dictionary of American Law*. He used historical allusions and sometimes had vehement transitions. Justice Story who was on the receiving end of several arguments said of Emmet that, "he kindled as he spoke." In the same text, from a distinguished 19th-century judge we learn that "you were struck with his power. He seems like a piece of immense machinery moving with the greatest regularity and smoothness, yet as if restraining its gigantic power."

Discussions about trial practice usually involve precepts, and invariably the precepts are worth listening to and even jotting down. When it comes to the lawyer's emotions during the trial, for example, we learn that he is to betray nothing. In the same way, the lawyer, when it comes to any contested point, should always act as if he has won the point. If the jury is fooled by this, then the lawyer has in fact won. Perception is all. The list can go on and would eventually get to nuggets such as the precept that the lawyer should never ask a question to which he does not already know the answer. The problem with learning by precepts is that they can fail you when you most need them. For example, what we don't hear from the precept givers is how hard it can be not to ask the question that brings you down a blind alley. In the same way, what happens when rules collide? One rule is to never let a witness explain. But there's also the rule that says that a lawyer should never appear to avoid a subject. Learning by way of example has its own weaknesses, but the ratio to insight is greater for it than for learning by way of precepts. Execution is always an issue, but knowing about successful styles and practices from reading about successful lawyers gives the lawyer willing to use his imagination help in answering the question of how to persuade a jury. Glibness, it turns out, is not the answer.

HOPE AND DREAD: THE NATURE OF LEGAL RESEARCH

We don't hear much about lawyers researching the law, though we should, if only to better understand what Felix Frankfurter was getting at in his *Law and Politics* when he wrote that legal research "requires the poetic quality of the imagination that sees significance and relation where others are indifferent or see unrelatedness." There's little mention of it in autobiography and memoir. Moreover, legal novels—that is, novels written by and about lawyers—rarely show the lawyer at his desk or in the library looking for law. The lawyers we find in these plot-driven novels are more apt to be looking for love or running from bad guys rather than researching. An exception is Robert Traver's *Anatomy of a Murder*, which, fifty years on and still the best novel about lawyers and the legal system, dared to take the reader into the law library for a Eureka moment—two simultaneous Eureka moments, to be accurate–and to pivot the novel and the protagonist's professional and personal lives on looking for law and having his love for the profession rekindled. How we research the law has changed dramatically since the time of *Anatomy of a Murder*, but the importance of legal research to the lawyer's life hasn't. It is still the act that links us to the profession.

For there to be any chance at a Eureka moment, rare enough as it is, the lawyer must necessarily engage in legal research. Not all do. We know anecdotally and from studies that senior lawyers in large law firms free themselves of the research chore and use armies of young associates hired for this very reason to do what the senior lawyer no longer feels required to do. Other lawyers may decide to forego research because they are bored, lazy, or indifferent to the law as found in judicial opinions, statutes, and regulations—our three sources of law. Insiders know that there is even a class of lawyer who abdicates his responsibilities and submits pleadings only barely researched, if researched at all, relying on the judge to figure it out.

Legal research had once been about books and about how to find what you needed in those books. The 19th century was the age of the treatise. William Blackstone's *Commentaries on the Laws of England*, which dominated 18th-century legal education and practice, gave way to Kent's *Commentaries*, Dane's *Abridgement*, and the work of treatise writers such as Justice Joseph Story, who wrote treatises on nearly every topic. As quoted in the second volume of *The Cambridge History of Law in America*, Abraham Lincoln, both a country and corporate lawyer in his career, noted in 1858 that the way to success "was to read Blackstone's *Commentaries*, Chitty's *Pleading*, Greenleaf's *Evidence*, Story's *Equity Pleading*, get a license and go to the practice and still keep reading."

Treatises early on were cited as though they had the force of law. They expounded their principles and then tied them to reported decisions, usually from the largest and most active jurisdictions. This was something of a stop-gap measure to the constant complaint that the law reports were not disseminated widely enough. This led one critic in 1823, for example, to observe in *The North American Review* that "we deem it a scandal to the profession that the reports of the decisions of the federal courts have so limited circulation and cannot but publish our astonishment that they are to be found in so very few of the county law libraries in Massachusetts." We find an example of this in Nevada and the first year of the state's Supreme Court, 1865. In *Travis v. Epstein*, for example, the court laments its limited resources, writing, "from the want of access to a good library, we have not been able to give this part of the subject such an examination as we could have desired." In another case, *Cox v. Smith*, the court qualified its analysis with the lament and complaint that it did not have as many available reports as counsel writing the brief did. The result was that its conclusion was consistent with the law only "so far as the reports referred to were accessible to us."

As the century wore on and as the country expanded westward, more and more reports were published and made available to the bench and bar. The states themselves more often published their reports in an official form, while publishing companies recognized the growing market and began publishing the reports privately. John West of the West Publishing Company had the idea for regional reporters, such as the *Atlantic Report, Northeast*

Reporter, Pacific Reporter and the like, which published the appellate decisions from geographical regions. West Publishing also published its version of the United States Supreme Court decisions, the *Supreme Court Reporter*, and the decisions of the circuit courts of appeal and the district courts in the *Federal Reporter* and the *Federal Supplement* respectively.

Soon, ironically, the problem became how to make sense of and use all this law. On the educational side, with the number of law schools beginning to increase in the 19th century, the response, begun at Harvard, was to introduce casebooks and the scientific method to facilitate the analyses and extraction of legal principles. The problem for practitioners was to find the law that could help them in this ever-expanding body of published case law. It was here that John West came to the rescue of American law with his digest system (borrowed from others) which sought to organize all of the case law that was emerging at an ever increasing pace from the state and federal courts. The goal was to make it easy or easier for lawyers to find the principles of law they were looking for, not in treatises, but in the decisions themselves of their own jurisdictions.

The West digest system was the star of legal research as it was taught in law schools before the information revolution. It still is, with additional instruction on how to search the databases for what is needed. But before the revolution, in those hardcopy times, the books were showcases. When legal research instructors, for example, taught what was known as the bibliographic method to introduce students to one research tool at a time, West's Publishing's regional reporters, its various federal reporters, its digest volumes, and its magnificent *Corpus Juris Secundum* led the way. I may be one of the few lawyers to admit that while in school the "treasure hunt" exercises devised by librarians to familiarize students with all the different books were actually fun. The other principal teaching method that law librarians have used in teaching students legal research skills, known as the integrated process oriented approach, led even more directly to West Publishing publications when students needed to find, analyze, and apply the law for their projects.

It is a commonplace to observe that the ability with electronic databases to search for cases by keywords has transformed research. I used the digest system before everything went electronic and recall how often my volumes of the *Federal Reporter* and the *Supreme Court Reporter* covered nearly all the space on my work table, piled one upon another—sometimes four or five layers of books—with the quotation from a case that I'd hope to find only faintly calling to me to discover it. Today multiple computer screens and easily printed documents substitute for a mountain of books. With the wizardry of WESTLAW, I can simply click on the indexed key number as it is set out in the beginning of the case and then, with one more click, choose my data base, which is either going to be all federal cases or cases from my Ninth Circuit. I then get a list of all the headnotes from all the cases in which the key number appears. I can then begin reading through these mini-paragraph descriptions of the facts and the law applied to determine which of the cases I should read as I go searching into the next round of inquiry.

There is of course no established routine to get to the right cases and the right quotable language. I would start at a distance at the beginning of the search and steadily move closer to what I could use, but there was too much looking, going back and looking again, and then following a different path, and then only to look back again, to think that the process was laid out inherently and just needed to be followed from one book to the next mechanically. And certainly, because there was no set pattern to the search, the emotional responses of elation and disappointment appeared and receded as I went along. In a case that helped me, I might find a citation to another case which, I was convinced, would provide the language I needed to lock down my argument once I got to it. But it often happened that, when I got there, I found out either that the facts were sufficiently different so as to undercut the usefulness of the case or that the case which had led me there had not gotten the holding quite right. Frustrated, all I could do was travel down another path of cases and the cases cited therein. Hard copy or electronic database, the frustration was, and still is today when I research, the same.

What has not changed is the nature of research, at least for lawyers. Research for lawyers is not an academic exercise because there is a real client and real money at stake. It is a fiction that lawyers bring disinterestedness to their research. Advocacy does not tolerate disinterested analysis. Once a lawyer is looking for law that helps his or her client, detachment gives way and partisanship takes over. How much it takes over depends on the lawyer's personality and the attachment to the client. The result in part is that the lawyer researching reads an opinion for what it offers him or her, not for what it offers as an explication of how law works.

There is an emotional rollercoaster ride that invariably goes with every sustained bit of research. Computerized research has not changed that aspect of research. The emotions follow in general terms whether the research is in support of a position that the lawyer is asserting or whether it is to test and if necessary rebut the cases and analysis asserted in a responsive pleading by the opposition. The difference between the former and the latter is hoping to find something that helps and dreading to find something that hurts. Hope and dread, the twin pillars of legal research.

I AM RIGHT BECAUSE I SAY I AM

Oddly enough, given the significance of the topic, almost nothing has been written about the phenomenon of judicial ego and arrogance that gets at its significance. We have all seen examples of both, yet commentators rarely take on the topic of these twin excrescences. For something so important, there should be discussion, not in the courtroom of course, where judges rule and would not allow it anyway, but in the general discourse about the legal profession and the fair administration of justice. We need not worry about the ethical rule keeping lawyers from criticizing judges, which applies to lawyers criticizing judicial performance in their pending matters. Besides, a discussion of judicial ego and arrogance is not even criticism per se. It is just an exploration of the phenomenon known as "black robe-itis."

There have been several formulations or definitions of black robe-itis. Many go to the idea that the disease, if we can call it that, allows judges to let their own sense of self-importance cloud their good judgment. More define it as a phenomenon in which judges believe that their judicial appointments have made them god-like creatures unapproachable by mere humans. An especially good formulation appears in what is known informally as the federal judge song by a group of lawyers billing themselves as the Bar and Grill singers. One apparently unhappy federal judge described the song in an opinion as "a derisive ditty going around the courthouse" set to the music of "Happy Together" by the Turtles. It captures the sensibility in question nicely. We can sing along to "[i]magine me as God. I do/ I think about it day and night./ It feels so right/ To be a federal district judge and know that I'm/ Appointed forever." The chorus is even better: "I'm a federal judge/ And I'm smarter than you/ For all my life./ I can do whatever I want to do/ For all my life."

Black robe-itis is a voluntary condition. It is not a set of attitudes or beliefs that judges are required to follow upon their appointments as judges.

A key element, in fact, speaks to this voluntary nature of black robe-itis. It is that judges with it believe that their elevation to the bench has given them particular insight and something approaching infallibility. Lower court judges by definition would hardly feel themselves entitled to claim infallibility, though they do, given that their rulings are subject to appellate review. Robert Jackson wittily noted in his 1953 opinion in *Brown v. Allen* that even U.S. Supreme Court justices such as himself should be wary of believing in their own infallibility. "We are final not because we are infallible," he once wrote, "we are infallible because we are final."

We have had several accounts from judges describing how they decide cases. None of these judges even remotely suggests that the result he arrived at must be correct because he is, after all, the judge. How could they when they are presenting the method of analysis and the factors to be considered in making a decision? These judges describing the decision-making process, such as Frank Coffin who served on the U.S. Court of Appeals for the First Circuit, are describing an aspect of modesty that judges necessarily need in trying to sort their way to what they consider to be the best result.

Black robe-itis has been cited by many as an explanation for the unfortunately large number of examples of judicial rudeness, arrogance, and egotism. This is of course right and will be considered elsewhere. My real interest here is in the way black robe-itis deludes a judge into thinking that he is invariably right just because he is the judge. It is obvious that being appointed a judge—say, a federal judge—does not make the person appointed any smarter or insightful. It does not make him a better writer, nor does it bestow greater reasoning skills than were there before. A body of heretofore-unknown legal knowledge and acumen does not suddenly get grafted onto the newly appointed judge. Federal judges do attend a version of judge school for a few weeks, but there they learn judicial fundamentals and office management techniques, not secrets of the universe. If only that were the case.

I once got myself into more than a spot of bother when I confronted some federal judges with what they must have considered heresy in making the argument that the appointment process does not change who the appointee is. I had given a talk to an audience containing several federal judges and spent only a brief time outlining what I consider to be this obvious point before talking about a book I had written on the importance of personality to the careers of four different Supreme Court Justices. I found out later from one of the judges—the only one of the group not afflicted with black robe-itis—that the others were furious with me for my view. In various ways those offended judges let me know over the next few years when I appeared before them that my view was, to put it politely, misguided. What I experienced reflected badly on the federal judiciary and, ironically, underscored the validity of my point.

It is a remarkable exercise in self-delusion for a judge to display any symptoms of black robe-itis. Anyone who has seen a judge with black robe-itis deal with contending views in an argument knows that the judge so afflicted substitutes an intellectual process marked by modesty, as described by someone such as Judge Coffin, for a display of know-nothingness. It is ironic that the judge with black robe-itis reveals himself on the decision-making front when he engages, or tries to engage, with lawyers in open court—though engagement means trying to deflect argument so as to not have to explain any reasoning. Anyone without black robe-itis would be embarrassed to try this move to trump without engaging, but that is a hallmark of black robe-itis, a certain shamelessness that conveys to others that they have no role in the process.

Black robe-itis must be wonderfully comforting for those who have it. It detaches them from all that goes on around them and frees them from accountability. It is a bubble existence. Inside the bubble are only the judge and his law clerks. It is an amusing mark of black robe-itis that judges act as though they are smarter than their law clerks when, in fact, this is true in only the rarest exceptions. The explanation is simple enough. The law clerk was chosen by way of meritocracy. The judge was chosen because he knew a power broker who knew the appointment decision maker. To confuse merit with success is a mark of black robe-itis delusionalism.

Also, it is not as though only judges can do what judges do. Judges are just lawyers in robes with different functions in the legal process. Our judiciary bears no resemblance to the judiciary of many European countries in which young lawyers choose the judicial path early on and are trained for years in a type of civil service system for the continental version of a judge. Judges in our version have everything in common with lawyers except what they wear and what they do in the process. They use the same reasoning skills and the like. This squarely rebuts any argument that what judges do is special.

But, of course, it is this element of commonality that black robe-itis judges have to reject. It is galling to see a black robe-itis judge not engage lawyers when those lawyers have done their jobs and brought legitimate argument to bear on an issue. The judicial process, contrary to what all black robe-itis judges believe, is a collaborative process. Judges do not decide—or issue fiats—in a vacuum. This explains the principle we find in the reports that lawyers are almost as important to the process as judges. Judges are a bit more important because they make the decisions. Those decisions, we should not forget, are a function of the contributions of the lawyers.

On one level—important to me, for example—black robe-itis as it shows itself in the decision-making process delivers a fresh insult to lawyers each time it presents itself. For the lawyers, it is not that their arguments have been rejected that matters. This happens all the time and is just a part of practicing law. Rather, what matters is the rejection of the lawyers' standing to inquire into the law and try to reason through it. It is to dismiss as futile and irrelevant the intellectual component of lawyers—their very right of existence.

While I am always wary of setting out generalizations or formulas, my experience has been that the existence and extent of black robe-itis runs in relation to a judge's appreciation of law as an intellectual undertaking in which it is the honest, respectful process of inquiry that matters most. Nothing can be right unless the reasoning supports it. A respect for reasoning runs counter to at least this judicial decision-making version of black robe-itis. The belief that reasoning matters means that reasoning is respected. If reasoning is respected, those who employ reasoning need to be respected. The answer is not right because a judge who believes himself fleshed with power by the nature of an appointment declares it right. It is right—or as right as it can seem to be at that time, that place, and with the particular facts of a case—because the reasoning leads us to conclude that it is the best answer. Is it a coincidence, we have to ask, that our greatest judges have taken the approach of intellectual modesty and emphasis on reasoning? What made Henry Friendly so great? What makes Richard

Posner so great? For both, it is taking each case as a new puzzle in the law and working through all the applicable law for reasoning to give the best result, without regard to what that result might be. It is the reasoning they are willing to put on display that guides them—not ego, not black robe-itis.

INTRODUCTION TO JUSTICE

Introductions are the preferred approach by judges looking to go beyond the generic and personalize the opinion. References to popular culture play well, perhaps even better, depending on the audience, than literary allusions. Frank Easterbrook as an example shows that he has a sense of humor when he writes in the trademark case *Jay Franco & Sons, Inc. v. Franel* that "[t]he same year that Huey Lewis and the News informed America that it's 'Hip to Be Square,' [plaintiff] sought to trademark the circular beach towel." In the same way and for a similar result, Janice Brown of the District of Columbia Circuit in the financial fraud case *United States ex rel. K & R Limited Partnership v. Massachusetts Housing Finance Agency* involving intention began, "forty years ago Jimi Hendrix trilled his plaintive query: 'Is this love, baby, or is it . . . [just] confusion?' In this False Claims Act case, we face a similar question involving a mortgage subsidy program initiated in that era: Is this fraud, or is it . . . just confusion?"

But introductions designed to comment on a case do not always use allusions to popular culture or to literature. This way the judge does not have to worry about the stature of the quoted writer, whether the audience even recognizes the writer or the quoted matter, or, most important of all, how apt the quotation is. For the judge seeking to distinguish his opinion with introductions that can be employed to make any number of points, the question always is how smart or effective the observations in the opening paragraph are.

Striking, dramatic, and attention getting openings often represent the best of a judge's writing. A brief introductory paragraph that has elegance and a touch of the epigram comes from Frank Easterbrook of the Seventh Circuit and puts his literary gifts on display. In *United States v. Bartlett*, a case involving three police officers and their violations of the rights of victims to be free of unreasonable searches and seizures, Easterbrook rather than "the court" recited the shocking details of an officer's brutal treatment of suspects with fine narrative skill: "The distance between civilization and barbarity, and the time needed to pass from one state to the other is depressingly short. Police officers in Milwaukee proved this the morning of October 24, 2004."

A colleague of Judge Easterbrook's on the Seventh (until he passed away recently), Judge Terence Evans, strikes in a similar manner in a prison conditions case in *Gillis v. Litscher*. He opens with a carefully painted picture: "[s]tripped naked in a small cell with nothing except a toilet; forced to sleep on a concrete floor or slab; denied any human contact; fed nothing but 'nutriloaf;' and given just a modicum of toilet paper—four squares—only a few times. Although this might sound like a stay at a Soviet gulag in the 1930s, it is, according to the claims in this case, Wisconsin in 2002. Whether these conditions are, as a matter of law, only 'uncomfortable, but not unconstitutional' as the State contends, is the issue we consider in this case."

Empathy, that much-discussed judicial quality, shines through in another introduction from Judge Evans. It comes from a felon-in-possession-of-a-weapon case, *United States v. Wise*, though what got his attention was not the presented issue of whether the sentencing enhancement imposed in the district court was proper. He opened the opinion, "[i]t is an event almost too painful to recount: a four-year-old discharged a gun he found lying around the house, killing his two-year-old cousin." In a like manner but from another court, Judge Maryanne Barry of the Third Circuit shows empathy in the immigration case of *Sheriff v. United States* testing the bounds of what is known as humanitarian asylum. She begins the opinion, "[t]his is a case of almost unimaginable horrors inflicted on a Liberian woman by supporters of former Liberian president, Charles Taylor," before cataloging incidents of murder, torture, abduction, and rape.

Judges can use introductions to show sensitivity to what a case is really about. Take the case of *United States v. Letts*, in which we learn that the defendant's life had early on shown promise and solid citizen performance through fourteen years of honorable military service, before depression, isolation, and personal loss unhinged him and he ended up involved in a large drug conspiracy. The court captures the human tragedy, the waste, by noting in the first sentence that "[t]he facts of [defendant's] life that gave rise to this case read somewhat like a morality play." On a matter far less serious but still with significant implications, the court in a case involving parking spaces gives a sensible take on how something as insignificant as a parking space could prompt someone to go to court to vindicate a right. The message is that we can't be high handed and scoff at the quotidian. The court noted in *Astralia Condominium Ass'n v. Secretary* that "[o]urs is a society in which people live, work, relax, and shop in apartment complexes, office towers, industrial parks, stadia, and malls that stretch as far as the eye can see." We get more than we need to know about driving the streets of the urban, rather than the suburban, world when the court in the drug case *United States v.Harris* notes that, "[t]his case arises from a peculiar example of urban entrepreneurship—the drive-by drug bazaar." It can indeed be an ugly world. There is commentary on the devolution of society, as when *Doorbal v. Department of Corrections* begins with, "[t]his appeal involves a spree of murder and mayhem so heinous and bizarre that one would expect to see it only in a crime drama on television, but the only issue of law borders on the frivolous."

Sometimes there is a little fun to be poked. Sometimes the litigants get the skewer. "Some people are impossible to please," the court begins in *Alvrarez v. Royal Atlantic Developers, Inc.,* a Title VII employment retaliation case, describing the standards imposed on the plaintiff that led to her always failing. This particular boss, who is impossible to please, has another telling trait. "And it seems that the judgment she passes [on employees] is always unfavorable." In the legal malpractice case *Redwood v.Dobson*, the court opens with "[t]his is a grudge match," making it clear that both sides should be blushing with shame. "This is the kind of case that could give a car salesman a bad name," the court begins in *United States v.Tahzib* , a case involving tax evasion, embezzlement, and a luxury car salesman. In the bankruptcy fraud case *In re Meyers* we find that, "[e]very now and then we encounter an appeal where just about everyone appears to have behaved badly." In the Title VII retaliation case *Brewer v. Trustees of University of Illinois* we're not sure what to make of the introduction's tone, though my guess is on the sarcastic. "This case," we learn, "concerns the corrupt, Machiavellian world of permit parking at the University of Illinois's Urbana–Champaign campus, and the ill fortune of a student who became involved in it." Tone is an issue again in the sentencing case of *United States v. Nelson*, in which a very serious issue is balanced against a lame joke in the beginning. The court asks, "[W]hat is the meaning of life? Or perhaps more pointedly, what is the equivalent of a term of life imprisonment for sentencing purposes?" Another opening that should go the way of extinction tries all too hard to link that which can't be put together for a joke, though perhaps jurisdictional devotees would chuckle. "This case," the court begins in *Rhode Island Fisherman's Alliance, Inc. v. Rhode Island Department of Environmental Management*, "brings us face to face with two exotic creatures: the American lobster and a state-law claim that may or may not contain an embedded federal question sufficient to ground a claim of original jurisdiction under 28 U.S.C. §1331 (commonly known as 'federal question' jurisdiction)."

Courts sometimes don't mind pointing out ironies. The reader can judge how sharp the ironies are. In the mail fraud case *United States v. Otero* involving a postal worker, the court poked gently at what he hopes is irony. "While neither rain nor sleet nor snow could keep the residents along Postal Highway Contract Route 64 in Los Lunas, New Mexico from receiving their mail, the temptations of mail fraud and credit card theft were a different story." The irony is stronger when the United States sued a jet engine contractor under the False Claims Act. The court began *United States v. United Technologies Corp.* by noting that "[f]ighter jet engines propel planes faster than the speed of sound, a sight that may be as exhilarating to watch as it must be to experience. Not so the procurement process for awarding contracts to make jet engines." This same judge in the Medicare case *Henry Ford Health System v. Department of Health and Human Services* involving the Henry Ford Hospital found a similar irony that needed to be noted and exploited the connection to the car maker himself. "'My effort is in the direction of simplicity,' once wrote the namesake of the Henry Ford Hospital. Mr. Ford apparently had nothing to do with the creation of the Medicare program."

But of all the reasons that judges enhance their opinions with specially crafted introductions, the chief reason remains to lure the reader into the case. Often the judge is trying to show at the beginning that he is worth reading and does this by showing off a few skills, such as the apt use of a quotation or some other cleverness. Sometimes the judge wants to lay bare the emotional issues undergirding a case to draw the reader in. Sometimes the emphasis is on teasing out ironies to show that the judge understands life and law on many levels. Mostly, though, a good introduction tries to draw the reader in by promising, or at least suggesting, that the opinion has a good story to tell. To let the reader know that the authoring judge has a natural story telling talent makes the reader want to read on. This is what happens, for example, when William Bauer of the Seventh Circuit opens *Bakery Machinery & Fabrication, Inc. v. Traditional Baking Incorporated* about the consequences of a lawyer apparently deciding that he did not want to follow any of the court's orders or deadlines with, "[t]his is an example of how the sins of the lawyer can be visited upon the client." The reader knows from the formulation turning on *sins* and *visiting* that a good story will follow. Getting the reader to read on, after all, is the point of the exercise.

JUDICIAL WRITING

The problem with judicial writing is that, with only few exceptions, it is not written by judges. We have long known that in the federal system the rise of the law clerk has meant the decline in judge-written opinions, so that today only a few judges write their own opinions. Law clerks first rose to dominate the Supreme Court beginning some sixty years ago, and in the last few decades they have also come to dominate with their growing numbers both the district courts and the circuit courts of appeals. What we have not directly confronted, though, are the consequences of having law clerks speak for their bosses.

Some have complained about the style and substance of opinions written by law clerks, but I think this misses the mark. The usual complaints are that the opinions are too long, too heavily footnoted, and too steeped in a law review sensibility. Opinions written by judges before the rise of the law clerk are, in contrast, much shorter, tighter, and more inclined to resolve issues with a more workman like approach. The opinions are the last word, the summing up, following the judge's engagement with the issues, law, and argument. Judges had little interest in displaying what was known to all and seemed to be writing more directly for the audience of the lawyers in the case. Put differently, law clerks in writing their opinions make more of them than they need to.

Not surprisingly, the judges recognize the talent of their law clerks and in many cases bow to it. In oral histories from Article III judges from around the country, many acknowledge that their law clerks are brighter and better writers than they. They defend themselves by insisting that they hold the decision-making reins. For them, they still qualify as writers because of the level of editorial control they exert over the final product. Ironically, law clerks have perhaps set too high a bar and have intimidated those judges who want to write. The test, though, is not whether a judge can match a clerk-written opinion. Some of them were law clerks themselves and of course can meet the standard. The test is whether the judge wants to grapple with the case at hand and submit to the transformative power of writing. Luther Swygert, first a district judge and then a judge on the Seventh Circuit, put it nicely when he noted in his oral history for the Seventh Circuit, "one thing, of course, that happens—and I know has happened to me and I am sure has happened to a lot of other appeals judges—is that once you start to write and get into it you change your mind. I think the ratio is high for the possibility of the writer of the opinion to change his mind, much higher than the other two people [on the panel] if they are in agreement. They tend not to get into the depth as the writer of the opinion does."

It is not, however, business as usual throughout the *Federal Reporter, Third Series*. A few judges have different interests in mind and, rather than rigidly following the five-part organization, structure their opinions to best advance their goal of explaining how law works. Richard Posner of the Seventh Circuit more than any other judge uses opinions to explore the reasoning behind legal principles and explain their applications to the issues at hand. With a gift of composition, and especially a gift of exposition, he moves the reader quickly to what is at issue and then with headlong enthusiasm sorts it all out, giving us little essays on the constellation of issues that the case presents. That Posner uses no footnotes only strengthens the idea that he is aiming for the essayistic approach. Beyond using a direct, distinctive, and engaging voice, he also embraces casual, colloquial language and pointedly rejects legal language and legalisms whenever they would otherwise appear. Legal rules in his opinions, rather than being abstract principles mechanically applied, reflect the way we live and what we think is fair, efficient, and socially beneficial. It all seems effortless, the mark, ironically, of an opinion written and rewritten many times, all by the same hand. Posner's complete engagement leads to a depth of analysis not found anywhere. It is inquiry coupled with analysis and exposition, all guided by a comprehensive understanding of how law works, both specifically and generally.

Judges can also be intimidated by the opinions of some of our greatest judges who made it a point to always write their own. It would indeed be hard to measure up to the work of Holmes, Hand, and Posner, our three greatest practitioners of the genre. But of course that is not the point. Judges contribute to the tradition of the opinion—in an age in which law professors writing in law reviews tend to deploy ideological weaponry rather than explain how law works—when they engage with the law. Their voice, the experienced voice, is the voice law clerks cannot assume.

There are three principal arguments at issue. The first is that none of it much matters because no one reads judicial opinions anyway. In his oral history for the District of Columbia Circuit, Robert Bork noted that he was sure that "nobody ever reads those opinions, ever. Maybe the parties, maybe the counsel does." This argument not only does not consider the history and tradition of judicial opinions in the American democracy, it does not consider opinions as a genre of expository literature. More to the point, opinions are where we go to declare ourselves. American history, we can fairly say, has been played out and described in our judicial opinions.

The second argument, that law clerks need to write opinions because of ever-increasing case loads, has an easy answer. Far too many opinions are published, filling the *Federal Supplement* and the *Federal Reporter* at alarming rates. Some judges are not fond of this trend. As district judge Richard Mills put it in his oral history, "I have a very strong feeling about some of these cases that are filed in *Federal Supplement*. It is just absolute trash, it is garbage to put in orders and motions and other things that are clearly not precedential. It is all a rehash of old settled law. It is nothing more than an ego trip to have your name in print. I find it very offensive to me because I believe printed opinions ought to be for that which adds to the body of law and not just reiterated. But there's too much unprecedential opinion writing that goes into the hard volumes. These attorneys have to pay tremendous amounts of money for all those books. Every year you're talking about eight, ten volumes, and there's not twenty-five percent of it that is really of value, is really worth something."

The third argument, that judges can write opinions without actually writing them because of their level of direction and editorial control, has its own short answer. Judges, even though they otherwise create the rules for what they do, do not set the standard for determining authorship. The standard that applies elsewhere, especially in the intellectual world, applies to judges and their opinions as well. Readers in this world and in the general literary world trust and expect that the person whose name crowns the text wrote the text. In the intellectual world at least, heads would roll if authors were only titularly involved in what goes out under their name.

Having judges write their own opinions thus solves two problems. It would, first, bring the number of published opinions back to manageable levels. Second, it would bring intellectual honesty back into law. Law as found in our courts is the rarest of activities. It has an intellectual component, but it is not an academic discipline. It is linked, unlike academic disciplines, to the way people live. Voices in the law matter. We are engaging in legal fictions of a sort if we say that a judge in a judicial opinion wrote this or that unless that is the case. The job of judging is declaring not just results but how the law works. If the judges won't tell us, who will?

Benefits flow from having judges write their own opinions. Both the bar and the lower courts, for example, would better understand the thinking and inclinations of judges who declare themselves on the page. But beyond being more transparent, the law would also become more predictable, since the only constant in the process would be the judges themselves. Moreover, the obligation to write would advance a self-selection process for judicial appointment, deterring those less inclined to full engagement and identifying those who embrace the full dimensions of the judicial post.

I recognize that, taken to its logical conclusion, my regime if implemented would change confirmation hearings for the Supreme Court. It would make the first question to a lower court candidate seeking promotion to the High Court, "So, judge, do you do your own work?" My standard, I must insist, is not unusually high. The question, as I say, is not whether federal judicial nominees can do the work of Holmes, Hand, or Posner. It is merely whether they do their own work.

LAUGH OUT LOUD

Who would have thought that, as we traverse what Cardozo called the Sahara of the judicial opinion, we would find the occasional bubbling spring providing relief in the form of humor? It takes many forms, ranging from tired jokes to sly wit to satire so powerful as to make us laugh. To invoke Samuel Johnson, we can say that, while it might not be done well, it is a surprise to find it done at all.

The oddities and curiosities that dot the *Federal Reporter* do not qualify as humor if intention is a requirement, but they amuse nonetheless. One example is the trademark dispute case *Louis Vuitton Malletier v. Haute Diggity Dog* brought by luxury handbag maker Louis Vuitton against the maker of plush dog chew toys for using the name "Chewy Vuiton." Another would be the copyright infringement case *JWC Investments, Inc. v. Novelty, Inc.* involving the plush doll known as Pull My Finger Fred. Fred is a white, middle-aged, overweight man with black hair and a receding hairline who sits in an armchair wearing a tank top and blue pants. His talent is that he farts when the extended finger on his right hand is pulled and makes "somewhat crude, somewhat funny statements about the bodily noises he emits, such as 'Did somebody step on a duck?' or 'Silent but deadly.'" His plush doll rival, Fartman, has the same physical and sartorial characteristics and also sits in an armchair. He too farts when his extended finger is pulled and comments on his emissions.

The nature of the cases themselves sometimes provide humor with their ludicrous claims. In an example from the D.C. Circuit, a group of lactose-intolerant individuals filed a class-action lawsuit against nine sellers of milk. The court in *Mills v. Giant of Maryland, LLC* politely called the suit unusual. The claim was that the plaintiffs consumed milk before they were aware of their lactose intolerance and, as a result, suffered temporary gas and stomach discomfort. In the plaintiffs' world, the milk sellers should have put warnings on the labels to inform consumers that some individuals might be intolerant of milk. Lunacy, too, can make us smile. In a D.C. Circuit case *United States v.Papagano* the defendant, according to a court, "had a goal: to collect two of every kind of computer or, as he phrased it, to build the 'Noah's Ark of Computer land.' Unable to buy such a collection, he decided to steal it. Over 10 years, he pilfered 19,709 pieces of computer equipment from his employer, the Naval Research Laboratory." No word on how many lawyers the defendant had.

Judges seeking to amuse have their own motives. Sometimes the humor is just a byproduct of indignation, frustration, and a view that the world has fallen into chaos. Terence Evans of the Seventh Circuit begins the Lanham Act case *Georgia-Pacific v. Kimberly-Clark* this way: "Toilet paper. This case is about toilet paper." After describing the impressive litigation efforts of the parties, Georgia Pacific and Kimberly-Clark, Evans wryly notes, "[t]hat's quite a record considering, again, that this case is about toilet paper." In a class action attorneys' fees case, for example, Judge Carnes of the Eleventh Circuit in *Kenny A. v. Perdue* uses humor as a pitchfork to chide the attorneys for the plaintiff class by invoking the well-known phenomenon of financial insatiability. The opinion begins, "[w]hen asked how much money would be enough for him, John D. Rockefeller reportedly said: 'Just a little bit more.' The attorneys for the plaintiff class want more than just a little bit more." Not surprisingly, the lawyers did not get their little bit more.

Judges can be drawn to what might be called one-liners that deliver a humorous punch. In the Eleventh Circuit sentence review case *United States v. Shaw* involving a defendant who started with a blaze of criminality at thirteen and just kept on going, Judge Carnes uses hyperbole for trenchant effect in the one-line arena. He notes first that the defendant's "rap sheet is long enough to require extra postage" before identifying the sad fact that the defendant's repeated arrests and various prison terms over a fifteen year period make it look as though the defendant "is determined to serve a life sentence, albeit on the installment plan." The question before the court was "whether the current installment is a reasonable one."

In contrast, we can find instances of more subtle and even erudite humor in the advance sheets. One that dazzles comes in the bankruptcy case *In re Porto* involving in part a botched hair transplant, in which the court in a footnote invokes Alexander Pope's *The Rape of the Lock*. The ironic

edge can be so sharp as to produce a laugh for those who know their 19th
-century American literature. In a case about stolen paintings, the court notes
in *United States v. Ternus* that "Ralph Waldo Emerson once said, 'Though
we travel the world over to find the beautiful, we must carry it with us or
we find it not,'" before pointing sharply to the irony that "[s]omeone took
that advice too literally, carrying away four old masters' paintings from
the Musee des Beaux-Arts in Nice, France." Perhaps the best comes in the
Ninth Circuit case *Love v. Associated Newpapers, Ltd.* in which Mike Love
of the Beach Boys sued former band member Brian Wilson and a British
newspaper that distributed a CD of Brian Wilson's solo performances of
Beach Boys songs as part of a promotion campaign for Wilson's British tour.
The issue was whether the Lanham Act could be invoked extraterritorially.
Judge Thomas concluded the introduction portion of his opinion by stating, blandly enough, that, "the central issue before us is whether American
claims for relief can be asserted on the basis of conduct that only occurred
in Great Britain." He follows this with the unremarkable, "the defendants
think not." The next sentence joins the issue and jumps off the page with
its playful knowingness: "Love wishes they could all be California torts."

One judge cleverly and amusingly uses Shakespeare to add a bit of spice
to an opinion. In the freedom of speech case *Villegas v. Gilroy Garlic Festival
Association*, the judge notes that 120,000 visitors attend the festival each
year and that since its inception more than 3 million people have attended,
to partake, as described in the festival's promotional materials, in food laced
with over two tons of garlic. This prompts the judge to wryly note that in
holding the garlic festival, the city was disregarding Shakespeare's admonition in *A Midsummer's Night Dream*, which in a footnote is set out: "And,
most dear actors, eat no onions nor garlic, for we are to utter sweet breath."

Puns are supposedly the enemies of erudition, but they deserve some
attention. They are a matter of taste and some would argue that, even when
done well, they do not rise to the level of humor. I'm declaring myself by
asserting that the following puns made me laugh. They both come from
the pen of Richard Posner of the Seventh Circuit. In the fall from ladder
case *Schmude v. Tricam Industries, Inc.* we find, "the gravity of [the plaintiff's] injury may have been due to the fact that he weighs 350 pounds,"
and in a suit against a motel for bed bug infested rooms, *Mathias v. Accor*

Economy Lodging, Inc., Posner remarks of the plaintiff, after he had been moved twice by motel management following his complaints, that it was "odd that at that point he did not flee the motel."

There are attempts at humor that do not succeed, some less than others. Consider Judge Torruella's use in the First Circuit case of *Fairest-Knight v. Marine World Distributors, Inc.* of a well-worn amusing observation. "This case, involving the saga of an extremely frustrated boat owner, provides further support for the occasionally expressed view that the two happiest days of a boat owner's life are the day he buys his boat and the day he sells it." And Judge Cardamone falls even flatter in the Second Circuit Wild Bird Conservation Act case *United States v. Cullen* involving the rare Black Sparrowhawk. After noting that there have been few, if any, prosecutions of the Act, Cardamone as part of his general observation that the case before the court was unusual in various ways, goes esoteric on us. He tells us that, "judicial opinions often characterize an odd provision of the law or an ingenious argument as a 'rare bird' (*rara avis*). But in this case we have before us as the subject matter literally a *rara avis in teris* or a rare bird on the earth." Long walk, little joke.

That there are as many misses as hits makes us appreciate an explosion even more. In a civil case from the Seventh Circuit, *Gonzalez-Servin v. Ford Motor Co.*, the plaintiff's lawyer cleverly got around contrary precedent by simply ignoring it. He never mentioned the case in multiple submissions, all of which followed the publication of the damning precedent. This is a recognized phenomenon in the profession, judging from the several opinions in which lawyers are described as metaphorically acting as ostriches. Richard Posner rehabilitates the reputation of the ostrich in his opinion by noting that ostriches do not really hide their heads in the sand as an avoidance mechanism, but he takes the public's understanding of what ostriches do, or rather their misunderstanding, and makes sure that the plaintiff's lawyer gets the point. On the last page of the opinion he places two black and white images, each taking up nearly half the page. On the top is an ostrich with its head in the sand. On the bottom, there is a man dressed in a business suit (our lawyer presumably) with his head in the sand. LOL.

There has long been a debate about whether humor is suitable in judicial opinions. The general view is that when the humor comes too much at a litigant's expense it loses sight of an opinion's purpose and has become just an occasion for the judge to stretch his humor chops. The other view is that humor can add to an opinion by revealing the opinion writer's level of engagement. Anything toward that end is seen as good. Humor also reminds us that the judicial opinion is a genre of literature not strait-jacketed by directives in opinion writing manuals and that the opinion in part reflects the opinion writer's view of the world to give more ironic weight to the opinion. Sometimes the facts of a case, reflecting as they do the way we live, present juxtapositions and ironies that must be mentioned, not just on the theory that no good joke should go unused, but on the theory that the opinion writer understands life—what we sometimes grandly call the human condition.

LAWYERS GONE BAD

We should not confuse the public's general dislike of lawyers with the ever-increasing number of lawyers disciplined for misconduct. There is an overlap, to be sure, but lawyers have always been disliked while our plague of misconduct has more modern roots, though not because there is anything particularly different about today's profession. What lawyers do in their offices and in court has not changed much over our history. Complexity of work does not make it fundamentally different. Office work will be office work, and court work will be court work. The change has been not with what lawyers do, but with who they are. An argument that the center of the legal profession is not holding could start with sanctionable misconduct in all its forms.

Consistent with the theme of making lawyers more aware of the misdeeds of their fellow lawyers and to use those misdeeds as objects lessons of what lawyers should not be doing, many state bar journals publish the facts and results of disciplinary proceedings. My state does this in the *California Bar Journal* in a section every month titled DISCIPLINE. The well-known problem areas are well represented, usually each month.

I have friends who report reading the section hoping to see enemies in trouble, perhaps even vanquished by way of disbarment, that heaviest of sanctions. Other friends tell me that reading about what other lawyers have done produces a type of paranoia or, worse, a shock of recognition. Some see themselves in the factual recitations, much in the same way that some hypochondriacs conclude that they must have whatever disease being described because some of the symptoms seem familiar to them—at least they think they do. The concern is not with plainly sanctionable conduct relating to money but conduct such as not giving a file enough attention or not communicating enough with the clients; conduct that can reach critical mass with particular clients and lead to trouble.

The universe of misconduct is not all that large or interesting. There are no surprises in the statistics. Even the statistic that the vast majority of disciplinary sanctions involve either solo practitioners or lawyers in small firms does not produce the interesting conspiracy angle that we might have expected. All we find when we look behind the statistic is that solo practitioners and small firm lawyers are the ones with the most client contact and with the most opportunity to offend with unmonitored access to trust accounts. The actionable conduct falls into several categories such as not keeping the client informed, not returning phone calls (as part of a clever strategy), neglecting cases, disregarding suspension orders, misappropriation of money, getting an unrelated (or related) criminal conviction, over-billing, and failure to cooperate with the bar when being investigated. In looking through WESTLAW headnotes on disbarment found in 45k59.14, my favorite involves the lawyer whose misconduct even included defrauding his mother, his principal client. Talk about a lawyer with issues. The headnote reads: "[d]isbarment was appropriate sanction for attorney's cumulative misconduct, which included disobeying court orders, filing frivolous claims, engaging in disruptive conduct, and seriously interfering with the administration of justice, in connection with his representation of client, his efforts to disrupt foreclosure sale of his condominium apartment, and his fraudulent and dishonest conduct directed at his mother, who had been his principal client for the past ten to 15 years; attorney's pattern of predatory and deceitful conduct demonstrated his total contempt of his ethical obligations, the law, court rules and procedure, and even basic civility."

Facts underlying sanctionable conduct have become as predictable as the conduct itself. In what might be a majority of cases, the offending conduct was related to a substance or alcohol abuse problem, financial problems, or stress, all of which can be described as the lawyer's personal life spiraling out of control. In the bar discipline world, most everything falls under the heading of "need or greed."

To the credit of the bar, the underlying factors are considered in disciplinary proceedings. Substance abuse, for example, is usually described as a mitigating circumstance, especially if the lawyer has begun to address the problem. It is something of an irony that the bar when judging its own takes a far more tolerant view than society generally in recognizing these causal relationships.

As part of the sensitivity to the effect of substance abuse on a lawyer's conduct, one line of reasoning has been that this just shows that lawyers are just like everyone else. We even have a law review article, "The Humanization of Lawyers" by Fred Zacharias in *Professional Lawyer Symposium*, making this point. To argue that lawyers have problems with alcohol, drugs, marriages, and mental health issues consistent with the problems of the general population might be missing the point, though, if we look to the more important issue of how lawyers respond to their misconduct once it has been discovered and prosecuted in a disciplinary proceeding.

Most lawyers "get it," so to speak, especially if the complaint involves something that does not tend to lead to disbarment, at least the first time around. The lawyers acknowledge responsibility and discipline, follow the bar remedial program, and are not heard from again. The more serious the offense, the more likely that the lawyer will adopt a full defensive if not offensive mode and demonstrate that he does not get it. Here, we find the self-serving explanations and rationalizations and the position generally that the lawyer is not at fault. If there is fault, it belongs elsewhere, with the client even.

In asking what lessons can be learned from their studies of lawyer misconduct and discipline, researchers tell us what we already knew or at least suspected—that misbehaving lawyers do not see themselves as misbehaving, either at the time or once caught. There is such banality in what the lawyers have been up to and their rationalizations and explanations for their conduct that it is passing strange to hear scholars discuss the so-called powerful psychological motivations leading lawyers into trouble.

Lawyers have to work almost as hard to be disbarred as they do to get admitted. Disbarment is, of course, different from all other sanctions such as reprimand, probation, or suspension. It represents being cast out, though a surprisingly high percentage of disbarred lawyers after time reapply and get readmitted. Lifetime disbarment is a rare animal. Disbarment is for high-end misconduct, such as massive over-billing, or for serial offenders and their repeated, remorseless conduct.

The two leading books on lawyer misconduct, *Lawyers in the Dock* and *Lawyers on Trial*, are both by Richard L. Abel of UCLA. Each takes a handful of disciplinary cases and examines both the conduct itself and what happened at the disciplinary hearings. We see lawyers at their worst in the hearings that Abel covers. They might also be the worst lawyers (getting there as they did), but the arguments they make in response are rooted in conspiracy theory, grandiosity, entitlement, and near-unfathomable arrogance. We know from their first words (they usually represent themselves) both where they are going and that we do not want to follow along. These lawyers resemble white-collar criminals and their responses to getting caught. To this we can add that the lawyers at their hearings have the patter of fraudsters trying to sell.

All of it (or almost all, to use a lawyer's caution) comes back to a perception of self as a professional and its essential premise that lawyering is about the client and that the question should not (or rarely) get to be how the lawyer is personally benefitted. The lawyer is instead professionally benefitted by way of the client. The professional benefit to the lawyer is measured differently. It is a paradox or irony that 19th -century commentators wanted to make the practice of law more into a profession by distinguishing it from a business. Different, higher standards applied to a profession. Today the practices of some lawyers—big and small—may have all the trappings of a profession but are nonetheless using business-based ethics rather than professional ethics. Moreover, lawyers often see clients as the enemy in the fight over the client's money, using the full range of sharp practices against them

Looking just at the numbers, misconduct in the legal profession today is different from what it was fifty or sixty years ago. Richard Abel, as part of his history of bar discipline in California, reports that only a few lawyers each year were disbarred in California in the 1950s and 1960s. Making more of lawyer misconduct and beefing up misconduct investigations and prosecutions—so much so that California now has a bar court—certainly helps explains why a higher percentage of lawyers today offend than in the 1950s and 1960s. But we need more explanations, such as whether the general shift in the culture to narcissism has affected how lawyers think about themselves and their misconduct and, more to the point, whether the emphasis in legal education on the Socratic method and on the lawyer-as-master-of-the-universe sensibility contributes to the outrageous arrogance that underlies so much lawyer misconduct.

LAWYERS WRITING

There's more than one problem with the term "legal writing." To begin with, the term covers too much ground and lumps together writing by both judges and lawyers. Both types of course share the common subject of law, but little else. Because one advocates and one reasons and resolves, we should use the terms "judicial writing" and "lawyer writing" as a way of reminding us of the purposes of each type of writing. The bigger problem with the term "legal writing" stems from the misconception about the way that facts and ideas in law are expressed. Does the law require its own type of writing—this legal writing that we hear so much about? We can answer the question by asking if there is anything particularly special about writing about the law that distinguishes it from writing—expository prose—generally.

Those writing in the law, whether judges or lawyers, have always wanted the public to think that the law demands its own special language of sorts. Jefferson got at one aspect of this when he complained in a letter from 1817 that lawyers were "making every other word a 'said' or 'aforesaid' and saying everything two or three times, so that nobody but we of the craft can untwist the diction and find out what it means." There is the heavy use of Latin in maxims such as the maxims (or canons) of statutory construction that the profession stubbornly clings to and continues in the labels we give doctrine, as in *res ipse loquitur*. Then there is the specialized jargon that has also been a feature of the language of the law. An item in the 18th-century English *Spectator* of 1712 by an "author uncertain" captures the spirit nicely in the form of a citizen describing a visit to Westminster Hall and the lawyerly language that set him off. He writes in No. 551 that once court began, one lawyer addressed the court with "when this matter was last *stirred* before your lordships; the next humbly moved to *quash* an indictment; another complained that his adversary had *snapped* a judgment; the next informed the Court that his client was *stripped* of his possessions; another begged leave to acquaint their lordships that they had been *saddled with costs*. At last up got a grave serjeant [barrister], and told us his client had been *hung up* a whole term by a writ of error. At this I could stand it no longer, but came hither and resolved to apply myself to your Honour to interpose with these gentlemen, that they would leave off such low and unnatural expressions; for surely, though the lawyers subscribe to hideous French and false Latin, yet they should let their clients have a little decent and proper English for their money."

As amusing and as damning as this passage is, legal writers do in fact even today seemingly go out of their way to make their prose distant and disembodied, as if to confer authority on it this way, and by making a fetish of supposed precision.

The Plain English Movement that has been the law's response to the opacity and verbosity of legal language is worth charting to recognize its dimensions and, as I'll argue, its limitations. It began for practitioners in the 1960s and applied techniques that had long been applied by composition instructors for sentence and paragraph construction. David Melinkoff began in 1963 what might be called the first phase of the Plain English Movement with *The Language of the Law*, his learned, historical tour of legal writing going back centuries and to its roots in England in which he argues that the prolixity, obscuring, and bulkiness of legal writing can be stripped away without doing violence to the legal principles at issue. Richard Wydick for the second phase in the next decade then published his influential law review article that was then expanded in 1978 into his even more influential *Plain English for Lawyers*. His chapters took on fundamental composition topics: omitting surplus words; using base verbs, not nominalizations; preferring the active voice; using short sentences; arranging your words with care; choosing your words with care; avoiding language quirks, and punctuating carefully. Only four topics related specifically to lawyers. Two considered special problems of drafting of documents, while the two that considered more traditional prose directed lawyers not to use redundant legal phrases and not to use legalisms. Wydick's book thus had more in common with a book such as *The Elements of Style* by Strunk and White than with anything aimed at lawyers. *The Elements of Style*, which marked an important development in prose instruction when praised by E.B. White in a 1959 *New Yorker* article and then revised by White himself and published later that year, broke free of books, such as Eric Partridge's exceedingly popular *Usage and Abusage*, first complained about usage and then gave guidance on the proper way to do things. It could have been called *A Hint of Elegance*. Important sections address simplicity, clarity, and an active voice, though there is also guidance of usage sort helping writers to avoid choosing what might be popular but nonetheless incorrect.

Bryan Garner has conceived of himself as the third phase of the Plain English Movement with his many books and articles that stress grammar, punctuation, and style. The problem is that the third phase of the Plain English Movement should instead be the assertion that there is nothing particularly special about law and that what lawyers and judges write is just plain old English, not what Garner has in mind. The third phase should not be mere reformulation of the second phase, as practiced by Garner. Garner here is not the only offender, just the most visible—he does seem to be everywhere. He has been joined by a legion of contributors to professional journals and articles providing bite-sized bits of grammar and punctuation. They too should be criticized. The titles of some journal articles tell all: "If I Were A Lawyer: Tense In Legal Writing;" "That's The Way It Is: 'That' And 'Which' In Legal Writing;" "Five Tips for Good Legal Writing;" "Improve Your Legal Writing with Five Simple Rules;" "Cutting the Clutter: Three Steps to More Concise Writing;" "Do's, Don'ts, and Maybes: Legal Writing Grammar;" "Do's, Don'ts, and Maybes: Legal Writing Punctuation;" and "Rhetoric in Legal Writing." Garner tries at times to distinguish himself from practitioners teaching writing mechanics and to consider the grander idea of style in the way that Strunk and White consider the subject in *The Elements of Style*. But there is nothing particularly new or useful in what Garner describes, however. More might be gained in probing how style works by unpacking the best bits of good writers, but Garner prefers to stay on the surface. Whether it is on the compositional or stylistic fronts, Garner perpetuates the idea that legal writing is somehow special and ironically makes matters worse. There might not be enough money in it for legal writing CLE providers to abandon the specialness notion and instead urge lawyers to recognize that legal writing is just writing (and perhaps encouraging them to read more), but it would be better for the profession.

In truth, there's nothing special about legal writing—though law schools and practitioners would argue differently. It's just expository prose. On this, if on nothing else, I agree with Justice Scalia, who told an audience at the Harvard Club in Manhattan in 2008 that he did not believe that legal writing exists. "That is to say," he said, "I do not believe it exists as a separate genre of writing. Rather I think legal writing belongs to that large, undifferentiated, unglamorous category of writing known as nonfiction prose." These are bracing words for those who cling to the idea of so-called legal writing. To emphasize the point, Justice Scalia in the same talk noted that "someone who is a good legal writer would, but for the need to master a different substantive subject, be an equivalently good writer of history, economics, or, indeed, theology." It also follows, as history has borne out, that good writers in these subjects can make the switch and be good legal writers.

The development in the Plain English Movement that we have not gotten—yet, anyway—is the wide-spread dissemination of the idea that we should not think of the movement as a movement concerned with punctuation, sentence concision, of even paragraphing, but as a movement proclaiming that all of what lawyers write is just another example of expository writing. Maybe a decade or generation of constant reminder to lawyers would get the point across and initiate change. Such a message cuts against all of what lawyers are taught in school and what they learn in practice. The real question in what lawyers write is, or should be, what is the quality of the thinking being expressed? Our best judges have recognized that they should aim in their writing for the expository prose model, so why shouldn't lawyers? That model features an emphasis on the honest truth. The longer we stick with the label of "legal writing" and what it implies, the longer we keep ourselves from acknowledging what it is we should be doing.

LEGAL WRITING INSTRUCTION MISUNDERSTOOD

One way to look at the problem of lawyer writing is to suggest that, while the profession is asking the right questions about competence and ways to improve that competence, the profession is getting the answers either wrong or not quite right. Yes, lawyers are not particularly good writers, but not for the reasons endlessly listed by commentators. And yes, something can be done to improve lawyer writing. It's just not what educators and commentators have been pushing.

It's certainly easy to find examples of bad lawyer writing. Our cases, especially federal cases, are filled with examples of judges commenting on terrible lawyer writing. They point to and give examples of bad punctuation; lexical, syntactical, and logical errors; grammatical errors; redundancy; verbosity; run-on sentences; and, in my favorite description, "sheer gobbledygook." The writing that passes through my office from fellow defense lawyers and from Assistant United States Attorneys does not seem to be as bad as the writing pilloried in the *Federal Reporter*, though reading it prompts alternate rounds of amusement and despair. The usual suspects are all on display, such as not using the obligatory comma after city and state in an address or after the year in a date, misusing the adverbial conjunction *however*, and getting subject and verb agreement for words such as *jury* wrong. Usage mistakes abound, as in confusing *disinterested* and *uninterested* and not knowing that *principal* and *principle* have different meanings. Parallelism is just an eleven-letter word to these lawyers, if we make the doubtful assumption that they have heard it. One lawyer I am burdened with reading commits all of the above sins and goes further in not knowing the difference between *its* and *it's* and adding a possessive apostrophe to possessive pronouns themselves. The defense bar far more than the prosecution uses persuasion gimmicks such as italics or bold fonts or capital letters. The Assistant United States Attorneys at least for the most part write in developed paragraphs. Having layers of review in the United States Attorney's Office probably helps improve the final product. Defense lawyers have no such interest in at least trying to get things right. It would be nice to explain the phenomenon of bad defense lawyer writing by saying that defense lawyers resist the rules of grammar and punctuation in the same way that they resist the authority of the federal government in its prosecution, but that gives too much credit to the defense bar. Laziness, indifference, and ignorance are the better explanations.

In fashioning remedies, we need to look at what law school education and commentary in the profession have been up to. Law school legal writing has typically been built around the legal memorandum, which analyzes law on particular points. In law firms, the memoranda are often sent to the general counsel of the client to keep the client abreast of the legal work for which they are paying so dearly. The reason is that this is what young lawyers do, as backed up by the research. A Thomson West survey, for example, has indicated that in large firms a new associate can expect to spend 80 percent of his time researching, drafting, and writing documents. Between years 2–4, the figure drops to 70 percent, and for associates with more than five years, the figure drops to 40 percent. Consistent with the goals of the legal memorandum, legal writing instructors in part train students to research and analyze. They see their jobs as two-fold. They teach these written patterns of legal analysis—IRAC structured (Issue, Rule, Argument, Conclusion) or its variations—in memoranda of objective legal analysis, but they also teach the bits that go into the writing such as persuasive headings, readable sentences, and citation form. The IRAC instruction is designed to complement the case briefing that students are doing in their substantive law classes.

But why, if the issue is writing, are legal writing instructors bringing in substantive legal analysis? Why emphasize the legal memorandum at all? It's true that associates in the larger firms at least spent a fair amount of time with such research and analysis chores, but legal writing classes should not be trying to do the work of substantive law or substantive research classes. Knowing the law and knowing how to find it are unrelated to the job of writing about the results of legal research and analysis, which is what a legal memorandum does. Law schools simply divert themselves from confronting the essential issue of writing by trying to link so-called legal writing with other aspects of legal education—unless you think that what the students are writing is some special form of legal writing, which, of course, is the thinking that dominates both in legal education and the profession. To ask why we need legal writing as currently taught if the student knows how to research and knows the law and how to analyze it is to prove my point. To that person, writing up the results should be easy. Language skills taught in legal writing classes have nothing to do with legal reasoning or knowledge of the law. We should admit this and follow the consequences—the most significant of which is that writing should be taught as just writing. Bring on the composition instructors. If anything, legal writing instructors should be building courses around the top ten legal writing tips delivered recently by federal district court judge Richard George Kopf on his website, *Hercules and the Umpire* (www.herculesandtheumpire.com). Instructors would not be able to replicate the irreverence and wit of his blog, but the list can be explored with profit. Some of the highlights are that the lawyer should start a brief with a concise and accurate statement of the facts and use the writing style found in the *Dick and Jane* books. The best briefs will not seem to contain legal writing but just writing. Briefs seeking to educate the judge will be received harshly. Hyperlink when possible. Burn anything that Bryan Garner has written. Don't "bitch slap" your opponent because it only makes the judge want to do the same to you, "but in super slow motion." Get a good editor. Never send the judge something "unless someone less dumb than you has read it first." These are good precepts all.

Lawyers are a different matter. Seeing them as versions of law students and subjecting them to reminders in professional journals about punctuation, grammar, and the like mistakes what it is lawyers need to hear about their writing. They need to be told a bit about the mechanical or composition issues, but primarily they need to be reminded at every turn that when they submit a brief to a judge they are writers trying to persuade an audience in the same way that any other writer is trying to persuade an audience. That the lawyer knows precisely who his audience is should make it easy for him to give that audience what it is looking for. What, after all, is the purpose of writing if not that?

We need to keep lawyer writing in perspective. Justice Scalia in his 2008 remarks to the Harvard Club in Manhattan said that his days teaching legal writing at the University of Virginia convinced him that students lacked the skills to write at all, to say nothing of legal writing. "To tell the truth," he said, "at as late a stage as law school, I doubt this skill can be taught." What can be conveyed, he continued, was the "realization that there is an immense difference between writing and good writing" and that it "takes time and sweat to convert the former into the latter." Of course, if students cannot be taught to write, then teaching lawyers to write is hardly likely. Scalia's idea of the writing someone can be taught might be different from what lawyers need to do with their writing. Scalia is a gifted writer. Those powerful dissents of his, which we can take to be his, display skills and a level of sophistication that few writers can match. But lawyers in their writing are not trying to match—nor could they—Scalia's skills. The power of a brief to persuade, even if written by the finest writer imaginable, is greatly overrated. What the lawyer writes is determined by the facts and by the law, both of which the lawyer has almost no control over. Presenting whatever best commends an argument is the challenge for the lawyer in his writing. Being more modest about what the lawyer can do in a brief helps the lawyer present his case more effectively and, perhaps ironically, it calls into question the apparatus of legal writing instruction in law school and professional commentary on legal writing. Simple, direct, targeted—those are the distinguishing characteristics of good legal writing, if we must use that term. Put differently, these are the characteristics of just plain good writing.

To encourage such writing, we have to accept lawyer writing for what it is, not for what we want to fancy it up to be. If a lawyer sees himself as a writer and accepts a writer's responsibilities, all of the details such as punctuation and grammar problems will drop away. Any writer knows he has to fix those problems to have presentable prose. Getting lawyers to see themselves as writers gives them the incentive to handle the details while keeping their eyes on the prize—the audience.

LITERARY ALLUSIONS

It is with their use of literary allusions that judges in part try to establish themselves as writers. There is good reason for this. The apt literary quotation enhances an opinion, giving it depth and texture. But ours is not an age in which we should loosen our critical standards as to whether quoting literature is done well because we are surprised to find that judges are doing it at all. We are past that and can make no allowances just because the writer is a judge. As readers, we have the right to apply to the judges using allusions all the tests we apply to others. If anything, because judges are going beyond the traditional confines of the judicial opinion genre when they use literary allusions, we need to be persuaded that the allusions are more than just rhetorical flourishes spliced onto an opinion. A judicial writer as peacock diminishes the law and the opinion as a genre. What, then, do we think when, in looking through two hundred odd recent volumes of the *Federal Reporter,* Third Series, we encounter references to or quotations from writers such as Ben Franklin, James M. Cain, LudwigWittgenstein, Franz Kafka, Leo Tolstoy, Mark Twain, Samuel Johnson, Homer, A. E. Housman, Charles Dickens, Charles Sandburg, Robert Frost, Albert Camus, T.S. Eliot, Marcus Tullius Cicero, William Shakespeare, Ralph Waldo Emerson, Alexander Pope, Samuel Butler, Lewis Carroll, Gertrude Stein, and Abraham Lincoln? (Shakespeare by far leads as the most quoted writer, and for this and other reasons he is discussed in a separate essay.)

Judges always run the risk of misfiring when they use literary allusions. Often, the allusion does not go far in illuminating whatever is at issue and instead prompts the reader to wonder about its inclusion. A reference to Thoreau and his famous pond in a dispute over a subdivision retention pond sounds promising, if it delivers insight. What we get instead is some high-end name-dropping in *Harvey v. Town of Merrillville*: "Henry David Thoreau found solace when he lived near Walden Pond. Homeowners perhaps seeking the same from a small pond in the Innsbrook subdivision in

Merillville, Indiana, claim to have found anything but. They allege that the retention pond their lots abut is a haven not for tranquility but for algae and mosquitoes, a source of flooding and frustration rather than inspiration and insight." Other judges stumble in believing that a thought becomes profound just because the name of a famous cultural observer is attached to it, producing an effect at odds with the intention. For example, in the social security case *Liskowitz v. Astrue* in which the issue was whether there were a significant number of suitable jobs that the claimant could perform, the court first sorted through both a mass of statistical evidence and a challenge to the statistical approach of that evidence. By this time the court had spent its enthusiasm for the subject and for the dueling statistical models. Having chosen one, the court sighs and sagely notes, invoking Wittgenstein for no apparent purpose, that "in administrative proceedings, no less than in ordinary life, 'explanations come to an end somewhere.'" There are, unfortunately, more examples of allusions mismatched to the judicial moment. In the failure to pay payroll tax case *United States v. Easterday*, the court begins, "this case illustrates the enduring truth of Ben Franklin's sage observation that 'nothing is certain but death and taxes.'" In the copyright infringement case *Coquico, Inc. v. Rodriguez* involving a popular stuffed animal rendering of the coqui, a tree frog indigenous to Puerto Rico, the court invokes the fairy tale from the Brothers Grimm in which a frog kissed by a beautiful princess turns into a handsome prince to note that the plaintiff–appellant "has not yet managed to turn the coqui into an imperial presence, [though it has] fashioned a popular stuffed-animal rendering of the coqui and, thus, turned the frog into dollars." In the large drug conspiracy case *United States v. Benbow*, the court begins by noting that "the facts underlying this case began like something out of a James Bond novel but soon morphed into an international drug conspiracy sting." And in the child custody case *Castro v. United States*, the dissent, throwing up its hand at what to do, opens with the quotation from Kings on King Solomon splitting the baby and noting, "we face a situation at least as old as the one faced by King Solomon, and one requiring his wisdom: what to do when two parents claim a child." In the habeas corpus ineffective assistance of counsel case *Richter v. Hickman*, in which the issue was the extent to which the defendant's lawyer conducted an adequate investigation, the court begins by quoting *The Art of War* for the proposition that "to not prepare is the greatest of crimes; to be prepared beforehand for any contingency is the greatest of virtues." Poorly used allusions all.

Certainly the well-chosen quotation in an introduction can identify a case's essence, which is usually different from the case's holding. The reference can be short and pointed, as in the Clean Air Act preemption case *National Association of Home Builders v. San Joaquin Valley Unified Air Pollution Control District*, in which the court writes that, "The residents of the San Joaquin Valley breathe 'an air that kills,'" and footnotes A.E. Housman's *A Shropshire Lad* (1903). Water, like air, receives special treatment. In *Consejo de Desarrollo Economico, Mexicali v. United States*, a case involving the only source of water in Imperial County, California, the All-American Canal, the court recognizes the importance of water to the area and eases into the question of what will happen if the canal is improved and no longer seeps highly valued water. In an impressive opening the court conveys the meaning of water in the west, writing that "Colorado Poet Laureate Thomas H. Fernil described the West by saying: 'Here is the land where life is written in water.' The legacy of the West is one of continual, and often bitter, controversies about water rights, both above and below the surface. In the West, 'whiskey is for drinking; water is for fighting over,' Mark Twain is said to have observed. Our water dispute brings us to the Mexican–California border and the plans of the United States Bureau of Reclamation to prevent the All-American Canal from seeping water-seepage upon which thousands of Mexicans rely."

A more involved use of a literary allusion delivers some powerful judicial commentary, if not chastisement, and a striking illustration of irony. In an arbitration case, the insight goes not so much to the legal issues, which are straightforward, but to the animating motives of the parties and what can be called a howling irony. *International Union of Operating Engineers v. County of Plumas* from the Ninth Circuit involves labor arbitration, but what distinguishes the case is that the defendant county, thinking that it would be a better forum for its defense, removed the case to federal court after the union had originally filed in the Superior Court of California. On appeal, the county then took the contrary tack and argued that the court did not have subject matter jurisdiction. Brazen yes, but also permitted, since the rule that parties cannot change their litigation positions once taken does not apply to the principle that jurisdictional issues can be raised at any time. It also meant that the plaintiff union had to change its position and argue for jurisdiction, after having argued against it before removal. The defendant was indeed correct that the district court did not have subject matter jurisdiction. But it was the galling litigation strategy on both sides and the irony of the result that prompted the court to invoke James M. Cain, master of the double-cross, at both the beginning and end of the opinion. In the opening paragraph the court observes that "James M. Cain, whose novels were often adapted into film noir, described his body of work by saying 'I write of the wish that comes true—for some reason, a terrifying concept.' The plight of Pumas County would have doubtless piqued his interest." To conclude the opinion, the court turns again to Cain to note that in the archetypical Cain novel "two parties wish an outcome and both endeavor to bring it to fruition—sometimes together and sometimes independently—usually employing less than savory means." The court, fairly appalled at the opportunism of the parties, then sends the case back to the district court before sending it back to the state court to give the district judge the chance to decide whether fees or other sanctions should be imposed for wasting that court's time. The court does this, "bearing in mind the admonition that one ought to temper the rule of law with poetic justice."

Literary allusions that have jaw-dropping effectiveness tend not to be so involved as the James Cain reference, though that allusion works wonderfully well. The jaw-dropping allusion seems to come out of nowhere and is so apt that the reader feels a gush of understanding tinged with excitement at having seen the idea put into action. Here's an example from a Richard Posner opinion, *United States v. Gladish,* in which the issue is the substantial element requirement in a criminal attempt statute. Posner takes the principle of law, that to be guilty of an attempt you must both intend the completed crime and take a substantial step toward its completion, and gives it life by invoking the "hollow men" of T.S. Eliot's poem to distinguish between those who would have completed a crime and those who are incapacitated from action because "Between the conception/ And the creation/ Between the emotion/ And the response/ Falls the shadow."

The power of the literary allusion, especially the jaw-dropping kind, comes from the reader's recognition of the interconnectedness of law and literature, not in any sort of critical theory way, but in the way that the writer is showing us that he understands both worlds and that these two worlds are really aspects of each other. Does it matter that a judge is sufficiently steeped in literature that he can connect in his own mind and then for the reader the connection between law and literature on a specific point? It does, because the connection between law and literature as expressed in the literary quotation is undergirded by the idea that law is a human creation and human tool for us to move through life. Literature is about the human. Law is also. In its own minor way, using the apt literary reference, especially if it is not the product of searching through *Bartlett's Familiar Quotations* (or some version thereof), illustrates this important idea.

MODESTLY PUT

Writing by lawyers to judges—briefs—is functionary, not imaginative or expressive. It is, we should recognize, a lot simpler than people make it out to be. At least that's what I think when I think of the goal of legal writing. Other legal writing by lawyers might have other goals, such as the goal of trying to intimidate the opposition with a screed disguised as a demand letter, but for brief writing, the staple of legal writing, there isn't much doubt as to the writer's goal—to offer palatable persuasion.

My goal in brief writing is to make things easy for the judge. The judge wants a question answered. Briefs are tools to help the judge do his job. Precedent persuades, not rhetoric. Judges simply won't be persuaded by anything other than solid principles of law and by a solid set of facts. To try and provide anything but solid law or solid facts risks becoming counterproductive. Nor is conciseness enough. I try to identify the point at issue as precisely as possible and cut away everything else. Arguments usually turn on fine, subtle points, and nothing is gained by rehashing the obvious issues and following a set of formalities, such as setting out the layers of law establishing standards of review or the like. I take my reader as knowledgeable and interested in distinguishing the finer points. My tone suggests the idea that, once the essential issue or point is identified and the law applied, the response is easy. The goal is to just set it out for the judge, making it easy for him to see the correctness of the analysis. It all bespeaks a certain modesty of approach. I'm not trying to argue that white is black and black is white, as Jonathan Swift said lawyers are apt to do. I'm just pointing to the obvious. The approach relies, of course, on having found the right law. If I have the law on my side, fewer cases are best to make the argument. The court is looking for sure footing in its decision making, and the right law, as precisely on point as possible, gives the court what it needs.

When the issue is not the law but the application of the facts to the law, I strive for an orderly presentation. I like to use cues, such as "first," "second," and so forth. Organizational markers hardly matter, however, if the factual descriptions cannot bear close scrutiny. I never shade the facts to help an argument because the shading would be discovered—with the other side gleefully pouncing on misstatements—and credibility lost. The whole brief writing approach looks to credibility. In giving the court a reason to follow my direction, I want to be seen as a reputable guide.

The finer points of style add to the basic approach, though I don't know how much. I do not believe much in blaring organizational aids such as subheadings. If I can narrow the issues in the way that I want, strong topic sentences are enough. When there are several distinct issues to be argued, I'll go with sections. I use no bullet points and I certainly employ no gimmicks of persuasion, no capitalized words, and no use of the bold font. I go light on parentheticals, though I like to use the dash. It might be a failing, but I am fond of pointing out paradoxes and ironies. I do not use trendy words or phrases. No *appropriate*, *impact*, *reset*, or *perfect storm*. I only rarely use literary allusions, making sure when I do that the reader will understand my reference. I aim for active constructions. I am fond of using the rhetorical device of antithesis, contrasting ideas or words in a balanced or parallel construction. Sentence length also becomes less of a worry with the strong control of a coordinate conjunction. I go lightly on case citations, avoiding string citations. I'll try to find the latest and best case for any particular point. I use the case law of my Ninth Circuit if available, though I feel more than comfortable roaming the other circuits for authority. I have my own pantheon of judges I will cite by name, as in "(Posner, J.)." Posner is the first and most important judge I'll cite to this way. I'll also cite by name to Frank Easterbrook, Michael Boudin, and Jon Newman. I trust that the judge or the judge's law clerks will recognize quality. The real issue in distinguishing the opponent's case law, though, is the tone. The urge is to be sharp, suggesting with the sharpness that the opponent is trying to pull a fast one on the court. But even when the opponent is doing just that, it is better, I have come to believe, to distinguish the case law more neutrally. Not drawing the judge into a pitched battle of screaming lawyers makes for a better reply.

While I get some pleasure and satisfaction when I write professionally, I do not much enjoy legal writing. I have in fact a dissatisfaction with it that runs deep. I consider it a chore and, in what might be a surprise to the reader, an affront to me as a person who likes to read and write. The problem is that I am forced to do it as a professional, not as the writer I see myself as. I am someone who has always been engaged in a writing project—articles, essays, book reviews, newspaper columns, or books. I take on the projects because I like to write and because writing is important to me. No matter what form I'm working in, I get the satisfaction of composition, to be sure, but I get something more. I get to find out what I think about something. It's never clear at the start of a project, especially a bigger project, how you think and feel about a topic or subject. Finding out is the fun. Writing is the interrelated engagement with the self and with the outside world. And from what I have read, others feel similarly about writing and self-discovery. This is where we test ourselves, by pushing new information (research) against what we thought was correct and then re-determining what we think in light of the new information. If we are true to inquiry and conduct research not just to confirm what we think, the process takes us back and forth and all over before we settle on what we think is true. Once there, the final writing can begin. Drafts represent our honest confrontations with ourselves.

There is, to be sure, satisfaction in lawyering with figuring out the argument that best helps the client. That satisfaction is different from the satisfaction that comes from having discovered what I think about something. Simply put, one is personal and the other professional. Cleverness is more directly associated with finding the best line of argument for a motion or brief. There is, I must admit, a certain satisfaction that comes from using cleverness. This cleverness, built of a foundation of understanding the law, is more about fitting pieces of a puzzle together. To say that this kind of satisfaction (even when supplemented by the satisfaction of putting the best structure and polish on the writing) is less rewarding than the satisfaction that comes from writing not as an advocate but for myself is not to denigrate or disparage legal writing. It is just to point to the limitation of legal writing from the practitioner's perspective.

I cannot avoid my substantive legal writing obligations. I put them off, though, and force myself to do them. It might well be that my struggle suggests that law is not for me. Maybe. It could also suggest what is the real nature of legal writing. There's not much of me in my legal writing. It's just something I do. I research and analyze the law and then write it up in a way that most advances my client's interests while staying within ethical borders. Kept at this distance, it's a professional obligation that is manageable. The reader, in sorting through the problem at hand, is looking for information and does not want to spend the time that is needed to distinguish information from zealotry. The reader does not want to deal with capitalized words, bold lettering, or arguments that strain at the truth. The judge is—or should be—on an engagement and self-discovery mission. To understand this is to better understand the practitioner's legal writing. Lawyers need to recognize that legal writing is not about them—which seems to be the default position—but about the reader. That lawyers tend toward arrogance, as I describe elsewhere, might have something to do with this.

The problem with legal writing is that it cannot escape what it is. Badly done, it frustrates a reader looking for meaning and pains and maddens a reader who does not want to see English used poorly, incorrectly, or indifferently. But even when written clearly and with a proper regard for usage, the language of legal writing can dispirit the reader because it lacks the writer's individual, personal involvement. We need to accept this fact, but first we need to acknowledge it.

MOVIES AND TELEVISION
IN JUDICIAL OPINIONS

Strolls through the advance sheets of West's *Federal Reporter* produce much to notice and talk about, even though relationship between the noteworthy and the rest is not as high as we might want it to be. On the one hand, judges too often in their opinions are just showing off or reaching for an easy popular cultural reference. On the other hand, though, judges more thoughtfully using these references are trying to show the relevance of those references and to locate themselves as writers in the genre of the judicial opinion. The opinions, after all, are all that appellate judges leave behind. Take for example the way that judges in the last five years or so have used film and television references in their opinions.

There should be no surprise that appellate judges would have an urge to use references to movies and television in their judicial opinions. In at least one instance the goal was to show off. This is what seems to have happened in *United States v. Syufy*, a Ninth Circuit anti-trust case involving movie theater owners in which Alex Kozinski, inspired by some version of movie magic, slipped into his now well-known opinion references to 215 movie titles. In the last couple of years of my browsing, judges have instead wanted to show that what they are doing connects to the way people live. Law is not applied in the abstract and cannot be uncoupled from the historic facts of the human comedy that is our lives, though rarely is there comedy of the amusing sort to be found.

In the main, though, television and film references are made to no particular effect. There is not much added value when the court in the bank robbery case *United States v. Montes* begins by noting that "[i]n a scene reminiscent of the long ago days of *Butch Cassidy and the Sundance Kid*, [the defendants] were involved in a bank robbery spree. Much like the now infamous characters, their careers as bank robbers were short-lived and came to an end when they were captured by authorities." A reference to *Chinatown* in southwest water case *Consejo de Desarrollo Economico, Mexicali v. U.S.*, on the other hand, adds a bit, though only atmospherically.

There can be references that surprise and satisfy. In the child pornography case *United States v. Kelley*, in which the issue is whether unsolicited e-mail (spam) can form the basis of probable cause, the dissent in a footnote directs us to television's *Monty Python's Flying Circus* not on the issue at hand but on the etymology of *spam*, perhaps just for fun. It turns out that the meaning comes from the famous Python sketch on the Hormel food product. The idea is that, in the same way that the increasingly loud chorus sung by the Python players on spam makes other conversation impossible, unsolicited commercial e-mail drowns out normal discourse on the Internet, or so the opinion reports in a footnote reference to a law review article by Adam Hamel.

The urge is to link the subject at hand with our more familiar world of popular culture. The better urge is to show connections, to give insight, while the baser urge is to show off, to suggest meaning but not deliver. In the habeas case *Williams v. Cavazos*, in which the issue turned on what happened in jury deliberations, Judge Reinhardt begins the opinion by setting out the dialogue of two jury deliberation scenes, one from *Twelve Angry Men* and one from the case at hand based on the testimony of one of the jurors. The same is true of an odd case involving a challenge to a Texas statute prohibiting horsemeat for human consumption. The court in *Empacadora de Carnes de Fresnillo v. Curry* begins with a jolt, noting that, "the lone cowboy riding his horse on a Texas trail is a cinematic icon. Not once in memory did the cowboy eat his horse, but film is an imperfect mirror for reality." The court added in a footnote, though, that thieves would occasionally eat the cowboy's horse, citing the 1956 film *Seven Men from Now*.

When the subject at hand is a movie, it would not be fair to the litigants to use the occasion for jokes (see Kozinski and his 215 movie references), though surely it takes some restraint to go easy on a reference to the movie at issue. Reaching perhaps the right balance was the court's mildly amusing observation toward irony in the case *Richlin v. Metro-Goldwyn-Mayer Pictures, Inc* involving the ownership of the 1962 film *The Pink Panther*. The court opens with, "Inspector Jacques Clouseau, famously unable to crack the simplest of murder cases, would most certainly be confounded by the case we face. While Inspector Clouseau searched for the answer to the question, 'Who did it?' we must search for the answer to the question, 'Who owns it?'"

More can be made of a movie reference. To give the reader some sense of what to expect when it comes to the difficulty in distinguishing the cops from the crooks in a robbery and extortion case because many of the actors in the events are both, the court points to *Training Day*, Denzel Washington's corrupt cop movie, and notes in *United States v.Haynes* that "in our case, life imitates art." It's a good point, useful in fact, so it is surprising to see it limited to footnote status. To put it in the body of the text, to lead with it, would have been better.

This is what one judge—Terence Evans of the Seventh Circuit—does in *United States v. Calabrese*, the case of a Chicago gangster who claimed in part that there was insufficient evidence for the jury's guilty verdict. Evans recites in the opening paragraph the applicable directive that the facts are to be reviewed in the light most favorable to the verdict and then, in his only deadpan moment, he adds, "and so viewed, the facts read like a Nicholas Pileggi/Martin Scorcese screenplay." This then sets the court off in two exuberant footnotes to describe the connections between the film *Goodfellas*, which was based on a nonfiction book by Pileggi, and the facts before the court. We learn about the film, the violent sociopath character played by Joe Pesci, and that Pesci won an Oscar for his work. And then Evans as a movie fan describes the film's first scene and the Ray Liotta character explaining how it all began by saying, "[t]o me, being a gangster was better than being president of the United States." The opinion's language lapses into certain casualness, even to sound like a *noir* crime novel, which is consistent with the theme that life imitates art. We read of triggermen and mob hits, for example. To further make this point, a second movie footnote points out that the facts described in the opinion are right out of a scene of *Goodfellas*, with the scene then described.

Judges are sometimes too eager to show that they watch television and movies and that they have a fan's enthusiasm for and devotion to a particular show. With Judge Evans, it is HBO's *The Wire*. In the drug case appeal of *United States v. Fiasche* that involved wiretaps and what is known as a "dope phone," Evans in a footnote explains that viewers of "the acclaimed HBO hit series, *The Wire*, know that these phones (usually called 'burners') are difficult to trace and a favored tool of drug dealers." And in a drug case in which the definition of *re-up* is an issue, Evans first goes to the dictionary for the usual meaning before going to its meaning in drug slang, quoting from *The Wire*, giving season and episode number.

There is more Judges Evans. He could not resist summarizing the plot of *My Cousin Vinny*, reciting some of its famous dialogue, in the habeas corpus case *Sutherland v. Gaetz* in which the defendant claimed that, because his lawyer had been locked up overnight during his trial for obstreperousness, he was denied his right to effective assistance of counsel. The court detailed just how the lawyer had angered the trial judge, and then in a footnote recounted the plot of *My Cousin Vinny* under the theory that readers may find the conduct of the lawyer at issue in the appeal reminiscent of the antics of the lawyer in the movie.

Judge Evans illustrates the problem with movie and television references of both too little and too much; too little because the evidence of the declared theme that life imitates art has only the courage of a footnote. But those footnotes reveal too much enthusiasm and too much personal pleasure being revealed. It is its own turn on narcissism.

Film and television, despite the unique power they have to affect us, are not perhaps the best places to turn to show the connections between life and law. Certainly the evidence as found in the reports shows that literature is better suited for the job. Movie and television references in opinions should continue. Opinion writers need to recognize, though, such references usually produce more amusement than insight for the reader.

NATURE OF LAWYERS AND LAWYERING

Even Shakespeare struggled to describe the nature of lawyers and lawyering, if we are to judge by the graveyard speech in *Hamlet*. We learn of quiddits, quillets, cases, tenures, tricks, vouchers, and recognizances, but only as part of Shakespeare's point that even a lawyer's manipulation of the world cannot spare him a trip to that undiscovered country from which no traveler returns. When we take to the problem we could keep our distance and take the demographic route and use statistics on the more than one million lawyers in the country. We could first divide and summarize all the different types of lawyer work there are and then, if we wanted to, fashion profiles of the lawyers themselves by age, race, education, geographic distribution, and the like. There would be value to this approach, but it hardly gets to the nature of lawyers and lawyering if we understand *nature* to refer to that which is most fundamental, most essential. But even with the right approach, we can only hint at the nature of lawyers and lawyering in fifteen hundred words such as these.

If only there were more than the shock of recognition in one-line declarations of who lawyers are and what they do. We can start, though, with brightly limned truth from various lawyer novelists writing about what they know. Pithiness has its place, as with Stephen Carter in his novel *New England White* having his protagonist declare, "I'm a lawyer. I'm rude for a living." Lisa Scottoline in *Everywhere That Mary Went* gets off two good observations plumbing to truth. "I'm a lawyer," her lawyer protagonist Mary says, "[w]e don't get paid to listen. We get paid to talk." In the second, we learn that it is more than just talk. "I'll make your life a living hell. I know how to do it, you understand? It's my job. I'm a lawyer." More substantively and connecting lawyers to their education, Scott Turow in *Limitations* writes of one character that, "[h]e is a lawyer, a master of distinctions."

A description of what lawyers do has to get at what they are really doing when they do something, not just describe the thing being done. To try a case, to draft a will, and to counsel a client can all be described from the outside and are in fact described this way in practice literature, but anyone who has done any of these tasks knows that much more is going on than what is described from the outside. Scott Turow, who impresses at every turn with his insight, describes for example in *Personal Injuries* a criminal lawyer's task in telling a client that he will be going to jail. He dispenses a lot of bad news, his character tells us. Only oncologists routinely delivering fatal diagnoses to patients have it harder. And it's true. "It was my responsibility," his character tell us, "many times every year to tell people—many of them kindly, okay human beings who'd made a single mistake or who suffered from character failings that did not prevent them from being loving parents or friends—it was my duty to tell these individuals that they were going to be scourged by their community, captured, and caged. Even worse, I often helped them explain these unimaginable facts to their spouses and children, most of whom inevitably felt, with some reason, that they were the true victims of the penal system." The truth delivered is hard on all involved, including the lawyer, who feels part of the burden of changing lives with his explanations.

Definitions can of course help, but soon enough we see their limitations. What does it mean to be an advocate, for example? Taking the word first as a noun and then as a verb, *advocate* applies to both who lawyers are and what they do. All true, but what we learn from the dictionary is dwarfed in insight by what John William Corrington in his short story "Nothing Succeeds" tells us about lawyers as advocates and the act of advocacy. He shows us that the lawyer as an advocate loses himself in the job. "It is of the essence of advocates," he tells us, "that they be able to take on at once the color of the place where they must work. It is not a conscious thing, or it would be useless. It is an inherent capacity by which he who would preserve or alter the status of a situation in which he is alien shifts his cognitions into the key dominant amongst the contenders with whom he deals." This is a dense but necessary quotation.

Corrington's point is that as part of their advocacy, advocates become part of what they are working on. The connection of course is to George

Orwell's "Shooting an Elephant" essay and its theme that the tyrant wears a mask and his face grows to fit it. You become what you do. Others have made this point about lawyers and their work, in different formulations and with different emphases, but none as penetratingly as Corrington. Consider a stone metaphor. A lawyer in a second short story, "Nothing Succeeds," laments—for all lawyers—that, "[o]ne of the results of aging in the law is that you are not easily gotten to. By the time you have been at it thirty or forty years, you have done so many things no one should have to do that something has drained out of you, to be replaced with the law, like a creature trapped in the mud which is hard pressed for a long, long time, leaching away the soft parts, making everything over. In stone." In yet a third short story, the litigator in "Actes and Monuments" uses his ruthlessness as a weapon against lawyers of more delicate sensibility and learns an essential lesson after a heart attack that prompts him to seek a new life. He learns that "such work tightens the viscera. One cannot play bloodster without gradually coming to possess the metabolism of a jaguar, a predator."

Weighed down with these insights, it is a relief to come across a different formulation that can perhaps make us smile. Kermit Roosevelt in *In the Shadow of the Law* notes that, "[a]fter a certain number of years, lawyers started to resemble their clients, either in analogy to the pattern of married couples or on the theory that you are what you eat."

Identity issues help explain why nearly all the lawyers in Lawrence Joseph's 1997 non-fictional *Lawyerland* are unhappy or worse. *Lawyerland* is a rare find for a lawyer looking to find out what other lawyers think about what they do. The book's conceit has Joseph as a lawyer himself (though he doubles as a poet) interviewing a number of lawyers he knows or has been led to from a wide variety of fields. The goal was to get honest, free-wheeling conversation about all the things that lawyers think about or talk to each other about. In a clever move, Joseph creates from his conversations a series of what might be called composite lawyers. What is most striking about the book is that the lawyers are marked by flashes of anger and hate and that their views on practicing law and the profession generally flow from their own particular places in the profession and in opposition to the places others find themselves in. The criminal defense lawyer, for example, displays passionate hatred toward the prosecutors who brought extra prosecutorial zeal against one of his clients. An insurance company defense lawyer, similarly, hates personal injury lawyers for the frivolous lawsuits they bring. The two labor lawyers—one representing fired workers and the other representing the firing companies—who meet with the author to explain what each of them does nearly begin brawling, so committed are they to their respective positions. The litigation positions they take translate into entire world views. They can't even stay in the same room at the same time—one walks out in a huff. And the two lawyers who decades before had worked together at a federal agency before taking different paths in the profession, one going to a corporate law firm and the other to his own small firm that represents plaintiffs of all stripes, begin their joint meeting with the author fondly enough, but before long they take umbrage at the suggestion of the other that they have abandoned, in their different ways, the ideals they shared when they worked together at the start of their careers. Fond remembrance turns into charged testiness.

How does it happen? Where does it happen? What are the warning signs? Can it be avoided? These are the essential questions for the profession, not whether it does happen. Kermit Roosevelt (*In the Shadow of the Law*) puts the transformation, the melding of the mask to the face, in the big firm context. Young associate Katja is struggling with her personal life being taken over by her law firm life, and the tricks she has used so far, such as sticking to a schedule of reading novels, are losing their effectiveness. She seeks out a thoughtful partner who explains that lawyers resisting the pull of the practice of law do one of two things. They can can become self-hating as they try to insist that they have interests outside the office—a legal profession version of the hyphenate, as in lawyer-painter or lawyer-collector—or they can give in and become assimilated, which translated into the language of popular culture means becoming part of the Borg. He has a good speech worth quoting in part. "If you commit yourself emotionally to the job, it will give you something in return," he says. "But it will consume your life. If you hold back, you may live outside your work, but you'll hate every minute you spend there. You have to give in. This is a big firm. You're in the machine now. It will process you. And when it's over, it won't have mattered if you loved Shakespeare or Coltrane or the Boston Red Sox. What you love doesn't matter to the law. Love is nothing here."

To return to Orwell and the problems he recognized in himself when he felt forced to kill the elephant, there was for him only one way out of his dilemma of becoming a policeman exercising force he did not believe in. He had been legally right in shooting the elephant, but that was not enough. He could not abide the implications of what he had done and had to flee the role to keep the mask from fitting his face permanently.

All of this leads to the most difficult question lawyers face—what to do about what lawyering does to them? Orwell's response to the pressures he felt probably won't fit many lawyers. Nor should it. There was an authoritarian military machine demanding conformity from Orwell. Not so for lawyers, even in the worst of Big Law firms. There is in law firms an artificial hierarchy among the lawyers, but it just that, artificial. Lawyers once admitted are all equal. If nothing else, this status imposes an obligation for a lawyer to establish his own relationship with the law and with the profession. Lives in the law cannot be delegated to others. Each lawyer must for himself confront the essential nature of lawyering, which is the ongoing struggle of lawyers, ironically, not to be transformed by the very acts of their lawyering. There are no easy answers, but answers are nonetheless required. Reading the lawyers writing fiction about their lawyer characters wearing suffocating masks is a start. The rest is up to each lawyer.

NIHILISTS AMONG US

Lack of civility sure, but it's nihilism that's the real threat to the legal profession. It's not good for anyone when lawyers act like jerks and gum up the works and make life unpleasant for judges and opposing lawyers. But to not believe in law, which comes about as an extension of not believing in the very nature of the legal profession . . . now that gets to the core of what's wrong with the legal profession today. That's the nihilist's way.

Nihilism is more than incivility. It is the major leagues of aggressively alienating behavior while incivility is the minor leagues. Incivility, as we know, has been a persistent if not growing problem in the profession for the last few decades. Commentators, judges, and lawyers began to take notice in the 1970s and 1980s and the profession began taking action beginning around 1990. Studies and surveys were conducted to identify its manifestations and to suggest ways to combat it. The 1991 study conducted by the Committee on Civility of the Seventh Federal Judicial Circuit is a good example of the profession's response to the incivility problem. The study got back fifteen hundred responses to its questionnaire and thousands of comments from lawyers and judges on what the problem looks like and how possibly to solve it. It was less than surprising to learn that acts of incivility come in all sizes. We learn of lawyers not responding to phone calls or letters, presenting mindless opposition to discovery requests, outright lying, using discovery as a weapon, scheduling matters when the other party is unavailable, taking extreme positions and blindly maintaining them in the face of uncontroverted contrary evidence, being consistently late, being less than honest in discovery disclosures, lying about conversations about other lawyers, deceiving without committing a direct falsehood, seeking postponements the day before deposition because of a "conflict," setting depositions without notice, using Rule 11 as a weapon, fighting about everything, attacking opposing lawyers rather than confronting the facts of the case, and generally practicing "S.O.B." law.

Incivility for lawyers has as its currency contempt and bad manners. Nihilism, incivility's dark cousin, on the other hand, dwells in the very rejection of the meaning of law. The nihilist lawyer does not believe in law, not in a grander political way, such as the well-known nihilistic attitude of totalitarian regimes toward law and justice, but in a smaller, more personal way. We find an example of this nihilism in the lawyer character of Todd Andrews in John Barth's 1956 novel *The Floating Opera*. Andrews has been identified by commentators for good reason as a nihilist based on his nihilistic view of the law and is used by Barth in the first of a series of novels in which he explores whether there is reason to believe in anything.

Andrews, our narrating protagonist, is a partner in a small Maryland law firm recounting in the novel the events of the day in which he had planned to commit suicide but ultimately changed his mind. On the law and the practice of law he is explicit. He doesn't believe in "that will-o'-the-wisp, the law," and tells us he has no interest in what law is. His attitude, he tells, us "allows for the defeat, even the punishment of the innocent, and at times the victory of the guilty." He accepts his basic irresponsibility. "I affirm, I insist upon my basic and ultimate irresponsibility. Yes, indeed." He engages in sophistry and practices casuistry. Winning or losing litigation is of no concern to him, he says, "and I think I've never made a secret of that fact to my clients. They come to me, as they come before the law, because *they* think they have a case. The law and I are uncommitted." He is "curious about things that the law can be made to do, but this disinterestedly, without involvement." Perhaps as a general reflection of his view of the law, the big probate matter that he is handling and which he succeeds in winning involves a bequest by the owner of a pickling company of one hundred pickle jars of his excrement that he had required to be saved from his last stay in the hospital. The details of what Andrews does to win are unpleasant and are best not discussed.

Judging by the way he engages with others, Andrews seems to have nothing in common with today's uncivil lawyers. He is polite, has a sense of humor, and gets along well with the lawyers he works with and opposes. These traits would certainly set him apart from other nihilist lawyers in a crowd. What links him with those other lawyers is that he like them does not believe in law. He's just more subtle about it. The other lawyers in the crowd—the worst offenders I am describing—show that they do not believe in law in other ways. Staggeringly, the nihilist lawyer does not believe in that which makes law work—language. The responses that lawyers routinely give to interrogatory requests and to document production requests are examples of this, though there are others. The requesting party anticipates the objection that the request is vague, ambiguous, and all the rest by setting out detailed definitions for most every word that can be interpreted broadly enough so that the responding party cannot say that it does not know what the requesting party is talking about. This, of course, does not stop the responding party from objecting to every interrogatory, no matter how clearly it is written, on the grounds that the interrogatory is vague, ambiguous, and unintelligible. That an interrogatory in unintelligible is the favored response to most everything.

The requesting party has every right to be insulted by the response that the request is unintelligible. Time, effort, and, most of all, intelligence have gone into the drafting of the interrogatories. Language matters and the drafter has worked hard at getting his language to work as hard for him as it can. The responding party, with a wink and nudge, contemptuously dismisses the interrogatories by saying that it can't for its life understand what the requesting party is talking about. It's done with a wink and a nudge because, when the tables are turned, the requesting party turned responding party is going to make the same vague, ambiguous, and unintelligible responses that had been given to it when it had made its interrogatory inquiries.

This phenomenon, this rejection of language and its ability to convey ideas and information, might be brushed aside because everyone knows that the discovery process exists more for show and billable hours than as a legitimate attempt at resolving disputes. But the nihilist lawyer takes the rejection of language to its logical conclusion when he persists in other contexts in asserting that he has no idea what the other side is talking about. To "meet and confer" should mean that the lawyers have gotten together to talk through their differences. Taking the unintelligible line when talking on the telephone or in person takes on a whole new meaning. It is now more clearly marked as an act of negation. Today's nihilism is expressed in failing to respond to calls, e-mails, and letters; claiming that letters and e-mails did not arrive; or claiming that packages arrived damaged and insisting on having them resent. The nihilist lawyer does not believe in communication and uses that absence of belief as a weapon. Only the client's desires exist for the nihilist lawyer. And once you factor in that the lawyer has likely abdicated his role as counselor and has done nothing to reign in the client and is instead a mere facilitator for the client's desires, then you have an even deeper nihilism.

Not believing in language allows the nihilist to engage in mischief on two levels. On one level, what the nihilist considers to be the failure of language operates to keep ideas from being discussed. In a recent case of mine I tried hard to persuade my nihilist opponent as we prepared for a court trial to stipulate to certain hardly debatable facts, knowing that if we didn't the court would be angry for wasting its time in proving these uncontested facts. My opponent would not budge, would not even respond to my e-mails. And sure enough, once I started proving these incontestable facts at trial, the judge became irate, took us into chambers, and insisted that we get together and stipulate to what was now an obvious set of incontestable facts. In the meeting that followed with my nihilist opponent I was treated to complaints that he could not stipulate because he did not know, exactly, what I wanted him to stipulate to. No matter what I said, or no matter what the court had said, my nihilist opponent would not engage. So on one level there was no way to breach the distance between the facts and what the lawyer wanted. On a second level, however, not believing in language meant that my nihilist opponent and myself were never able to engage as two lawyers sorting through an issue. His negation went beyond the facts of the trial to me as a lawyer. This is where he lived, in denying even my existence as a lawyer

What was true of my opponent is true of all lawyer nihilists—that they assert in all of what they do that nothing binds them professionally to opposing counsel. For these nihilists, there are no brothers and sisters at the bar, no professional colleagues. Those experiences that help bind lawyers together—law school, studying for the bar, the bar examination itself, first jobs, and all the rest—have no sway with them. They have no brothers, to invoke *Richard the Third*, they are themselves alone.

Our bad-acting, uncivil lawyers would argue that the dedication they show for their client's cause demonstrates that, rather than not believing in law, they believe in law completely. But that's a smoke screen. These nihilists devalue the law's highest values, a devaluing move consistent with a fundamental nihilistic attitude trait. These nihilists do not believe in lawyers. They do not believe in the legal profession. To do so would require shared values, which would include recognition and civility. They do not believe in law and the profession necessary for it to function.

PERSONALITY AND OFFICE SPACE

Everything about his office space reflects upon the lawyer—where the space is located, what kind of building it is in, and how it is furnished. Commentator Fred Williams in his *Journal of Dispute Resolution* article "The Law Office as Indicator and Amplifier of Professional Status" has suggested that "in seeing that his office space is appropriately designed and decorated, the lawyer fulfills at least two purposes: he gives a sense of the powers available to be exercised on the client's behalf by the attorney; and, he reminds himself of his obligation to appropriately exercise those powers." Not for the lawyers I know, I must say. They share the dominant view that an office's purpose is to shine a light on the lawyer's splendor.

Just what is an office for and how should it be maintained? Advice from a 19th-century judge to some graduating law students poised to go into practice can act as our window into the importance of the lawyer's office to his practice. We learn from Charles I. Walker's "Practical Suggestions" found in Joseph Wesley Donovan's 1881 *Modern Jury Trials and Advocates* that it can double as a guide not just to an historical period but to the issues that the offices raise and is worthy of extensive quotation. The description presents a modest approach to how an office presents the lawyer. First, we learn, the office must be orderly. "Although not as important as some other matters, I think the manner in which you keep your office is not unimportant. The lawyer should remember that 'Order is heaven's first law,' and order, perfect and complete, should reign in his office. His books and papers should be arranged so that there is a place for everything, and everything is to be found in its place. The time and worry saved to a man, by habits of a system of order, can hardly be exaggerated." Orderliness must then be matched by neatness, we learn. "Neatness, too, should prevail. Nothing is more disgusting than the office of a lawyer where the furniture is covered with as heavy coat of dust, the floor covered with old papers, and the spittoons filthy and disgusting with the result of the use of tobacco. If you are so far unfortunate as to be slaves either to the habit of smoking or chewing, establish it as a settled rule of your life, that you will do neither in your office. If you indulge in these habits there, then every visitor will feel also at liberty to indulge in the same filthy habits, and the result will be that your office will be offensive to more senses than one." Lastly, your furniture should reflect your station. "Your furniture should be neat and comfortable, and how expensive, should entirely depend upon your business. If the business authorizes it, a carpeted room, good chairs, and neatly covered tables, aid in giving character and dignity to a lawyer's office."

Certainly in the public's imagination good lawyers do not only come out of high rises. Paul Biegler's law office in the 1959 blockbuster movie version of Robert Traver's *Anatomy of a Murder*, set in Michigan's rural Upper Peninsula, was only his modest house with a section set aside for lawyering. This was actually an improvement for Biegler. In the novel, he lived and had his office above a dime store. In small, rural towns in the 1950s lawyers such as Biegler might not have thought that having an office above a dime store meant anything. It probably didn't. Twenty-five years ago I had an office above a liquor store on the busiest street in a small college town and no one thought twice about it. I know I didn't because I had made the twelve hundred recently remodeled square feet into just what I wanted the space to be.

Other lawyers have felt differently about what their office space might be saying about their success or lack of it. Scott Turow in his fine novel *Pleading Guilty* has his narrator, Mack Malloy, reflect on his good fortune to have caught the attention early in his career of a go-getter named Jake who ushered him into the worlds of practice and office space success by describing the office space hell that goes with failure. "Without Jake," he says to himself, "I'd probably be in some interior office space with cheap paneling, practicing on my own, scrambling around to the police courts and otherwise looking hungrily at the silent telephone."

Giving full reign to their personalities is not an unknown objective for lawyers in their office furnishings. Perry Mason of the original television series stamped his office with style and with marks of his personality. Mason had a great office in downtown Los Angeles, supposedly just west of Hill Street between 3rd and 4th Streets. He had a balcony (perhaps inspiring the balcony in *Boston Legal* four decades later) and a secret entrance for Paul Drake, his indispensable private investigator. He had a prominently displayed bust of Voltaire in his office as well, and perhaps emblematic of being the cleverest lawyer around, his office had no fewer than twelve walls, thanks to ingenious set designers. On the fictional side, Richard Dooling's darkly comic *White Man's Grave* gives us the most ferocious bankruptcy lawyer in Indianapolis, who takes the Hemingway approach to masculinity assertion. In the office we first find a banner proclaiming KING OF THE BEASTS still not taken down after a celebratory party. Then we read that "his desk and three enormous worktables were scattered with trophies from proceedings gone by." And finally, immediately to the lawyer's right, we see the head of a huge stuffed black bear that the killer bankruptcy lawyer had shot in Alaska and which "was mounted on the lid of a metal wastebasket."

Fiction cannot match real life sometimes, though. Melvin Belli, the King of Torts, as he was described in a 1954 *Life* magazine piece, worked in an office every bit as flamboyant as the red silk-lined suits and calf-high black snakeskin cowboy boots he wore to court. His appetites ran to "good wines, great tables, wide travels, and beautiful women." The office featured an enormous Bengal tiger-skin rug purchased from Elizabeth Taylor, a 17th-century globe, Nepalese tapestries, hundreds of rare books, a case of French Burgundy, and an 18th-century mahogany bar. And as a nice touch, the brick walls sported autographed photographs of friends from sports, show business, and politics. Of course there was also a life-sized self-portrait with a distinctly Napoleonic sensibility.

If anything, Belli gives cover for us all and our individualized urges to proclaim ourselves. In like manner, law firms use space allocation—both square footage and location—among lawyers and staff to deliver messages of hierarchy. *Double Billing: A Young Lawyer's Tale of Greed, Sex, Lies, and the Pursuit of a Swivel Chair*, Cameron Stracher's perceptive and keenly observant memoir of sorts about a young associate's Big Law experiences, helps sort through the layers of meaning as to how much and what kinds of space law firm inhabitants have. His first-person narrator tells us first about the office for the lawyers of their different ranks. "Light and space," he writes. "Like some principle of relativity, the more you had, the faster you were moving. Partners had the corner offices, the ones on the higher floors, the large southern exposures. Associates had offices with windows and played a frantic game of musical chairs when colleagues departed and their offices became available." A rung down in the hierarchy, the staff were condemned to life without windows. "Paralegals dwelled in the interior offices," we learn, "two to a room. Secretaries were grouped in threes and fours in 'stations' near their bosses, their faces visible to all who passed in the hallway, a four-foot wall obstructing only their computers." And then, perhaps invoking some Dante-esque hellish language, we find that "in the inner circle, airless and lightless, clanking with the machine drone of copiers, smelling of toner and grease, crowded with boxes and files, dwelled the messengers and file clerks. While the lawyers and paralegals had doors, and the secretaries at least had cubicles, these unfortunate denizens of the middle world were without a nameplate, a telephone, a place to sit. They leaned against bookshelves and hovered near the monstrous machines as the gears spat out paper like flies."

How a law office presents to the world and what it says about its individual lawyers has taken on a new twist with the developing trend of online law practices in which there is no actual office, only what is now called a "virtual law office." Certainly all the technology is there for a law practice to offer everything but the handshake that typical offices offer. With Skype, e-mail, and the rest, lawyers can talk to, communicate with, and even meet with their clients to provide them all that they need. Some states with badly written or archaic attorney residency requirements are struggling to indicate that there are no impediments to a web-based practice and virtual offices, but this seems to be just a detail as virtual law practices grow in size and increase in number. Technologically-based issues such as the ethical implications of cloud computing are not unique to virtual practices. In many ways, the brick-and-mortar law practice as we know it exists solely for the lawyer to be physically in the same room with clients and, of course, to impress them with those offices. A firm's website is now the functional equivalent of the downtown office building, at least as far as trying to impress the client goes.

Traditionalists will argue that there will always be a need to have big meetings with clients, or other lawyers, or both. Larger firms have been leading the way in using technology but holding out on the need for a physical location, likely because they believe that with their size nothing other than an office building will work. But, as more and more of what lawyers do today happens in front of a computer or some other technological portal, the meaning of the relationship between a lawyer and his office space comes into sharper focus as it gets challenged.

A deep irony accompanies the movement to virtual law offices. Lawyering in many ways is an individual activity, done by the lawyer alone. The multitude of ways that a lawyer can enhance himself with the aid of technology isolates the issue of how important law firms themselves, not just law firm office spaces, are to the practice of law. All of today's technology allows the solo practitioner or small firm to compete as never before with firms that have had resource advantages in the past. At the same time, that very technology and the enhanced lawyers it produces should make us wonder just why we need, from a lawyering point of view, law firms, certainly big law firms. If form follows function, perhaps office space, or the lack of an ultimate need for it, is telling us something about what the very function of lawyering is.

PRACTICE BEFORE AN UNHAPPY JUDGE

The best source for information on the phenomenon of federal judges who have resigned comes from the Federal Judicial Center and a study it commissioned in 1992 to scour available records to identify the particular reasons that judges over a two-hundred-year period gave for their resignations. The judges have of course cited a variety of reasons for resigning their commissions. The best-known resignations are best described as forced resignations, such as when former Illinois governor Otto Kerner resigned from the United States Court of Appeals for the Seventh Circuit in 1974 one step ahead of impeachment after having been convicted in 1973 of sixteen mail fraud counts in federal court. The voluntary resignations for issues relating to the normal processes of life are more interesting, as they tell us something about the job of judging and when the fit between the judge and the job is no longer tight. Based on what I've seen, we should have more resignations.

Some judges have resigned their positions only to take up new judicial positions or positions in government. One judge (actually a Justice), Charles Evans Hughes, had the good fortune to resign from the Supreme Court to run for president, and then, after losing, be reappointed to the Court, this time as Chief Justice. Some have resigned because of disabilities and others have resigned for age or health reasons. A fair number have resigned to return to the practice of law, while others have left for other types of employment. A distressing large or impressively small number of judges, depending on your point of view, have resigned rather than face the wrath of Congress. More general allegations of judicial misbehavior have led an even greater number of judges to resign.

Some reasons for leaving the bench have been with us since the beginning of the republic. Complaints about judicial salaries are like this. Resignations tied to inadequate salaries began as early as 1796, with

173

Nathaniel Pendleton resigning his position after six years, at the age of forty, because his salary was not great enough to educate his children. Similar explanations have followed through the decades. The contrast has always been with what the judges could make in private practice. When Simon Rifkin resigned in 1950, for example, word was that in his new law firm he would be making ten times his judicial salary of $15,000 per year. One district judge of the 19th century complained of the extensive travel required to meet the demands of the district, while a district judge leaving the bench in 1974 similarly complained that he did not like spending three months away from his family. One judge found that judicial service was just too tame for him. Another complained that, "the judicial life and duties proved less congenial than he expected." Another judge saw resignation as leading to freedom. Carl Rasch, who resigned in 1911 at the age of forty-five after just two years on the bench, told his local newspaper, "I feel like a man who has had a mighty load lifted from his shoulders. If I were ten or fifteen years older I might consider staying on the bench, but I am not yet ready for the constraint which hedges about this position. It doesn't comport with my temperament. I like to have my friends, a man on the bench cannot have real friends. When I meet a man I know and like, I want to slap him on the back if I feel that way and ask him to have a drink. You can't do that when you are a federal judge." For others it is a matter of principle. In the approximately twenty years that the Sentencing Guidelines were mandatory, which resulted in cabining judicial discretion at sentencing, many were heard to complain, but Irving Lawrence of the Southern District of California went further and resigned in opposition to the guidelines, believing them too harsh. "If I remain on the bench," he said, "I just can't, in good conscience, continue to do this." Some had greater goals to meet. For Justice John Hessin Clarke it was world peace. He resigned the High Court in 1922, at the age of sixty-five and after nine years of service, to promote American participation in the League of Nations. As described in *Guide to the United States Supreme Court*, he explained to the president that he would "'die happier' working for world peace rather than devoting his time to determining whether a drunken Indian had been deprived of his land or whether digging a ditch was unconstitutional or not."

That a federal judgeship is perhaps the most highly prized position in the profession does not mean it is the best job. It will be that for some, to be sure, but not for everyone. It may require too much time with books for some, as well as too much time with a pen or at the computer writing. And in the same way that the reading and writing demands of an appellate judgeship remain mere abstractions until the demands of the job kick in, the challenges that come with presiding over trials—boredom being the most obvious—do not present themselves until the new judge is on the bench and faced with what many consider to be the relentless tedium of trials.

Then there is the problem that comes with any lifetime appointment. It is perhaps surprising that, given that the appointment age has been steadily declining at both the trial and appellate levels, even more judges do not decide to leave the bench, just to do something else. Ours is not a system, such as found in Europe, in which judging is a career choice and path that young lawyers can pursue. Someone coming to the federal bench at forty—something of the norm today—can look forward to between thirty or forty years on the bench, at the same job, and living in the same bubble of isolation. People often change while the job does not.

Not only might a judge's interest in the profession change once on the bench for a bit, but the changes that might affect anyone else can also affect judges. It might not be changes with regard to money, the freedom to speak publicly, or the ability to socialize that affect the judge. It can just be that the judge changes in his personal life as he grows older. What about the judge who grows depressed, irritated, or unhappy that his life has not turned out as he hoped? Life's disappointments and their accompanying unhappiness, loneliness, boredom, resentment, jealousy, pessimism—just to name a few of the things that can happen to us along the way—visit judges as often as they visit others.

Judges who have resigned are to be respected for taking action against the forces that have led to their dissatisfaction on the bench. What must be true is that these judges who took the step of resigning cannot be the only judges who have complained about the forces and factors that prompted dissatisfaction. It is the nature of the job, for example, that the judges must deal with an isolation from the profession that they did not experience as practicing lawyers. And certainly any successful lawyer going to the bench will have a constant reminder that he has given up much financially to be a judge. Certainly the judges who resigned because the job turned out to be something other than what they expected cannot be the only ones to learn of a distance between reality and expectation.

This brings us to those judges who should resign but haven't. It is painful seeing a judge who, for purely personal reasons, in a matter of a just a few years falls from the obligations of the office. Every appearance before this kind of judge has you thinking afterwards—if not during—that he should just resign and stop inflicting unpleasantness on everyone else. Ironically, the oddly incentivized retirement scheme for federal judges makes it more difficult for those judges who should get out to do so. Retirement under 28 U.S.C. §371 (c) sets out the "Rule of 80" and the fifteen years of service that are ordinarily requirement to qualify for retirement. The retiring judge's age and at least fifteen years of service must total 80 for the judge to retire. The rule has flexibility built into it if the retiring judge is older than sixty-five, but not if younger. If older, the number of required years of service can be adjusted downward, so that, for example, a judge retiring at sixty-seven needs only thirteen years of service. For judges younger than sixty-five, the retirement scheme pushes them off a cliff and gives them nothing. Making enough money, though, should hardly be a problem for judges retiring in their prime years. In fact, it is getting back into the workplace that would likely fix much of what is wrong with their lives. It is the bubble that judges live in that curtails their ability to meet and interact with people and leads generally to the idea that judges are special. This idea has much to do with warping the judge's engagement with the profession and with life.

I know whereof I speak. I know a federal judge whostruggles with his loneliness (both in his job and his personal, unmarried life) and either cannot see that he is imposing his mood swings on those in the courtroom or does not care that he does. My guess is that he knows but does not care. The general rule of the need to change a losing game applies to federal judges as much as it does to anyone else. If the nature of judging, with its isolation, tedium, and desiccation exacerbates an unhappy and barren personal life, the answer is not to stay and hope things get better, since there is no reason to think that they will, but to leave and search out the people and experiences needed for a more fulfilling life. What, after all, does a job of prestige mean if the jobholder is unhappy at least in part because of the job?

The easy if not cowardly response to the problem is to double down, so to speak, on what the job allows a judge to get away with. It's a version of acting out as a plea for help, but at the same time rejecting the possibilities of help. If truth be told, it does not bother me for a moment that the judge I am describing is unhappy. He has brought it all upon himself. What matters is that the process, the fair administration of justice, suffers from mercurial rulings and for a prison-like atmosphere in his courtroom. Moreover, my professional life suffers because an appearance before an unhappy judge is the forced submission to live in someone else's world of pain. It's not for me, but I don't have a choice. Judges such as the one I am describing are just bullies of a sort, getting away with bad behavior—displays of temper, petulance, irritability, and abusiveness—because they can. It's wrong. The unhappy judge should just leave and let the rest of us get on with things.

PROFESSIONAL CYNICISM

At least we know what we are up against. For those who worry about the state of the profession on issues such as civility and the lawyer's role as counselor, we have been told that the solution is to recognize that the profession as we know it is dead. If we can do that, we can get on with the business of servicing monied interests and be treated in these changing times as the business consultants that lawyers have become. Why worry? Be happy—by changing the label and eliminating all those professional obligations. In a scorch-the-earth world, the argument runs, we should drop our obsession with the genteel and prowl the world with scowls on our faces.

We have long had those calling for the break up of the legal profession, but this new argument is different. In the past, critics have looked to autonomy and monopoly as distinguishing characteristics of the legal profession to argue that social, economic, and political trends have undermined the need for them. It no longer needs to be a world unto its own to succeed, the argument runs. Let's do away with entry barriers and let the market sort it out. The new wave of criticism in contrast has considered the ways that the profession is changing in the delivery of legal services and considers what the transformation means in relation to the notion of a profession. Several commentators in books and articles have gone this way, but academic Thomas Morgan deserves the most attention for the argument set out in his wonderfully titled articles "Calling Law a 'Profession' Only Confuses Thinking about the Challenges Lawyers Face" and "The Last Days of the American Lawyer" and in his 2010 *The Vanishing American Lawyer*, published by Oxford University Press. It is an argument based on a realism of what these new types of lawyers do—or want to do—and how that is not going to change. It can't even be considered surrender to the new forces. It is an embrace of these forces and an excited plea to modify our idea of the profession, to strengthen the identity of the new lawyer-trained operator. The troubling part for us is the idea that this is the way it should be. It accepts that lawyers don't have the obligation to try and reign in clients and that in litigation hardballing and scorching-the-earth are just fine. It accepts, if not advocates, our current configuration in which whatever professional sensibility there might be out there is trumped by the Big Law insular sensibility, the us-against-the-world approach that rejects the profession and embraces tribalism.

Morgan argues with vigor that from the time lawyers began their talk of professionalism and public service, they have always been more about money and themselves than anything else. For the idea of the profession, and professionalism, Morgan, as have many others, looks to Roscoe Pound's often repeated 1955 definition of a profession that "the term [professionalism] refers to a group of men pursuing a learned art as a common calling in the spirit of a public service—no less a public service because it may incidentally be a means of livelihood. Pursuit of the learned art in the spirit of a public service is the primary purpose. Gaining a livelihood is incidental, whereas in a business or trade it is the entire purpose." The American Bar Association thought in the 1980s that the definition still had bite and used it as part of its Commission on Professionalism. The thrust of the anti-profession argument goes right at the problem and declares the definition meaningless and to be just a label that makes lawyers feel good about themselves as they advise and align themselves with their clients. The idea for Morgan is that lawyers have used the rhetoric of professionalism "to defend practices that outside observers could easily see served the interest of lawyers but not the interest of the public or the interest of justice." Since what others call the legal profession has not acted much like a profession, Morgan argues, let's stop calling it and treating it like a profession. If we are more honest about what lawyers do individually and collectively, we can better recognize the changes such as globalization and atomization that are in store for what others call the legal profession. In the future, lawyers will be more like business consultants than anything else. Lawyers are economic actors, specially trained but driven by all the vices and virtues of a capitalist economic system. Talk of a profession or of professionalism just gets in the way of seeing what is before us.

The idea of professionalism is flattering to lawyers, he argues. The elements of what has been put forth as professionalism are all easily knocked down. Civility, for example, is just a personal choice, not something required by the profession, no matter how much nicer things would be if lawyers were nicer to each other. Such niceness, in fact, can run against the client's best interest, hardly making it a value to be promoted. Moreover, what others call the legal profession does not promote civility. While it is true, he acknowledges "that we share a common humanity and learn ethical conduct from others," he disagrees "with the implication that the only or even best understanding of good lawyer behavior is provided by other lawyers." Let's not confuse the lawyer as a person and what the lawyer does in his profession, runs the general theme. Equally important, the idea of professionalism, that the lawyer is supposed to act as a check on the client, is nonsense. The lawyer's job is to facilitate achieving the goals of a client and not acting as the client's conscience or moral advisor. The lawyer exists only for the client. A lawyer doing good things for a client is not a function of some nebulous concept of professionalism but a function of a particular lawyer using his skills for the benefit of the client. His conclusion is that "professionalism in the sense asserted by the ABA during the 19th and 20th centuries—and by . . . others today—should be seen as dead."

While not identified as such, Morgan's call to go easy on the idea of the profession is an accommodation to Big Law. It is his target audience and the sector of the profession growing and changing the most. The argument that Morgan makes too quickly gives up on the profession, perhaps because Morgan's understanding of it is too linked to the present.

The longer view of the profession shows that it has a history of a professional ideal which, if considered more fully, shows that recommitment to it rather than the abandonment of the profession as currently understood is the better way to go. Law was just one of several professions looking for credibility, legitimacy, and an authority of its own in the 19th century. The sciences in the second half of the 19th century ascended in status and law looked to the credibility that science's objective approach was getting and grafted onto that the importance of what might be called a community element in the name of voluntary association of members. This led to lawyers as professionals who "professed selfless and contractual service, membership in a strong association, and functional expertise modeled on the natural sciences." That, at least, is how Bruce A. Kimball describes it in his dazzling 1992 *The"True Professional Ideal" in America*. He points to a 19th-century jurist who, when trying to distinguish law from medicine, emphasized the association aspect of the profession. "Lawyers," we read, "are inclined to congregation—association, and if they are not positively clannish or cliquish, are frequently brought together in the practice of their profession, and learn to seek counsel . . . [T]he lawyer's habit of association of effort and thought, his disinclination to isolation, his consequent ability to see both sides of a question, his more liberal and tolerant notions of things render him a companion for lawyers as well as for others . . .The legal profession is thus always a brotherhood, and in this respect a direct contrast from the medical profession."

Those such as Morgan, in arguing that we should recognize that the idea of a legal profession no longer has currency, throw the professional baby out with the bath water in their calls for reform and accept the values implicit in Big Law size and the tribalism that goes with it. They get it wrong in arguing that we can do away with the outmoded idea of professionalism based on civility, which they say is, after all, optional. But civility is not a matter of personal choice, nor is it a stand-alone requirement of the profession. Instead, it is a function of the association element and exists by definition if the professional ideal is honored. Pointing out that those arguing against the idea of a profession are playing a mere verbal game helps the argument that law is a profession. More is needed, though it should not be based on just the argument for civility. We need to confront the core issue, which is that those who argue against the idea of a profession do so because they believe that lawyers should accept that they have become mere economic actors, business consultants with allegiances. They believe that the number of these such lawyers, housed in their respective Big Law bubbles, has reached the critical mass necessary to attack the very notion of a legal profession. We need instead to be brave enough to look to the size of law firms as the menace to the profession that it is. That the work of economic actors or business consultants is done by people who happen to be admitted to the bar does not transform their work into the practice of law, even if there are hundreds of them working out of the bubble of a Big Law firm. Those educated in the law don't have to practice law, but if they do, they have to do it properly. No redefinition allowed.

PROSECUTORS

There is a United States Attorney for each of the 94 districts around the country and accordingly 94 different United States Attorney's Offices (95 if you also count the one for the District of Columbia), though we can lump them together for discussion purposes and just refer to them as the United States Attorney's Office (USAO). The Assistant United States Attorneys (AUSAs) representing the government make use of this one office shorthand when they say, not without good reason, that the USAO is the biggest and best law firm in the country. The USAO attracts the highest quality applicants, either right out of law school or laterally from law firms. They've been to the best law schools and many have clerked for federal judges, even at the most prestigious levels of the circuit court and the United States Supreme Court. Part of the argument for the quality of the office relates to the work it does and to the special set of rules and expectations governing the prosecutors. The public places a special trust in the office. The best and best-known description of a prosecutor's duties in fact highlights the prosecutor's need to be able to distinguish among cases and among facts and to seek justice, wherever it may lead. Justice Sutherland's majority opinion in *Berger v. United States* of 1935 makes clear that there is nothing wrong with a prosecutor striking hard blows, so long as they are fair blows. "He may prosecute with earnestness and vigor—indeed, he should do so," the opinion states, but only in the pursuit of justice. The duty is to the innocent as well as to the guilty. "It is as much his duty to refrain from improper methods calculated to produce a wrongful conviction as it is to use every legitimate means to bring about a just one."

Despite the great trust that the public puts in AUSAs, we find in looking through the reports examples of prosecutors who cross the line and deliver something other than fair blows by attempting to use improper methods to secure convictions. Outside the courtroom this is usually done by keeping exculpatory evidence from the defense. During trials themselves, the favorite tactics are to comment on the defendant's silence, to use inflammatory language in closing argument, or to put his or his office's reputation behind a witness through vouching. Why an AUSA would even get close to the line, never mind crossing it, is a good question. Appellate courts in a number of cases have explicitly asked the question, sometimes rhetorically, sometimes not. In some cases, the judges point to overwhelming evidence to say that there was no need for what the government did. But of course there is never a need or a justification for crossing the line, and the courts often remind the government of this. Prosecutors, they point out, occupy a privileged place as representatives of the government. It has even been pointed out that prosecutors fill a quasi-judicial position in the criminal justice system. The cases explain that the government's success is not measured by wins, but by the fidelity to the principle of fair play. Hard blows, yes, but always fair blows. The opinions can be read as the judges slapping the government and demanding more maturity. The directive we hear in these cases is for the AUSA to stop being a jerk and a snarky bully and to get a hold on the bloodlust that is getting him into trouble and recognize that when you represent the government you give up the right to act out and to let your personality control you. An AUSA has special obligations. That the AUSA's counterpart opposing defense lawyer is not similarly restrained is not an excuse to make prosecuting into something that is about the AUSA personally and not the obligation.

There is no mystery as to why prosecutors are willing to cross ethical lines, at least according to one knowledgeable commentator. Prosecutor-turned-professor Bennett Gershman tells us that they want to win. "I was a prosecutor for ten years," he has noted. "I think I know something of the mind-set here. For the American prosecutor, the system is war. They see it as a total abstraction. They're going to win that war, and it's combat to the death." The better question is why some want to win so badly. Their charge is to do justice, and justice is done, we know, regardless of whether a jury convicts or acquits. The suggestion is that an element of the personal that goes beyond the desire to wear a white hat creeps into the desire to win for some prosecutors. For some it is an attraction to power. Tom Wolfe in *Bonfire of the Vanities* unforgettably describes a prosecutor's warped thrill with power when he moves into the mind of Assistant District

Attorney Lawrence Kramer, who is raging with resentment at his station in life as highlighted by the contrast between his life and that of Manhattanite master-of-the-universe Sherman McCoy , the great white whale he is prosecuting for a hit-and-run accident.

> [I]t was nothing less than the power . . . to which [he] . . . was totally given over. It was the power of the government over the freedom of its subjects. To think of it in the abstract made it seem so theoretical and academic, but to *feel* it—to see the *looks on their faces*—as they [the defendants] stare back at you, courier and conduit of the Power . . . and now to see *that little swallow of fright* in [McCoy's] perfect neck worth millions—well, the poet has never sung of that ecstasy or even dreamed of it, and no prosecutor, no judge, no cop, no income tax auditor will ever enlighten him, for we dare not even mention it to one another, do we? —and yet we *feel* it and we *know* it every time they look at us with those eyes that beg for mercy or, if not mercy, Lord, dumb luck or capricious generosity. (Just one break!) What are all the limestone faces of Fifth Avenue and all the marble halls and stuffed-leather libraries and all the riches of Wall Street in the face of *my* control of *your* destiny and your helplessness in the face of the Power?

Scott Turow, who served as an AUSA for several years in Chicago, is our guide to prosecutors good and bad. His remarkably successful *Presumed Innocent* has the best description found anywhere of a prosecutor who has been able to keep at bay the forces that corrupt and to see his job for what it is supposed to be. The insights come from narrator Rusty Sabich, high-ranking county prosecutor now on trial for killing a colleague, as he tells us about his experiences as a prosecutor. "In the beginning," he says,

> I often felt preoccupied, imagining how it would feel to sit there, held at the focus of scrutiny, ardently denounced before all who cared to listen, knowing that the most ordinary privileges of decent life—common trust, personal respect, and even liberty—were now like some cloak you had checked at the door and might never retrieve. I could

feel the fear, the hot frustration, the haunted separateness. Now, like ore deposits, the harder stuff of duty and obligation has settled in the veins where those softer feelings moved. I have a job to do. It is not that I have grown uncaring. Believe me. But this business of accusing, judging, punishing has gone on always; it is one of the great wheels turning beneath everything we do. I play my part. I am a functionary of our only universally recognized system of telling wrong from right, a bureaucrat of good and evil. This must be prohibited; not that. One would expect that after all these years of making charges, trying cases, watching defendants come and go, it might have all become a jumble. Somehow it has not.

That's the good prosecutor, a very disciplined, thoughtful, and even-keeled lawyer. If you have to be prosecuted, he's the one to have. Rusty Sabich finds, though, that he has not been lucky in the prosecutor his case has drawn and that he is being prosecuted not by his doppelganger but by a prosecutor from hell, Tommy Molto. That Sabich worked with Molto in the county district attorney's office and knows him well is far from comforting. "Tommy Molto was nicknamed the Mad Monk," Sabich tells us. "He is a former seminarian; five foot six inches if he is lucky, forty or fifty pounds overweight, badly pockmarked, nails bitten to the quick. A driven personality. The kind to stay up all night working on a brief, to go three months without taking off a weekend. A capable attorney, but he is burdened by a zealot's poverty of judgment." Striking succinctly, Turow writes that Molto is a "[s]allow little man, always lit by the eternal candle of one unending hatred or another." It is this hatred that is most troublesome.

We should always be worried about the exercise of prosecutorial power. It is perhaps ironic that in the case of AUSAs it is often true that their ambition to be something other than prosecutors makes them better prosecutors. That they tend not to be career prosecutors is an ironic hedge against those forces that bring the personal into play when it should instead be just the professional. Most AUSAs, especially those in large cities, stay for four to six years and then return to private practice. They could well return to the firm from which they came as young associates, when they had but two to three years experience, or they could go elsewhere. In either case, it is usually true that the returning AUSA returns with credit given by his law firm for his years as a prosecutor. This often means that the former AUSA returns as a partner or as a very senior associate essentially guaranteed partnership. The returning prosecutor now has trial experience at the highest level that few other lawyers in the firm have. Trial experience is what they went to the United States Attorney's Office for, working long hours and giving up a great deal of money in salary to get it. Returning to a law firm partnership makes it all worthwhile. The law firm is of course greatly benefitted, having been able to subcontract out the lawyer's trial experience. Everybody wins.

Perhaps the better chance of fairness in federal court should not rest on the irony of ambition. One idea is that there should be a version of term limits for prosecutors, all prosecutors. George V. Higgins, who like Turow served as an Assistant United States Attorney, has a character in one of his novels explain that working as a prosecutor for more than seven or eight years impairs judgment and instills a sense of righteousness. It would be good for all if just the opposite happened to career prosecutors, and, to be fair, there are career prosecutors who have moved more and more to fairness as they have gone through their careers. The problem is what Lord Acton described about absolute power corrupting absolutely. Too much happens before a case goes to trial to just rely on judges to right the balance when prosecutors go too far. There has to be an internal governor to keep prosecutors in check. Without such a check, the fair administration of justice will always be too dependent on chance.

THE SADDEST PLACE NO MORE

Lawyers at large firms have figured out that to get clients willing to pay big fees, they must put on a big show. For these Big Law clients, all that they see, hear, and feel in the reception area—no longer styled a waiting room—is designed to get them into the mood to spend money. It wasn't always this way. Once a lawyer's reception area was a dreaded place because of what would happen in the office proper. This led novelist Anthony Trollope in 19th-century England to write that a lawyer's waiting room is the saddest place on Earth. Over the centuries law practice waiting rooms have told us something about the practice in the same way that they have been sending messages to clients.

There was a time, in white shoe New York firms decades ago, when the goal was the shock and awe of seriousness and the message to clients that they have submitted themselves to the firm and its vision of the world. We read in Louis Auchincloss's short story "The Senior Partner's Ghost" from his collection *Tales of Manhattan*, for example, of a "dark paneled reception hall, whose tables, bare of magazines or even newspapers, testified to the sobriety of a client's wait." Perhaps not the saddest place, but close.

The alternate, up-to-date view of things stresses conspicuous consumption and ostentatious displays of wealth, and not just here in America. In the world of Big Law, it was out with the staid option of traditional dark wood and oriental rugs and in with the glittering and gleaming, so that when one of Auchincloss' fictional firms in his short story "Power in Trust" from *Powers of Attorney* nears a hundred lawyers and must find a new home it opts for "two great gleaming floors in a new glass cube at 65 Wall Street, with modern paintings and a marble staircase and a reception hall paneled in white and gold." Australia's leading lawyer novelist, Richard Beasley, describes a recognizable though antipodean approach in *Hell Has Harbour Views*. We learn that the cavernous, austere foyer in a huge firm of solicitors in a Sydney skyscraper was a space designed to impress, "to

189

tell people you're a success, to tell them you won't come cheaply." For the firm's clients, "this impression is overwhelmingly reinforced when they are lured into the panorama of Sydney Harbor once the lift doors open all those floors above. Receiving their legal bills does the trick too."

In Steve Martini's *Compelling Evidence*, a disgraced and expelled partner exiled to solo practitioner land has returned for an unsavory scrap of work. This gives him a chance to describe his former place of employment, now seen from a different perspective. In what is perhaps a reference to postmodernism and Frederic Jameson, who had so famously dissected the Boneventure Hotel in Los Angeles as part of his *Post Modernism or the Cultural Logic of Late Capitalism*, he tell us (deconstructs) what he sees as he waits. It is a long quotation but worth it. "In the far corner of the reception area are two deep-cushioned sofas that spread like twin dark clouds across the broad expanse of wall. Here the visitor feels the need to check his briefcase in favor of machete and pith helmet. The furnishings are lost in a jungle of ficus, philodendrons, ferns, and rubber plants, all rooted in hip-high planter boxes. A faint odor of moist earth permeates the area. I decline a seat on the sofa and instead muse about the spacious reception room, examining the rich wall hangings and two modern ceramics set on pedestals near the center of the room. They are new, since I left [the firm], the usual symbols of commercial affluence used to set the stage for what routinely follows in the private inner chambers of any large firm. They are employed like some artistic emetic to lubricate and ease the disgorging of substantial fees by clients who at times might wonder if they are receiving full value for their money."

The point is sufficiently important to deserve another good quotation. Sheldon Siegel, a corporate and securities practitioner with Sheppard, Mullin in San Francisco, begins *Special Circumstances* and his series of Mike Daley novels with a description of one of the city's largest firms which we hope, for Siegel's sake, is not based on his own firm's digs. Daley, as he is getting fired for underperforming, makes a few wonderful, skewering comments about the furnishings of the office space, which reflect in part the reason he did not fit in. "Our two-story rosewood-paneled reception area is about the size of a basketball court. A reception desk that is longer than a city bus sits at the south end of the forty-eighth floor, and I can see the Golden

Gate Bridge, Alcatraz Island and Sausalito through the glass enclosed conference room on the north wall." The furniture of the reception area tells all: "[T]he gray carpet, overstuffed leather chairs and antique coffee tables create the ambiance of a classic men's club, which is entirely appropriate since most of our attorneys and clients are white, male, and Republican."

We can agree that lawyers send messages with the look of their reception areas. The point is perhaps best made by going to the low-rent district. In *Kennedy for the Defense*, George V. Higgins's protagonist Jerry Kennedy, the self-proclaimed classiest sleazy lawyer in Boston, has his office in a building where you would not want to touch anything, and in the office itself the dishevelment continues. In the waiting room the furniture complements the riffraff waiting to pay retainers. He used to rent hideous furniture, Kennedy says, upholstered in green tweed, until a doctor-gone-bad client paid him in part with his own tacky office furniture, "six comfortable chairs upholstered tastefully in orange plastic. It is grained, like alligator hide, with chromium arms and little pieces of wood notched over the chrome. Six of them." In the fourth and last Kennedy novel, *Sandra Nichols Found Dead*, Kennedy has had some success and has moved offices to "a sublet condo space of about seven hundred square feet on the fourth floor of 20 Beacon Street opposite the State House." It has a prime location, and it is "quite elegant, really, all soft-gloss-paneled in honey-toned oak; thick carpeted; hushed; nicely furnished. It murmurs of class, and good breeding, and voices not raised." He never feels at home in the new digs, though, probably because of his identification with the criminal clients he has so long dealt with.

The contrast between Kennedy's low-rent reception area and those of Big Law firms that are near parodies of themselves acts as something of a jab at Big Law and its values and perhaps goes too far. A better example might be contrasting Big Law as found in the previous examples with what it was on Wall Street nearly one hundred years ago. By this time large (for their day) firms specialized in corporate work and work for big banks, as reported on by Morris Markey in a 1927 *New Yorker* article "The Trade of Law." Markey follows a lawyer friend's suggestion and visits him at his law firm, one of the twenty largest in the city. There are four name partners, seven junior partners, twenty-seven clerks and a group of thirty-five stenographers, typists, and file clerks. The firm's principal work involves bond issues, contracts, and a wide variety of corporate work. Office overhead is $250,000 a year. The partners clear $100,000 each, the junior partners six to twelve thousand each plus up to five percent of the firm's profits. Clerks, who would be associates in our day, started at fifteen hundred dollars a year and could be bumped up to eighteen hundred if they showed promise. They have no client contact and mostly research as they work their way up to drafting contracts or performing small corporate law tasks.

The article emphasizes throughout that the law office is abuzz with activity and that everyone there cares only about getting all the work done. For our purposes, the key passage in the article comes with a description of the reception area of this large law firm. Our reporter tells us that it is a large reception area with a thick green carpet on which "ranged huge leather settes, very comfortable looking, and desks at which young women labored assiduously over their typewriters. Tall cabinets stood against the walls, enclosed in glass and containing hundreds of thick volumes bound in yellow buckram." Reading this description today we are struck by the reception area doubling as a work area. In 1927 this fact is not mentioned; it is probably just assumed. Moreover, the outer work area doubling as a reception area has boys constantly moving through it carrying bundles of papers, all of which the visitor can see. The point for the visitor then was that the law firm was a place of work, only a place of work, with a reception that isn't really a reception area at all. No attention seems to be given to the client in the reception area. It comes close to being a statement that the client be damned. In contrast to Big Law reception areas of today, the reception area in 1927 was not a place of seduction but a place of work. If big fees were paid—and they were—it was for the work, not to maintain a life of office excess that appealed to the narcissism of clients willing to spend money to be part of the illusion promised by the reception area.

SEEING YOURSELF AND OTHERS

It would not be fair to expect movies and television to present to viewers the many-splendored variations of lawyer personalities that we in the profession have a chance to see. Stereotypes for the public will do, such as defense lawyers as pit bulls looking for a brawl or big firm lawyers as materialistic and even evil trying to maintain the status quo. Some truth, but not all. Only those on the inside appreciate the personality riches of the profession. Researchers looking into lawyer personality have helped the inquiry by looking to personality traits that distinguish lawyers from the general population. They have told us what we perhaps already knew from brief observation: that contrasted with the general population lawyers are more driven, aggressive, competitive, and materialistic; that they emphasize rights and obligations over emotions and interpersonal harmony; that they favor materialistic and pragmatic values over altruistic goals; and that they have higher than normal psychological stress. We need more. We need descriptions and observations from those who have moved among us to capture the essence of those other lawyers that we isolate when we say to a buddy or to ourselves that so and so is a this or that.

Scott Turow's *Pleading Guilty* is worth buying just for the thumbnail portraits narrating protagonist Mack Malloy gives us of the lawyers in his firm. Carl Pagnucci is an example. He is "stubbornly, subtly, but inalterably contrary," something most lawyers have run into. Further explained, Carl "regards agreement as a failure of his solemn obligation to exercise critical intelligence. There is always a probing question, a sly jest, a suggested alternative, always a way for him to put an ax to your tree. The guy is more than half a foot shorter than me and makes me feel no bigger than a flea." I know that guy, at least a few readers are saying to themselves.

Then there's Bert, who provides readers with a groan of anguished remembrances in dealing with his type. For Bert, "every case is a full-bore commitment. Got a client with a small problem, say, falsely representing that night is day, Bert will defend him without blinking. He is one of those lawyers who agrees with the other side about nothing. Everything leads to correspondence. Move the dep from two to one, Bert will send you a letter. Which bears no resemblance, by the way, to the conversation it claims to record. I say my client's having open-heart surgery and Bert's letter says the guy can't appear because he scheduled a doctor's appointment. With stunts like that, Bert's made enemies of half the trial lawyers in town."

Moving to the more general, we know instinctively and through experience that there's something to the idea that lawyers take on some of the distinguishing traits of their specialties. How much this is true is one of the better questions about the profession. Reducing things to their essences can, for sure, lead to both smiles and insights, though the smile factor lessens if you are among the target group, as when satirist Jeremy Blachman notes in his skewering *Anonymous Lawyer* that a firm's trust and estates section is where lawyers go to die. Steve Martini captures a particular trust and estates specialist in *Compelling Evidence* by observing that the lawyer "comes to this role well suited in appearance, a miserly-looking man with a craggy face and round wire-rimmed spectacles. If social reserve were a religion, [he] would be its high priest." We learn from big firm lawyer Sheldon Siegel in his *Special Circumstances* that divorce lawyers come in two species. His narrator Mike Daley is talking about a member of one of them, Sherman, whose genetic code might need readjusting, when he tells us that, "the really good ones steer their clients toward counseling and sometimes salvage marriages. Then there are people like Sherman, who relish the role of barracuda. He represents only men. He actually has a picture of a shark on his business cards. If you're going to war with your ex-wife, he's your guy."

Litigators deserve their own paragraph, or level of hell, depending on how you look at it. There's an amusing depiction of insurance defense lawyers in Steve Martini's *The Arraignment* brimming with truth worth noting. "When I turn to look at the lawyer," Martini's Paul Mondriani tells us, "he gives me the insurance eye, a play for dominance. There is much mutual sniffing here. This is well practiced by every indemnity lawyer I've ever met." We learn from William Bernhart in *Deadly Justice* the not particularly revealing observation that "litigators are obsessed with documents, especially when corporations are involved." But moving his finger to the jugular to take the pulse of the litigator in *Primary Justice* Bernhart has a partner hector an associate on the essence of litigation that has yet eluded the associate. "It's as if you don't know how to fight. You're not willing to be mean. I'll put it to you blunt, kid—in litigation sometimes you have to be a bully, and out-and-out asshole. When you're a litigator, you've got to remember that every second of misery you can bring to the opposition is a second that will make them consider settling. Being an asshole is *always* in your client's best interest." John William Corrington probes further and produces a jeweled insight distinguishing cut-throat litigators from mere lawyers in his short story "The Actes and Monuments." His litigator seeking redemption tells us, "I had had a certain gift with exceptionally sharp teeth. Yes, I had been cruel. I had enjoyed finding certain lawyers in the opposition, men I had known who were blessed with a kind of unwillingness to go for blood. They worked within the confines of their dignity, their gentleness, their inadequacy. But I worked elsewhere and won invariably."

Corporate lawyers come in for probably more than their fair share of grief in novels by and about lawyers. Jeremy Blachman lands the hardest and perhaps the foulest blow in *Anonymous Lawyer* when his narrator notes of his big firm's lawyers that, "everyone here has Asperger's syndrome to some extent—it's one of the markings of corporate lawyers." Sabin Willet in *Present Value* at one point takes the broader view of a law firm's corporate lawyers to detail common traits and characteristics. He writes that, "they were corporate lawyers to several large Boston-based firms. They were worriers, organizers, obsessors over detail, people who shot bolt upright at three a.m. because they couldn't recall if the extra copies of the contract had been FedExed to the client or only mailed. They shared a confidence that everything would go wrong if left to its own devices." He expands on their defining trait, the idea that each believed that he or she should not be the subject of criticism. Through this aversion to criticism, the corporate lawyers spoke the same language and had taken the same path to success. Described as "a burning passion right at the core of the liver," the principle of "I Must Never Be Subject to Criticism" did not flower in these lawyers only when they had been hired at their firms. Rather, the principle had been a driving part of their lives throughout making them who they are. It "was the essential element of each of their characters—that they should not be criticized. It had led each of them to a lifetime of good report cards. In schools, in entrance exams, in college, in law school, in job offers, in compensation. It led them to clothe their children a certain way and enroll them in certain schools; to live on certain streets in certain towns; to give to certain charities. It left them ever vigilant to fortifying all aspects of their lives against criticism—criticism that could come at any time from any quarter."

With this kind of powerful insight, it is easier to understand why lawyers take to the hills of fiction to throw their hand grenades at the profession. These lawyer novelists would otherwise have a lot to answer for from those in their professional circles who saw themselves in the novels if the lawyer novelists were not able to say that it was all made up or that the skewered characters were composites of several people. Bruised egos for lawyers who had been unflatteringly presented in novels lead to libel suits and strain within the firm. We have to be glad that these lawyer novelists have risked the lawsuits and given us the characters and descriptions. Even the lawyers with the unflattering personality types described in the fiction should perhaps be indebted to the lawyer novelists. They have had a chance to see themselves in the mirror, assuming they are willing to recognize the unflattering, and ask themselves if they like what they see. If they don't, they know what to do. For that, the rest of us can be grateful.

SERENDIPITOUS RESEARCH

Serendipitous research happens when the researcher is not looking for anything in particular and comes across information that becomes useful because it fits areas that he might be working on. This approach differs from random research, in which the researcher is actively and specifically researching one topic and discovers something unrelated that strikes the researcher as worthy of its own separate line of inquiry. Random research has led to any number of scientific discoveries. Looking for one thing, the scientist finds another. Perhaps serendipitous research is too whimsical a concept for lawyers. It shouldn't be. Other fields not only profit from serendipitous research but we find articles praising it. Historians, literary researchers, bibliophiles, and especially scientists all attest to the usefulness— what some might call the sublime usefulness—of serendipitous research. Yet legal researchers have held out against the serendipitous. As an example, Stacey L. Gordon in *Online Legal Research* writes that "[g]iven the vast amount, and variable quality, of available legal information, Internet surfing is not always an efficient research method. Serendipity and luck are often the only things responsible for relevant surfing discoveries. Although surfing the Internet and serendipitous findings certainly have value as entertainment and at times are even the only research option, they are not usually the most efficient use of research time."

Research is different from trying to keep up with developments in the law. Some specialties, such as taxation, of course, require lawyers to know how things change each year, and for those lawyers keeping abreast of changes in the law is mandatory. Many of those working in areas which do not change from year to year, except for new wrinkles here or there or the occasional landmark decision, still have an interest in keeping up with the latest developments and get their information from a variety of sources. Some read blogs written by practitioners in their area who delight in reporting on the latest developments. Some subscribe to newsletters or other specialty services from practice area specific organizations, such as criminal defense lawyer organizations. The hope, no matter how the lawyer keeps up with a specialty, is that he or she will see something that relates to a file currently being worked on—serendipitous research of a sort.

I profit every week from my own form of serendipitous research. Given that all I do is practice criminal defense in federal court, I subscribe to West's *Federal Reporter*, Third Series, not the hardcover version but the paperback advance sheets. These advance sheets make up my entire hardcopy law library except for some practice and statute books, quite a contrast to the early years of my practice and the dozens of practice volumes and treatises I owned. The advance sheets matter enormously to me. They arrive each week, on average four hundred to five hundred pages long, and represent all the reported opinions from the various United States Courts of Appeal. I thumb through the volume page by page, usually spending an hour or so with each volume. I look at each case, in part because I have an interest in the language and structure of judicial opinions, though I look more closely at the criminal cases because of my practice. There are three or four judges whose opinions I look at closely, and there is one, Richard Posner, whose opinions I read in each volume, regardless of subject matter. His opinions produce what only a few judges before him have produced in their work, a literary experience for the reader.

On average I will run across four or five criminal cases in each volume that bear heavily on active cases in my office, and on average I will run across ten or so principles of law that I note, either because I didn't know the principle of law, or at least as it is formulated in the opinion, and think it bears or will bear on the kinds of cases I have or because I know the principle but want a ready reference to its use in a recent opinion. I copy the particular pages I have noted to create a highly personal reference guide to what might be important in my work. Every month or so, I'll go through the pages I have collected to refresh myself on where I've been and what I've learned. With remarkable frequency I have come across rather exotic principles of law that have direct applications to cases I am working on. On one occasion in 2010, for example, I had gotten a drug case in which the indictment dated from 2004. The passage of six years triggered my interest in a defendant's right to a speedy trial, but I knew enough—though I've never had the precise issue—that there are balancing factors to be invoked that consider the cause of the delay and the prejudice to the defendant. Being a fugitive is a factor that weighs against a defendant, which was what my client was, technically at least. The case I happened to read involved both a five-year delay from indictment to arrest and fugitive status, but in the case the police knew where the defendant was throughout the five-year period. The case stood for the proposition that when the police know the where-abouts of a defendant but simply do not arrest, for whatever reason, the causation and delay factors cut in the defendant's favor. This was my case, since the records indicated that the police knew of my client's address at the time of the indictment and that his address did not change throughout the so-called fugitive period. The result here was that I happened to stumble in my weekly reading on the very case that I was able to use to argue that the case should be dismissed for a speedy trial violation. Serendipity.

The serendipitous research as I've described it gives a different gloss to research. It implies that reading and browsing for the lawyer are done with issues from pending cases rumbling around in the background. Maybe the better description is serendipitous reading. If it were done without the background noise, it would just be called reading, maintenance reading, or just educational reading. But would the point of law in question stick in the lawyer's mind if it didn't connect with something that the lawyer was working on or had perhaps worked on? Probably not. Browsing through judicial opinions has an element of education to it, but contrasting the way of reading opinions I have described with the way we all studied bar review material as we prepared for the big examination makes the point that in browsing we are looking more for the unusual, for the interesting bits, and for an engagement, even at a browsing distance, with the law as a vast set of principles fitting together to form the doctrines that give shape to our understanding of how law works.

Even though the world of research has been transformed by electronic databases and the use, or overuse, of keyword searching, it is still the legal doctrines which were imprinted onto our brains when we studied for the bar examination that shape the way we understand law. There's something about the intensity of bar examination preparation and the bar's almost exclusive emphasis on doctrine that gives what was studied in preparation for the bar such lasting influence over lawyers once they are in practice. In this sense, law librarians have gotten it wrong in arguing, as part of the discussion of the consequences of electronic research, that it is the West digest system that gives us a way to organize everything. What West Publishing provides has been described by Daniel Dabney, now the chief taxonomist at Thomsen Reuters, West Publishing's parent, as nothing less than a "universe of thinkable thoughts" by organizing the law by way of subjects and key numbers. Yet it's doctrine that we remember. And it is in browsing through opinions that we are reminded of both various doctrines and how those doctrines organize the law.

It would be better, as I argue elsewhere, if judges wrote their own opinions. Lawyers dipping into advance sheets for fun and profit would be better served by reading judges, who are more experienced than their law clerks in the law. The kinship between lawyers reading advance sheets and the judges writing them would be greater than the kinship lawyers might have with law clerks, a year or two out of school. But even as a second-best substitute, the clerk-written opinions edited by judges that we can read, or browse, in the advance sheets perform the valuable function, even if on a hit-or-miss basis or even serendipitously, of bringing lawyers closer to the law. When you get closer, you see all sorts of things either differently or for the first time.

SHAKESPEARE

The problems that go with the use of literary allusions generally apply even more particularly with allusions to Shakespeare. It is a consequence of Shakespeare being both the best and the best-known writer in the language. In our history of judicial opinions he has been alluded to more often by far than any other writer, usually with marginal effect and sometimes with great effect. It has been true as well with the way Shakespeare has been used in federal circuit opinions of the last few years. An apt allusion to Shakespeare tells us something about the law and in the process reflects well on the judge properly invoking him. An illusion poorly used, unfortunately, adds little to our understanding and reveals the judge to be something of a poser.

Shakespeare in these circuit court opinions is subject to the same excesses and abuses that he suffers from in opinions from other times and other courts. The culprits are those who want to use him but do not understand him. Most typically, well-known quotations from the plays are used as ornaments and for little effect. This happens, for example, when judges use "past is prologue," "consummation devoutly to be wished," "more in sorrow than in anger," "who steals my purse steal trash . . . ," "a rose by any other name would smell as sweet," "the quality of mercy is not strain'd," "brevity is the soul of wit," and "hoist with his own petard," though this last raises its own special problem. The quotations are used to suggest learnedness, but the quotations are so commonplace that their effect resolves more into preening. One example of using Shakespeare as a near cliché comes in *Rivera-Torres v. Rey-Hernandez* when the court opens with, "[T]he Bard of Avon once warned that 'delays have dangerous ends.' William Shakespeare, *The First Part of King Henry the Sixth* act 3, sc. 2." The court continues on the delay theme with the observation that, "[t]his case, in which the plaintiffs procrastinated for the better part of three years and cavalierly flouted the discovery deadlines announced by the district court, bears out that admonition. The tale follows." The point hardly seems worth the allusion.

We find the "hoist with his own petard" reference used a few times in this group of opinions. In one instance the quotation was used by one of the litigants. The quotation was actually misused, which prompts the court in *Disabled in Action of Pennsylvania v. Southeastern Pennsylvania Transportation Authority* to point out in a footnote that "in the pantheon of misused metaphors, 'hoist with his own petard' may be preeminent." The court then proceeds to explain that *petard* is a small bomb, but that its derivation comes from Middle French word, *peter*, which means to break wind. The court had gotten this information from *Webster's Third New International Dictionary* (1993). This then leads to the observation that, given this, the word "found favor with the master [Shakespeare] of the double entendre." Oddly, though, none of the leading editions of *Hamlet* glosses *petard* this way or makes any reference to a double entendre. The editors of the Penguin, Pelican, Signet, Norton Critical, and Oxford editions all interpret the passage in the same way. Rosencratz and Guildenstern in the play are escorting Hamlet to England and carrying a letter from the Danish king instructing the letter's recipient to strike off Hamlet's head. At sea Hamlet has stealthily acquired the letter and replaced it with a forgery purporting to be from the king instructing the English officials receiving the letter to put the bearers of the letter (Rosencrantz and Guildenstern) to sudden death. To underscore the irony that the two supposed friends of Hamlet now turned traitor to him will deliver the directive for their own deaths, Hamlet refers to the irony of a engineer, glossed as a demolition expert, blowing himself up with his own bomb, otherwise known as a *petar* or *pertard*, depending on the edition. Despite this set of facts and explanation, the court in *Disabled in Action* apparently thinks Shakespeare is making a joke with the idea of an engineer blowing himself up with his own fart, but, putting aside the fact that no one else has suggested this, this does violence to the gloss on an engineer as a demolition expert.

The judge's misreading of the "hoist by his own petard" quotation should embarrass the judge a bit because it shows him trying so very hard to be clever, but it pales on the embarrassment meter to what should attach to Jay Bybee of the Ninth Circuit for a howlingly incorrect allusion to Antony's famous speech in *Julius Caesar* in which his refrain that "Brutus is an honorable man" builds in the level of its irony. Bybee did not understand the speech and that Antony moves from irony to mockery and instead uses the reference to Antony's statement that "Brutus is an honorable man" to illustrate what is meant by vouching for a witness's credibility. An entire mob in *Julius Caesar* understood what Antony was saying. Not so much with Judge Bybee.

Having seen ho-hum and even incorrect uses of Shakespeare in judicial opinions, we can turn to the more serious attempts to use Shakespeare. An impressive invocation occurs when one court in the disability case *Desmond v. Mukasey* considers whether sleeping qualifies as a major life activity in the way that walking, seeing, hearing, speaking, and breathing do. In concluding that sleeping without question qualifies, the court first quotes a longish paragraph from a scientific test that considers sleeping in terms of evolutionary biology before adding the final word from *Macbeth*, "sleep that knits up the ravell'd sleave of care, The death of each day's life, sore labour's bath, Balm of hurt minds, great nature's second course, Chief nourisher in life's feast." Aptly done. The battle always is between Shakespeare done poorly or oddly and with Shakespeare done well.

When done well, reference to Shakespeare can add texture and, paradoxically, a more concrete understanding of an abstraction. Take the issue of knowing the future. Criminal statutes can attach liability when a defendant knows that certain events will occur. In a sex trafficking case, *United States v. Todd*, for example, the statute requires that in the hiring of employees the defendant knew that force, fraud, or coercion would be used to cause the victims to engage in commercial sex. In sorting through whether there was sufficient evidence for the jury to find that there was such knowledge, the court had to get closer to what was meant by *knowledge*. There is knowledge of the future, on the one hand, and then there is the knowledge of what the future will hold with regard to patterns of conduct that had been engaged in before. The statute looked to the latter. It could hardly look to the former, to a knowledge of the future, since time unfolds in its own way and beyond our control. To make the point, the court quotes Shakespeare. "As William Shakespeare said in Sonnet 115 of time, its 'million'd accidents creep in' and nothing is completely stable, no plan is beyond alteration." *Bartlett's Familiar Quotations* could not have been used for this quotation. It springs from deeper knowledge.

A recent Seventh Circuit opinion shows Shakespeare being used with great effect. It comes from the habeas corpus case *Holmes v. Levenhagen*, in which the issue was the ability of the defendant who had psychiatric problems to assist his lawyer at trial. The defendant could answer certain questions rationally when queried by experts, but at the same time he could not be budged from a number of what the appellate court called "his crazy beliefs." The opinion sorts through the evidence and tests for schizophrenia—and in the process dispels the common misconception that is refers to a split personality—to show that the defendant was not sufficiently able to assist his lawyer. What mattered most was that "a sight, a sound, that would elicit no reaction from a sane person can separate a schizophrenic from his rational mind." This is, as the court points out, the definition of *schizophrenia* that the American Psychiatric Association uses. Then a reference to *Hamlet* gels the point and allows us to imagine in our mind's eye how the schizophrenic acts as illustrated by Ophelia. The court writes, "Claudius in *Hamlet* had it right when he said: 'Poor Ophelia/ Divided from herself and her fair judgment,/ Without the which we are pictures, or mere beasts.'" With this the reader can see that forcing the defendant to stand trial in his condition would be the definition of unfairness.

This brings us back to Antony's speech in *Julius Caesar* and its misuse as an illustration of the government in a criminal case vouching for a witness. No one familiar with the play could have misunderstood Antony's meaning in saying that Brutus is an honorable man. It is one of the most recognized scenes in all of Shakespeare. To use the speech and get its meaning wrong offends the soul, but it does produce its own reward by showing the judge in the worst light imaginable, as a poser. It is a jaw-dropping moment of a very different sort. To consider its opposite, the judge aptly using Shakespeare as with the Ophelia reference or the reference to sleep, is to understand the fusion of life and law.

SO, HOW DID I DO?

Pride, vanity, and ego—just a few words that might be used in description and analyses of lawyers. Hero, all-conquering warrior, master of the universe, just a few ways lawyers—litigators especially—describe themselves, at least to themselves. Maybe it is just the nature of the work. Any honest trial lawyer would have to admit to having that thrilling feeling that comes after beating up on a witness or getting the jury to lean forward and listen. It is the equivalent of what stand-up comics describe when they say that they "killed out there," referring to slaying an audience with laughter. Appellate lawyers, normally the more sedate ones, to be sure, are not immune to this feeling. Just ask any one of them after an effective argument how they did.

West Publishing understands this and sells the framed first page of a judicial opinion as it appears in its reporter pages. What lawyer wouldn't want to display his trophy kill for all to see, especially clients? What better way to advertise success and ability, especially if on the framed page the client can read the court's praise of the lawyer? In the recent Ninth Circuit en banc case *Lolong v. Gonzalez*, the court's first footnote read, "although we do not often comment on the quality of arguments, we would like to thank both counsel for aiding the court through their excellent advocacy in briefing and during oral argument." Heady stuff.

In the reports we do find the occasional encomium to a lawyer's performance, but more often we find performance criticisms that lawyers would never want their clients—to say nothing of their mothers—to see. The criticisms can be withering, scathing, and, to us at least (because we have a character flaw that prompts us to enjoy the sufferings of other lawyers) amusing.

Lawyers coming to the appellate opinions of their cases hoping for not just the right result but for references to what they had thought standout was lawyering can have their egos first deflated and then crushed with language cutting to the quick. Consider the prosecutor in *United States v. Foster* who falls victim to Frank Easterbrook's lash and reads that, "to call the performance of the United States Attorney's Office in this case a disappointment would be a gross understatement." This is what happens to other lawyers, not to us, we tell ourselves.

Performance assessments can expose to the world those lawyers called out on their audaciousness, their chutzpah. Oral arguments can be tense, anxious affairs for lawyers, and some allowance must be made for that. It is good to read in this regard that appellate judges allow some room for this, as when we read in the Richard Posner opinion *McClesky v. Astrue* that "the government's rather wild arguments were made by its lawyer only at oral argument, so perhaps should be forgiven." But to say one thing in a brief and then to take the opposite position at argument can stun, and not in a good way, as when Posner in the Title VII case *EEOC v. V&J Foods, Inc.* wrote, "[w]e were astonished when [defendant's] lawyer told us at argument that [the restaurant's general manager's] conduct toward [plaintiff restaurant employee] was not sexual harassment, though in his brief he had acknowledged that it was." Similarly, no good can come from a judge, again Posner, noting that the appellate lawyer had made an argument with a straight face.

The warning that should be posted on the doors to the appellate courtroom is not Dante's direful "abandon all hope ye who enter here." It is merely that the lawyer as well as the case will be judged. Judgment can be delivered on how well you know your field. What are a bankruptcy lawyer's clients to think when in the *Federal Reporter* we find a judge, Posner again, who notes in *Boyer v. Crown Stock Distribution, Inc.* that "when we asked the trustee's lawyer at argument who would be entitled to the money obtained by him in excess of what new Crown's creditors are owed, he surprised us (he is a bankruptcy lawyer, after all) by saying that he did not know."

An appellate opinion bears resemblance to a report card on what went on below. Trial judges look at them this way and sometimes do not take well to getting low marks or even failing, even though they have job security. They worry about their reputations, as do lawyers. We like to think that we can also recover from a bruised reputation, but in reading some accounts of lawyer performance we have to wonder. What can be said, for example, about a Deputy Federal Defender in *United States v. Herrera-Zuniga* whose briefing on sentencing reads, as the court put it, more like a prosecutor's argument in favor of a harsher sentence. The conviction in this Sixth Circuit case was for illegal reentry and the client had been deported twice and had been convicted five times of drunken driving. The court gave a higher than guideline sentence because of the defendant's criminal history. Defense counsel for his part submitted a sentencing memorandum that made no arguments for leniency and, astonishingly, included a letter he had written to his client in which he told the client that he was worthless, a danger to society, and not worthy of anything but the most severe punishment. The client had left him, he explained in his letter, without expressible sympathy, which unfortunately left him "almost unable to advocate on your behalf." The court of appeals (Clay, J.) thought the lawyer had gone too far in using *almost* and *sua sponte* raised the ineffective assistance of counsel issue and directed counsel to provide a copy of the opinion to his client, with the expectation, we can only assume, that the defendant would raise the claim in a habeas corpus petition.

In the civil rights and RICO case *Stanard v. Nygren* from the Seventh Circuit, the plaintiff's lawyer struggled with the "short and plain statement" pleading rule and ultimately had his motion to amend his second complaint denied and his case dismissed because of missed deadlines, ignored instructions, and an error-filled and incomprehensible complaint. The appellate court (Sykes, J.), after naming plaintiff's [and appellant's] counsel, pointed to the complaint's incoherence and explained that its "rampant grammatical, syntactical, and typographical errors contributed to an overall sense of unintelligibility." It then quoted some of the offending passages, including what the court described as a "staggering and incomprehensible 345-word sentence." Then, after affirming the trial judge's decision, the appellate court noted without irony that trial counsel turned appellate counsel failed to file a reasonably coherent brief on appeal. After again naming the lawyer, the court described counsel's approach as alarmingly deficient.

Bad reports cards in our Internet age can be bad for business. In the Seventh Circuit criminal case *United States v. Carter*, the defendant's appellate lawyer astonished the court by simply not showing up for oral argument. He called the day of argument to say that he would not be appearing in court, this even though his office was catty-corner to the courthouse. He then did not answer his phone and declined to return voice messages left by court staff. He also took a "thoughtless approach to preparing his main brief," itself inexecusable, all of which led the court to become a consumer advocate and write that "other clients, present or potential, ought to be aware." The court's intentions were perhaps revealed when it used the lawyer's name sixteen times in the opinion.

Two Texas lawyers might have a difficult time explaining to their respective clients why the judge thought that both were dolts. We are traveling beyond the confines of recent *Federal Reporter*, Third Series cases and going to the Southern District of Texas in 2001, but for good reason. The lawyers can tell their respective clients that the judge is a jerk, for which there is ample evidence, but nevertheless, to be singled out for such scathing criticism is hard to explain away. The unhappy judge in *Bradshaw v. Unity Marine Corporation, Inc.* writes, "[b]efore proceeding further, the Court notes that this case involves two extremely likable lawyers, who have together delivered some of the most amateurish pleadings ever to cross the hallowed causeway into Galveston, an effort which leads the Court to surmise but one plausible explanation. Both attorneys have obviously entered into a secret pact—complete with hats, handshakes, and cryptic words—to draft their pleadings entirely in crayon on the backs of gravy-stained paper place mats, in the hope that the Court would be so charmed by their child-like efforts that their utter dearth of legal authorities in their briefing would go unnoticed. Whatever actually occurred, the Court is now faced with the daunting task of deciphering their submissions. With Big Chief tablet readied, thick black pencil in hand, and a devil-may-care laugh in the face of death, life on the razor's edge sense of exhilaration, the Court begins."

Not surprisingly, opinions describing bad lawyering sometimes end with the court stating that it is sending a copy of the opinion to the state bar for inquiry into whether further disciplinary actions should be taken. Heavy deed. The temptation for lawyers looking to hide is to say that critical judges want someone to beat up on, but the opinions suggest otherwise. They represent appellate judges left with no choice but to expose inexcusably bad lawyering. The descriptions and complaints are always delivered in measured tones. It's the work, not the lawyer himself, except perhaps for the guy who, like Bartleby, "preferred not to" when it came to representing his client. Object lessons, perhaps. I see them more as reports of sadness at the legal profession's diminishment—of noble purpose undermined by indifference. The moral? Pity the lawyer who does not care about or for his profession.

TAKING INSTRUCTION FROM OTHERS

A look at what has been going on with the legal profession in our cousin common law countries of Australia and England can help us get some perspective on the strengths and weaknesses of our own, at least from the point of view of the lawyers. That we can learn from them is a bit ironic, given that lawyers in both countries want to be more like us. There are pushes in each country to lessen or eliminate the distinction between barristers and solicitors so that their respective professions look more like ours in which all lawyers are equal and have equal rights of audience in the courts. But learn we can, for the distance that barristers have from their clients has some appeal, though it must be balanced against its cost.

England and Australia produce lawyers in different ways. In England and Australia, future lawyers study law as undergraduates in classes giving broad overviews of various subjects. It is not until graduation in England that students choose which type of lawyer they want to be. Those who want to be solicitors enroll in a one-year Legal Practice Course while those aiming to be barristers enroll in a one-year Bar Vocational Course. This distinction in study mirrors the distinction in what the two groups do. As a shorthand, solicitors are office lawyers and barristers are trial advocates. For future solicitors, the Legal Practice Course is followed by a two-year period of learning on the job—known as a training contract—before moving on in the usual case to work for a firm of solicitors. Future English barristers, on the other hand, enter a year's pupilage in one of the Inns of Court and then hope to gain a tenancy at one of the chambers where barristers as solo practitioners club together for organization and expenses. In Australia, on the other hand, barristers do not branch off from solicitors straightaway. All law graduates must satisfy competence in a number of practice areas, done usually while working for a solicitor, to qualify as solicitors. After qualifying as a solicitor, someone interested in becoming a barrister has to pass a number of area examinations and then enter into a reading engagement usually lasting a year to learn the ropes of the job. The barrister entry requirements vary from state to state, but most include the examination and reader requirements following solicitor admission. And then, once in practice in their chambers, barristers in both countries have their lives controlled, so to speak, by their relationship with a clerk in chambers who acts as a broker on the barrister's behalf with solicitors who might want to hire the barrister. The barrister's relationship once engaged is with the solicitor, not with the client, though England in particular has been pushing to break down this barrier and allow certain types of qualified clients direct access to barristers. In both countries there has been an erosion of the barrister's monopoly over advocacy, with solicitors more and more increasing their rights of audience in a move that smacks of the American preference for lawyers once admitted to have rights equal to those of all other admitted lawyers.

Contrasts between our legal profession and legal system with the legal professions and systems of other countries such as England and Australia have mostly emphasized our belief in giving the public wider access to the court system. We follow the so-called American rule in which each side in litigation—with exceptions, of course—bears its own legal fees. In England and Australia, costs, which include legal fees, are assessed against the losing party, chilling, some would argue, the ability of individuals of modest means or less in these countries to bring suit. The more important contrast, from the lawyer's point of view, however, is with the relationship between the barrister, the solicitor, and the client. For cases going to trial in Australia or England it is the solicitor who does all the preparatory work. He then briefs the barrister on both the facts and the law. The barrister is then cabined by what the solicitor has given him by way of the facts of the case, primarily in the form of witness statements. The solicitor thus instructs the barrister in the case. If something comes up touching on something that the barrister has not been instructed on, the barrister has to then turn to the solicitor for further instruction. Because he has usually had little or no contact with the client (that's what solicitors are for) the barrister's relationship to the case is really with the file, with the briefs and his instructions. Decisions about how to handle a trial are a function of the documents that the barrister has been given. There are no facts to be changed or added to. He can't try to get at facts in cross-examination that he has not been instructed on, nor can he in direct examination bring out more than what the instructions direct. It all a done deal, so to speak, by the time the barrister gets the file, which is often right before trial.

The implications of this model, every American trial lawyer immediately recognizes, are staggering. The lawyer's role is diluted and diminished, if by *role* we mean a lawyer's personal involvement in the case, especially if involvement, as it often does, means the extent to which a lawyer has taken on the client's cause and, going further, identifies with the client. Consider an extreme example of identification. This is famed trial lawyer Gerry Spence telling us about his level of involvement in a case. Brace yourselves. In his *Gunning for Justice* Spence writes, "It is I, always, not the client, on trial. I have seen many clients asleep while the jury is out and I pace the floor in misery. The jury accepts or rejects me, not my case. I make the case. I am the director, the producer, its principal actor—it is my courtroom, my judge, my jury—it is I, and when the jury says no, it is the ultimate rejection because they are not saying no to just an idea, but they are saying no to all of me since I have put all of me in the pit. It is the final rejection, like a mortally wounded animal must feel when the bullet rammed through its guts where the entry wound is small, just the size of a nice neat forty-five." This, of course, goes too far but does get at what most lawyers feel as advocates, though to a lesser degree.

This is not to say that barristers are not able to make spirited presentations out of what has been given to them. Nor is it to say that barristers do not infuse their personalities into their trial work. British barrister and novelist David Crigman in *In Death We Trust*, *The Molecule Man*, and *What's The Truth Got To Do With It?* has given us an obnoxious and arrogant barrister character in Ronan Cadagan equal to the worst America has to offer (no names please). He is obsessed with trying to prove himself superior to everyone else, which he believes is best done by winning all his cases. He is even willing to go beyond what is acceptable by leapfrogging the solicitor and engaging more directly with the client. In one novel in which Cadagan is defending in a criminal matter, he even gives a version of The Lecture made famous by Robert Traver's *Anatomy of a Murder* to the client so as to reshape the instructions he has been given.

There is a certain purity in the English and Australian barrister systems that minimizes or even eliminates the barrister's contact with the client. The solicitor intermediary spares the barrister all the messiness of dealing with people and their problems, prompting some commentators to argue that the system helped create the semblance of a priesthood of the law. This, however, has never been our model. Efforts to cocoon lawyers in their work runs counter to our idea of what representation is. Even if it were available to us, turning trial advocacy into what can be described as a version of an academic exercise in the way of the barristers, English or Australian, is not what lawyers would want. But if there were only a way to give our lawyers more distance from their clients, more intellectual space, more of a chance to effect but not be affected? The comparison between the United States and England and Australia at least prompts that question.

A 2011 study of Australian legal barristers has given us at least one reason to think more about the barrister model as opposed to our model of representation. The study recruited 924 solicitors and 756 barristers and asked questions about psychological stress levels as they related to depression. When it came to how often in the past thirty days the respondents had experienced moderate stress, high distress, or very high distress, solicitors reported in for each of the three levels at rates significantly higher than those of the general population. Barristers, on the other hand, had rates for each of the three categories only slightly higher than those of the general population.

The result that life with minimized client contact makes life easier for barristers might prompt some lawyers to think the barrister approach is preferable. As much as I struggle with clients (and I like people, I should note), I could never see myself being limited in my advocacy to what someone had prepared for me. Nor, I suspect, would most lawyers. What I contributed to the case would be too cabined. I would be unable to do all that I could do, whatever that means. We may not want the level of involvement that Gerry Spence describes, but we want involvement nonetheless. This, then, seems to be the core issue, the nature of the beast, so to speak. To have an effect on what we do, we have to be affected by the act of doing it. The client wins.

THINKING LIKE A LAWYER

As lawyers, we are perhaps most fond of the idea that we think in a way that is different from the way everyone else (non-lawyers) thinks. Legal education trumpets the specialness of "thinking like a lawyer," as it is called, and the Socratic method most responsible for analytical insights that we are privy to. Anyone who has been around smart people knows that lawyers have no monopoly on rigorous thinking, the distinguishing feature of "thinking like a lawyer." Lawyers should know this and perhaps do, though few want to take the shine off the intellectualism that they have arrogated to themselves. In truth, it is called "thinking like a lawyer" only because lawyers assigned it that term.

Historically, lawyers engaged in the process of thinking through the legal issues that their cases presented long before that process was called "thinking like a lawyer," though one commentator, Jeffrey Lipshaw in his article "Models and Games" has argued that "thinking like a lawyer" is "a cultural phenomenon of the last 150 years or so"—raising the interesting question whether, taking this approach, Daniel Webster or Joseph Story, to use just two examples, thought like lawyers. But that is just an aside. The reputation for 18th- and 19th- century lawyers for rhetorical flourishes as part of advocacy has obscured this. Looking to an opinion from this period that tracks the arguments of the lawyers shows that the lawyers have brought to bear an active intelligence and disciplined reasoning skills. The great English essayist William Hazlit in the beginning of the 19th century nicely describes at least one variation of a lawyer's mind at work. Of the well-known British barrister Thorne Tooke, Hazlitt writes in *The Spirit of the Age* that Tooke "had the mind of a lawyer . . . a rigid and constant habit of attending to every word and clause in a sentence. . . Mr. Tooke, in fact, treated words, as the chemists do substances; he separated those which are compounded of others from those which are not decompoundable. He did not explain the obscure by the more obscure, but the difficult by the plain, the complex by the simple."

"Thinking like a lawyer" has its own definitions, even though it is so often linked to the Socratic method. The 2007 Carnegie study of legal education gives us a definition that looks with detachment to process, stating that to think like a lawyer "means redefining messy situations of actual or potential conflict as opportunities for advancing a client's cause through legal argument before a judge or through negotiation." If we look instead to the moving parts within, we read that the indoctrinated law student can "discriminate between the relevant and irrelevant facts of a case, to draw just distinctions between things apparently similar, and to discover true analogies between things apparently dissimilar . . ." That at least was how James Barr Ames, turn-of-the-20th-century Harvard Law School dean, described legal reasoning in his *Lectures on Legal History*. Then there's the separate but simultaneous thinking trick, set out by Thomas Reed Powell, again of Harvard. Thurman Arnold in *The Symbols of Government* quotes Powell as saying that, "[i]f you think you can think about a thing that is inextricably attached to something else without thinking of the thing which it is attached to, then you have a legal mind." Add skepticism and intellectual detachment and you know you are there, until we encounter Judge Ruggero Aldisert of the United States Court of Appeals for the Third Circuit in his article "Logic for Law Students," that is. He finds that there is a better way to describe and define legal reasoning. For him it means, simply enough, "employing logic to construct arguments."

The most important book on the subject of thinking like a lawyer (the explicit goal of the method) questions whether there is in fact such a thing. Frederick Schauer writes in the first paragraph of his *Thinking Like A Lawyer: A New Introduction to Legal Reasoning* that "whether lawyers think, reason, and argue differently from ordinary folk is a question and not an axiom."

Schauer argues that in many ways there is nothing special about the traits of thinking like a lawyer. He has been joined by several other commentators making this point. Schauer has just been the best in thinking through it. Thinking analytically and rigorously, dealing with facts and evidence, understanding the full context of an event or fact, seeing the other side of an argument, reasoning by analogy—these are skills that apply to any number of jobs or professions, not just to lawyers. But we need to be precise. There are, it is true, forms of reasoning that, though they have been traditionally associated with legal reasoning, apply far more to judicial decision making than to any form of "thinking like a lawyer." These would include making decisions according to rules, treating certain sources as authoritative, respecting precedent even when it appears to dictate the wrong outcome, being sensitive to the burdens of proof, and being attuned to questions of decision-making jurisdiction.

But all this might be beside the point. The real question is not so much whether the method lawyers are trained in is much different from the method of rigorous thinking that others in other disciplines engage in. The question for lawyers becomes how much they engage in rigorous thinking—call it what you will—at all after being trained to apply a disciplined inquisitive method to the problem or facts at issue. Put differently, can "thinking like a lawyer" withstand the world of practice? We want to think that "thinking like a lawyer" stays with us throughout our careers, but does it? Does our commitment to partisanship and to clients permit it? It would, of course, be greatly ironic if it couldn't withstand the pressures of practice, given the professed aims of the method, but we must acknowledge that in our profession today all the forces after law school work against the exercise of "thinking like a lawyer." The practice of law as we know it in America is about taking sides, not about sorting through facts with an approach neutral in its preferences. Lawyers do not practice the way that barristers do, for example, working exclusively as court advocates and moving from one case to the next without regard to the client, following the application of forensic reasoning wherever it takes him or her. To read the novels of British barrister Jonathan Davies shows the purer barrister advocate in action and the way that the barrister in analyzing a problem has more freedom to follow the reasoning where it leads. The barrister approach is cold, detached analysis.

Our American lawyers approach things differently. The legal profession is defined in part by the hemispheres of corporate clients and individual clients, but that's only the beginning of it. There are any number of specialties in which lawyers take one side and do not stray. It is unusual, for example, for a plaintiff's personal injury lawyer also to represent in other cases insurance companies defending against personal injury claims. Criminal defense lawyers and prosecutors stay in their own camps over their careers. If anything, prosecutors might go on to represent insurance companies in defense work and criminal defense lawyers might represent personal injury plaintiffs. Whatever lawyers learned in school has not kept them from narrowing and embracing certain beliefs, a not surprising idea considering that a lawyer's loyalty and belief in a position reflect not independent judgment but who the client is. It remains a good question—posed by researchers but not persuasively answered—whether lawyers choose certain work and certain clients because of affinity and identification issues or whether they find themselves with that work and then develop affinity and identification. Knowing, as we do from a recent study "Do Lawyers Really Believe Their Own Hype and Should They?" by Zev Eigen and Yair Listokin, that students randomly assigned moot court parties end up overwhelmingly believing that the merits favor their side does not solve the causation riddle, though it does suggest that "thinking like a lawyer" gets swallowed up by the practice of law. A quick test shows the truth of this. Are lawyers more driven by passion and partisanship in their cases or by a keenness for the analysis and a willingness to acknowledge a losing hand? "Thinking like a lawyer" might have been great in law school, even though it was misnamed, but after law school such thinking just gets in the way.

TYPOGRAPHICAL ERRORS

Typographical errors, known to all and accepted as part of life by most, sometimes lead to humor, at least as reported in published collections of them (there are such things) and in blogs featuring them as a genre of humor all their own. It's the difference between singing for your package and signing for it, that sort of thing. Funnytypos.com reports on the amusing typo and extends further to consider cousins misspellings and bad grammar. Malapropisms, because of the wit we find in them, usually have separate promoters. But not everyone draws attention to typos for their humor. Librarytypos.blogspot.com takes a sterner view and its bloggers declare that they are "a group of librarians from all over the world with a common interest—keeping our online catalogs free of errors." Leave it to the law to take the phenomenon of the offhand, casual, and unintended typographical error, wrestle it to the ground, and force it to give in and give up all of its possible significance.

Typos have significance in substantive law. In cyberlaw, for example, the nicely named *typosquatting* relies on mistakes made by web users when typing a trademark-protected website address into a web browser. These typosquatters use qwerty typos, letter swaps, and sticky keys to generate traffic on high-traffic trademark-protected domain names. Data showing, for example, that users often type *landswend* for *landsend* leads to a typo-based website parasitically drawing traffic. That the Anticybersquatting Consumers Protection Act has a clause to deter typosquatting does not seem to be enough, though.

The cases indicate that employers have little tolerance for employees with typo problems. That a newspaper editor missed his own typos and those of others when editing their work, not surprisingly, became part of a non-discriminatory termination case when the *Dallas Morning News* pared its work force and ended up in litigation. That the editor also wore shorts and tennis shoes to an interview with former Secretary of State Madeleine

Albright also supported the termination. In some cases a problem with typos is one of many problems. The list of defects in one federal age discrimination case that were considered to be legitimate, non-discriminatory reasons for termination included failing to answer the phone, failing to respond to e-mails, failure to follow directions, hostile interaction with coworkers, and, of course, introducing typos into the work of others. We also find typos to be an issue when plaintiff employees allege a hostile work environment. In one case the employer was alleged to have spoken to the plaintiff in a demeaning and condescending voice in front of co-workers and reprimanded her for minor typos in her work.

Typos, as aberrations almost by definition, have an identity marker aspect to them. That the same typos appear in the same places in separate documents can only mean that one document was copied from the other. The same principle applies to databases. In a Florida case, for example, the plaintiff had irrefutable evidence that its competitor had appropriated its database of customer information when the typos in the plaintiff's database were matched identically by the typos in the competitor's database. In the same way, law firms to their embarrassment have been exposed as double billers because of matching typos. In a number of cases in which a firm's fees were challenged, the usual result was that the firm conceded double billing when a second set of bills matched, typo for typo, another set of bills.

The range of judicial responses to briefs peppered with typos comes from recent interviews with several Supreme Court Justices published in *Scribes*. Justice Stevens didn't think twice about them, while Justice Scalia thought that typos in a brief suggested deeper, underlying problems. He didn't explain his plainly tenuous reasoning. From lower court judges we see references to "just a typo," but we also find instances in which lawyers are excoriated and even sanctioned for inadequate briefs sporting a host of problems, always, of course, including typos. When admonishing one lawyer, the court in *In Re High Sulphur* notes that the submitted brief is "riddled with typos and grammar mistakes, and it does not contain even one citation to the record." We find the most common response to sloppy writing in a case such as *Dana v. Holder*, in which the court faults petitioner's lawyer for filing a brief that contained numerous typographical and grammatical errors and then merely "reminds counsel of her obligation to review and proofread a brief before filing.

Judges have certainly accepted the idea that there is a relationship between the quality of a lawyer's work and his typo count. That the typo has become for some a metaphor for poor writing gets further support from at least one case in which a district judge remanded for clarification an administrative law judge's ruling in a social security disability case because the opinion failed to set out the judge's reasoning and because the opinion was riddled with obvious typos.

The natural impulse for most lawyers to catch and fix their typos for some can develop into a major project. What else can we think when courts have cut legal fees because of too much time spent in the typo wars? In one case from the Northern District of Illinois, two hours to correct typos in a motion and reply brief were struck as unnecessary in a sanctions fee petition. But in a case from the District of New Jersey, the court in a fee shifting case allowed five hours to edit a thirty-six-page document to be sure it was free of typos and grammatical errors. The prevailing party had asked for 37.6 hours, which the court found clearly excessive. In one Fair Debt Collection Practices Act case at least, judgment was rendered that checking for typos in a debt collection letter does not qualify as an attorney's work. The statute requires that an attorney sending a dunning letter must have direct and personal involvement in the mailing of letters. Merely putting the debt collector's letter on the lawyer's letterhead, with the lawyer checking amounts and fixing typos, was insufficient for this purpose, the court ruled.

Hubbub over a typographical error even became a dramatic turning point in *The Associates* (1979) by *The Paper Chase* novelist John Jay Osborne about a young lawyer's professional coming of age in a New York white shoe firm in the late 1970s. The villain of the piece is monomaniacal partner Wellington Rolls (of course), the chore is proofreading an SEC Registration Statement, and the culprit is an ampersand in an investment bank's hallowed name. But it's not what you think. The ampersand looks just fine, except that, unbeknownst to the novel's hero, it should be upside down rather than right side up. The nutty partner, having caught the mistake in the last stages of review, then uses the error as an occasion to heap some territorial-based abuse on the young associate. In what might be an echo of a Kingsfield moment from *The Paper Chase*, the partner ridicules and insults. "You moron," the partner screams, "you do not deserve to call yourself a lawyer." All for a mistake that the young associate had no way of knowing he was making. No wonder he strikes off on his own at novel's end.

While I will leave explicating the causal relationship to others, it seems that the view big law firms have toward typos has influenced the views of the courts and the profession on the subject. I've been told that lawyers at large law firms have been known to make the argument when trying to demonstrate superiority to their rivals that their rivals can't be that smart because their briefs have typos (or just one) in them. Thus do intelligence and proofreading skills get confused. Imagine the conclusion to be drawn from a stain on a lawyer's tie. Jeremy Blachman describes this sensibility in his wonderfully funny big firm satire *Anonymous Lawyer*, narrated by a New York firm's hiring partner. He boasts that the firm catches any misspelling, which we can equate to a typo, "within three and a half minutes of when it is typed, under the regulations." Anything else suggests incompetence. Typos for this firm are a sign of weakness. They must be searched out and destroyed.

Measuring intelligence by a typo count, though, confuses superficiality with substance. It's just too easy taking the measure of a lawyer by considering how nicely pressed his suit is. We call a lawyer an empty suit when we know there's nothing there beyond appearance. It's nice to read clean text, unmarred by typos, but we shouldn't make a fetish of it. The substantive law doesn't when it comes to an otherwise valid search warrant that in its description of the place to be search has typographical errors. If the law has the good sense to read for substance, so should we. Put differently, it's fair to point out an excessive number of typos, but it is not fair to measure competence in court submissions by the number of these superficial errors.

WHAT AM I WORTH?

It has been true from the beginning that fees help define a lawyer's professional life. Money earned has, for example, long provided status to lawyers as they take the measure of each other. There's something about the biggest. Justice Robert Jackson, a highly successful practitioner from the Buffalo, New York, area in the 1920s and 1930s before going to Washington, remarked in his oral history that all the lawyers he knew agreed that the lawyer who commanded the highest fees was considered the best lawyer and the leader of the bar. But money has gone further and helped define their existence as professionals. We get a joking version of this from famous 20th-century trial lawyer Max Steuer, who saw law as a paying proposition and dived into a case fee first, so to speak. When a prominent swindler sought to retain him, Steuer, as reported in Otto Obermaier's entry on him in Roger K. Newman's *The Yale Biographical Dictionary of Law*, cut short the man's explication of his predicament and exclaimed, "I can't think till I have the money." We find a more cutting and more memorable version of this idea in Shakespeare, when he described "the breath of the unfee'd lawyer," by which he meant the emptiness of a lawyer's advice when it is not being paid for. The public looks at lawyer fees from its point of view, not the lawyer's. For the public, greed has become almost synonymous with lawyers.

The default rule is that fees be reasonable. When the fee moves far enough from reasonable, the lawyer can find himself being sued by the client. The factors to be considered to determine an excessive fee include the time and labor involved; the novelty and difficulty of the question; the skill requisite to perform the work properly; losing out on other work because of accepting the case; the customary fee; whether the fee is contingent; time limitations imposed by client or circumstances; amount involved and result obtained; the experience, reputation and ability of the lawyer; the undesirability factor of the case; and the nature and length of the professional relationship with the client. Only the rarest disputes end up in court, leaving the lawyers to be tempered in their quests for fees only by the question of what they can get away with. Some have the smell of audacity to them. A lawyer could not recover legal fees for work in allegedly discovering a safe deposit box and a passbook in a probate matter when the lawyer knew all along where the box and passbook were. Charging $70,000 for filing a single document to confess judgment in an action was $60,000 too much. And charging $150,000 for several weeks of largely administrative work locating and collecting bank records in connection to the preparation of a will is clearly excessive. These fees are rooted in fraud and do not reflect the darkness in the lawyer's ambition, greed, and desire that can produce unconscionably high fees.

We primarily use three types of fee arrangements. There is the well-known contingency fee in which the lawyer does not earn a fee unless the client prevails, but we also use the flat fee and the hourly fee. With contingency fees, plaintiffs without cash but with good claims are able to find lawyers, opening and democratizing the legal system. That plaintiffs' lawyers can earn fees of one third or even one half of settlements, without regard to the actual time spent on a file, might strike some as conferring a windfall of sorts on the lawyers, but given the good that they do, we willingly accept what might strike some as a disproportionate reward. This is even more true of plaintiffs' lawyers in class action litigation. We accept the notion that the only efficient way to redress relatively small injuries to a large number of similarly situated plaintiffs is through a class action. We further accept that the lawyers representing the class profit disproportionally in this version of the contingency fee agreement, this even though the system encourages defendants to propose settlements that favor the lawyers over the class. We accept all of this because the basic efficiency cannot be denied. We also accept the idea that the Equal Justice Act encourages lawyers to take civil rights and other types of cases on a contingency by providing for legal fees so long as the plaintiff prevails, which is interpreted to mean being successful on any significant issue in the litigation that achieves some of the benefit sought by the party. These fee-shifting statutes are exceptions to the so-called American rule that each side in litigation bears its own legal fees. This rule rejects the loser-pays approach of countries such as England and Australia. American plaintiffs like this rule because it makes it easier for them to take their case to court. Making the loser pay the legal fees of the winner makes for a powerful deterrent for those thinking of suing.

The flat fee, in contrast, is a sum of money for the lawyer's work in a case. There is, to be sure, a lighter side to flat fee as found in entries in *The Yale Biographical Dictionary of American Law* in the sense that lawyers have joked about them. Hugo Black was known to cry if he had to move certain Alabama juries, but "not for less than $25,000," he said. Percy Foreman of Texas, we also learn, wanted to be known for his expensive fees. "It doesn't matter if my client is guilty," Foreman said, "by the time he's paid my fee I've punished him enough." New Dealer insider Tom Corcoran had the best explanation for high fees, at least in part because it allowed lawyers to take them as far as they wanted. He famously noted, "[w]hen you're charging fees, charge then high. The world takes you at your own valuation. You decide whether you're Tiffany or Woolworth."

Looked at broadly, there seems to be no easy answer as to the best fee arrangement. The billable hour, the flat fee, and the contingency fee all have their supporters, but all three also have their detractors. Critics argue that contingency fees are built on an inherent conflict of interest and that the arrangement can lead to windfall rewards for the lawyers. The flat fee has been criticized because it can pay the lawyer either too much or too little. And the billable hour has been criticized because of its susceptibility to abuse. It has also been criticized because it does not produce enough revenue. There are calls for an emerging fourth type of fee arrangement, called the value added agreement, which can take the billable hour approach and give lawyers extra money for good results using a multiplier.

What is a lawyer's work worth? Put differently, can a lawyer's fee ever be too much? We know that fees cannot be exorbitant and still be considered reasonable, but what does *exorbitant* mean? Just how relative a term is it? What do we make, for example, of the famous anecdote about famed New York lawyer Elihu Root (1845–1937)? His reputation was so great, we are told, that the president of one corporate client confronted him when he was eating breakfast to protest that one of Root's partners, rather than

Root himself, had reviewed one of his corporation's contracts. He gave the contract to Root, who promptly but carefully read and it and agreed with its adequacy. Root then added $25,000 to the bill, without protest. Good work if you can find it.

The core, near philosophical issues raised by these questions can have simple, if not simplistic answers for some. Contingent fees are justified, lawyers would argue, by the social good that such fee arrangements provide. Lawyers, in selecting the cases they believe have merit, become the filter for the cases that end up being filed in court. Yet courts have been telling us that contingent fees in class action cases are getting harder to justify because of the disproportionate rewards that the lawyers reap. This has led judges to review more aggressively the percentage of the settlement going to the lawyers. That class action suits have a social value can hardly be doubted. What they are worth to lawyers is a separate question. And on the billable hour front, lawyers, being lawyers, would say that the only consideration should be what the market will bear. In this marketplace, clients pay for whatever they think has value. Clients might be willing to pay extra because they think a lawyer has a special skill, a particular reputation, or certain influence that even other lawyers similarly placed do not. This can hardly be argued with.

That at least some lawyers earn a great deal of money is hard to escape. Senior partners in large firms in cities such as Los Angeles and New York now routinely earn one to two million dollars per year. A new echelon of big firm lawyer has emerged which bills at more than one thousand dollars per hour. Lead lawyers in class action litigation lay claim to a hefty percentage of large settlements, even when the individual class members get next to nothing, and first year associates at large firms hired right out of school make more—sometimes significantly more—than the $165,000 that federal judges earn. There's certainly nothing new about lawyers earning money. But now that they make so much money, the implications that flow from that money as it relates to the public, the profession, and to the individual lawyers themselves seem more important than ever. Fees, to be sure, are not antithetical to the legal profession, since we could hardly have a profession without them. But fees nonetheless pose the biggest challenges to a profession struggling with a cancerous impulse to devolve into being just a business and lawyers nothing more than tradesmen or, as some say, economic actors. Put differently, to understand lawyers and their fees is to understand the profession itself and where we find ourselves today.

WHAT WOULD SOCRATES THINK?

The Socratic method as practiced by law school professors will perhaps always be associated with Professor Kingsfield's description of the method (if only I could do his voice) in the movie *The Paper Chase*. He tells his first year contracts class that his little questions will spin the tumblers of their minds. "We do brain surgery here," he tells the students. "You teach yourselves the law, but I train your mind. You come in here with a skull full of mush, and you leave thinking like a lawyer." In Kingsfield, the Socratic method is defined by his chilling imperiousness. He berates and humiliates the students when they fail to keep up with him, all under the general theory that such treatment will toughen the students and give them the advantage when they engage in combat in practice. In one of the most famous scenes of the film, Kingsfield asks our first-year student protagonist, James T. Hart, to come to the front of the class when he refuses to engage in the method when called upon and passes instead. From the lectern, Kingsfield gives Hart a dime and tells him to call his mother and tell her that he will never become a lawyer. There is only one way and one method. It sounds promising, even sounds exciting. In practice, of course, things have not turned out so well, to the point that a dissident group has been arguing that the Socratic method as practiced warps new lawyers and gives them throughout their careers a sense of themselves and others that leads away from what Socrates intended in the first place.

The three common complaints are that the method does not teach students the wide range of skills they will need as practitioners, that the method advances ideological and political agendas, and that the method imposes harmful psychological effects on students. The complaints about the effects of the method on a student's view of interpersonal relationships and a general professional sensibility are particularly striking. As examples, Roger E. Schechter in "Changing Law Schools to Make Less Nasty Lawyers" has argued that a Socratic teacher "communicates an unspoken but nonetheless powerful message that mean-spirited wise-cracks, and even temper tantrums, are entirely appropriate behavior," while Paul T. Hayden in "Applying Client-Lawyer Models in Legal Education" argues that students learn from their instructors that "a super-competent lawyer is brusque, dominating, and often condescending to those less competent (a category that certainly includes clients)."

The argument is not that students should not be tested with inquiries that make them stretch, perhaps uncomfortably. Even with Socrates there were the birthing pains of reasoning. Rather, it is that there is a grand and perhaps risible irony in the way law schools treat their students and the way Socrates did. Socrates only modestly asserted his own wisdom, arguing that he was wiser than others only because he knew the limits of his knowledge. Not surprisingly, a standard definition of the Socratic method, as found in *The Penguin Dictionary of Philosophy,* is that it "consists in asking questions that will prompt reflection, which in turn will produce knowledge—or awareness of one's own ignorance." Modesty and an awareness of what they do not know are hardly traits of Kingsfield's successors. They send out into the world lawyers similarly constituted. In the grandest irony of all, they go out into the world of practice and seek to intimidate others as they were intimidated themselves. After all, in their minds they have become the masters entitled to ask the questions.

The real problem for the Socratic method to continue with its original packaging might not lie with the complaints pointed to by the dissidents. It is with the approach's reputation for brutality and its anti-nurturing approach to legal education. Staple that it still is at law schools, some think that the reputation of the Socratic method now needs to be redefined and rebranded, rounding the sharp edges, so as to persuade potential law students that theirs will not be an educational experience defined by pain and suffering. The University of Chicago Law School, for example, includes on its website the article "The Socratic Method" written by one of its professors, Elizabeth Garrett, intended to confront the enemy. The strategy is to emphasize that the Kingsfield performance in *The Paper Chase* is "an exaggerated and outdated caricature of the Socratic Method." No more are the days of the "relentless Socratic professor who ended every sentence with a question mark." The newer version prefers to use the Socratic method "to foster as much active learning as possible." For the new Socratic method, "the effort is a cooperative one in which the teacher and students work to understand an issue more completely." In seeking to play down the ferociousness of the Socratic method as it has been practiced, the website article uses dilution and calls it "participatory learning."

It has to be admitted that, no matter how the Socratic method is styled, when it is used properly in legal education it leads to ego bruising and certain emotional unpleasantness. There are to be sure problems with the Socratic method as currently used, but not because law schools have softened and caved in to consumer complaints to fashion a more user-friendly version. Rather, the problem, ironically enough, could well be with the professors themselves distorting the approach into something it was not intended to be. This does not seem to have been the problem with "Bull" Warren and the Kingsfield character based on him and played by John Houseman. Imperiousness might be a well laid charge, but not egomania. Egomania now, though, seems to be the rage. Warren, it can be noted by way of curiosity, was indeed a tough customer. For a 1937 *Life Magazine* piece on the Harvard Law School a photographer was dispatched to get pictures of the campus, classrooms, students, and some of the famous professors. He approached Warren, who told him that if he didn't leave him alone he would punch him in the nose. The magazine got something of a last laugh by including in the piece a photograph of the portrait of Warren hanging at the law school.

Scott Turow, in his fine *One L: The Turbulent True Story of a First Year at Harvard Law School*, provides a key insight into the ego dynamic at work. He writes that his first take on the method as practiced was enthusiastic. "The truth was," he tells us, "that I had been gripped, even thrilled, by the class. [The instructor], for all the melodrama and intimidation, had been magnificent, electric, in full possession of himself and the students. The points he'd made had had a wonderful clarity and directness. He was, as claimed, an exceptional teacher." Others were similarly taken with the method and this particular instructor, but by year's end open hostility had broken out, spurred by an ugly incident of humiliation. Turow's insight into the method as practiced comes when he understands, for this instructor at least, that a need to show off—to always be right, and to exploit his position—lies at the core of the persona he wants to project in the classroom. "He had had twenty years to learn [the material]; we were new to it, vulnerable—and captive. If you came to class, you had no choice but to watch those flamboyant demonstrations, possessing no real standard by which to know if they deserved the kind of open admiration [the instructor] seemed to expect. On the whole, I had the sense that [the instructor] was using the classroom to live out some strange vision of himself and that struck me as a misappropriation of a teacher's power."

Rather ironically, the most eloquent and powerful defense of the Socratic method turns not on the usefulness of having learned to think like a lawyer but on the very brutality in the traditional approach that has sent our generation of law professors fleeing from it. Paul Carrington, distinguished law professor and 1952 Harvard Law School graduate, takes a swat at political correctness and the consumer-friendly version of the Socratic method currently favored and argues in a 2010 *Journal of Legal Education* essay that it was the harshness of the Socratic method as practiced by Warren and others that toughened students and produced perhaps unexpected results. He draws a direct connection to Army Boot Camp, from which he had also graduated, and the *espirit de corps* that the painful, agonizing, and humiliating process produces among those who completed it. For Carrington, the real virtue of the Socratic method as properly practiced was that it gave students values separate from the value of thinking like a lawyer. The anguish, anxiety, and embarrassment sometimes produced by the well wielded pedagogical tool represented the price that students had to pay to mature intellectually and to establish the sense of a morally autonomous self that arms them to fight in the legal trenches. The moral lessons of the Socratic method mattered the most because they were the ones which would be tested the most in the practice of law.

There is a clear connection between Carrington's defense of the Socratic method as practiced by "Bull" Warren and the virtues of a legal education as described by Oliver Wendell Holmes in his various commencement addresses. Professors such as Warren taught law in what Holmes described as the "grand manner" and as part of a belief that lawyers could live greatly in the law. To do so, they needed to be armed with moral courage. As Holmes had put it in his address "The Use of Law Schools," "it seems to me that nearly all the education which men can get is moral, not intellectual. The main part of intellectual education is not the acquisition of facts, but learning to make the facts live." For this the Socratic method is best suited, but only when the instructors—and students—understand its true objective.

WHY ARE WE (LAWYERS) SO DISLIKED?

It is hard to know why the public dislikes and even hates lawyers as much as it does, though our tendencies toward arrogance, egotism, and narcissism might have something to do with it. When we add aggressiveness, competitiveness, and smugness to the mix, we get either a personality that only a mother can love or, if we listen to lawyers defending themselves on the arrogance charge, traits necessary for combat. This raises the causation issue, whether the practice of law prompts lawyers to develop these personality traits or whether individuals with these traits seek law out because in law they can be who they really want to be. That lawyers tend to see themselves as the smarter and wiser version of the human species, however, can hardly be denied. Whether we see them on television or read about them in the newspaper, lawyers are everywhere testing the limits of reasonableness and rationality—all in pursuit, they say, of zealous representation. This in part gives us such a bad name. It's the world seen only the lawyer's way, the arrogant way.

Lawyers in America have long been disliked. In our earliest years, the public disliked lawyers in part because they were hardly, if at all, trained. Some states had laws banning lawyers. Daniel Boorstin, a leading historian of the period—and also trained as a lawyer—writes in *The Americans: The Colonial Experience* that in colonial America "distrust of lawyers became an institution." Lawyers got past the laws banning them but the public's dislike continued. As the century progressed, new reasons to dislike lawyers emerged. Lawyers were seen as greedy and as manipulators of the system. One 19th-century commentator, Fred B. Perkins, in the magazine *The Galaxy* explained that the legal profession was attacked because it "is a human attempt at a remedy for human defects, and partakes therefore of the very weaknesses that it seeks to aid." Making money at the expense of both the client and justice did not help the bar's reputation, he added. There was also jealousy and irritation that lawyers persisted with their insistence on lawyer-speak to keep the public at a distance. Being associated with despised causes and people did not help either. In the 20th century, the increase in professional standards for lawyers beginning in the early decades did not do much to make lawyers any less disliked. The increasing role that lawyers have played in society has gone on to make lawyers even more disliked, though not in all places. Lawyer cartoons in *The New Yorker* have from the magazine's start in 1925 rooted their jokes not in venomous dislike of lawyers but in poking gentle fun at the self-centeredness of lawyers and the growing proliferation of lawyers and lawyerly moments in our society. That the audience of *The New Yorker* probably has a higher percentage of lawyers might explain this some.

It is also likely that the public's growing awareness of what lawyers do has increased its dislike of them. One of the consequences of the information age is that the lawyer's staple of what can be described as the legalistic approach is better known, though probably not better appreciated. Margaret Raymond has perceptively pointed out in her law review article "On Legalistic Behavior, The Advocacy Privilege, and Why People Hate Lawyers" that one aspect of the legalistic approach is excessive parsing of language to avoid answering the intended question. She writes that "[w]hile ordinary people interpret language in a cooperative way, trying to understand how the speaker intended to use language and to be responsive to the spirit of the inquiry, the lawyer relying on [his legalistic approach] acts selfishly, rejecting the reciprocal social obligation of communication and comprehension in favor of a unilateral insistence on proper questions by his adversary." For example, if a lawyer is asked, "Do you know what time it is?" he would say "yes" but not give the time, forcing the questioner to ask the second question as to the actual time. This approach explains the derisive jokes that turn on President Clinton's parsing of a question and answering that it all depends on the meaning of "is." Such an approach is hardly endearing.

The lawyer jokes of the last few decades have represented a type of assault on lawyers, though, to be fair, we can find equally caustic jokes about lawyers in England going back centuries. While some might point out that it takes a lawyer or, worse yet, a legal academic, to look for serious meaning in jokes, Mark Galanter in his 2006 *Lowering the Bar: Lawyer Jokes and Legal Culture* usefully points out that we can put lawyer jokes into nine basic categories. Some stretch across the decades and even centuries, while others have a modern flavor to them and feature themes that began to appear beginning in the 1980s. The first group is the enduring core and the second the new territories, as Galanter puts it. The enduring core jokes consider five major themes: lawyers as liars, as economic predators, as partners with the devil, as strife instigators, and as enemies of justice. The four new territory themes turn on lawyers as betrayers of trust, as morally deficient, as objects of scorn, and as (ouch!) targets of extinction.

Not just the nature but why we have lawyer jokes has come in for much psychoanalyzing of sorts by the profession, judging by the work of legal academics. One explanation is that in a world divided between lawyers and everyone else, lawyer jokes perform a bonding function for the general population. Some see lawyers as being responsible for many if not all of society's ills. They do, after all, seem to be everywhere and involved in everything, so why not blame them for most everything, especially those things for which they are the defenders and mouthpieces? Even when they act as so-called commentators when events such as celebrity trials take over television, lawyers present themselves as advocates, seeing just one side when the viewer wants something more balanced, more edifying.

Putting aside the idea that the public sees lawyers as easy targets and wants to blame or at least associate them with all of what is wrong with the world, the dynamics of the attorney–client relationship likely figure prominently, though perhaps without much discussion, in both the public's reaction to lawyers and the depth of that reaction. It is, most of all, a relationship characterized by its own type of intimacy. This puts greater demands on lawyers to meet expectations. Disappointed clients have been known to turn on their lawyers quickly and with ferocity.

One clue to what is going on with the public is that the themes of the so-called new territory jokes which began to emerge in the 1980s are strikingly different from the themes of the enduring lawyer jokes. The themes of the enduring lawyer jokes often turn on the tensions inherent in some of the basic functions of lawyers in the adversary system. Being responsible for advancing one side of truth, for example, can get distorted in a joke into a claim that lawyers are facilitating lies or are in fact lying themselves. The links between lawyers and clients, especially clients with monied interests, can be distorted into claims that lawyers are economic predators, instigators of strife, enemies of justices, and allies of the devil. In contrast, the themes of the new territory lawyer jokes go much more to the personal. Being accused of being morally deficient or betraying trust find root not in what lawyers do but in who they are. Not surprisingly, the jokes that target lawyers for extinction are most troubling to lawyers because they sense that personal element. It does not get much more personal.

It is perhaps not a coincidence that these new themes beginning in the 1980s correlate to a significant increase in the number of lawyers and the beginning of all those lawyer television shows. The audience for these shows would have known of Perry Mason as a distant black and white memory, if that. For them it was the flash and sleek rapaciousness of *L.A. Law* and the rest that held their attention. But it runs deeper than this. The great change over the last forty years has been that the public knows lawyers as never before. Whatever mystery or mystique lawyers and the profession ever had, as part of the cache of a learned profession, for example, has been eaten away by the explosion of lawyers in the popular culture, which includes advertising, with lawyers in an unmediated environment, so to speak, just selling themselves.

Lawyers—the public has come to know them all too well. Its dislike of them may be a variation of the idea that familiarity breeds contempt. In contrast, there is still some mystique to the medical profession. Doctors are not yet seen as just like everyone else. This is what has happened to lawyers. Moreover, physicians are seen as possessing special skill and knowledge. The public has increasingly come to believe that what lawyers sell is themselves, their personalities. "I will fight for you" is the tag line of countless lawyer advertisements. "Hire me because I have the personality of a pit bull," the advertisement is really saying. The public understands personality and recognizes its limitations. Reduced to just a snarl rather than to examples of expertise and knowledge worthy of respect, the lawyer is the perfect example of familiarity suitable to contempt.

YOU DON'T SAY?

A surprising amount of what might be called gratuitous commentary in recent circuit court opinions makes for amusing if not puzzling reading. It is *sui generis*, but we'll use "gratuitous commentary" as our shorthand referent. Its subject matter varies enormously and includes sports of all types, slang, geography, history, astronomy, and children's toys, just to mention a few subjects from the last few years' worth of the *Federal Reporter*, Third Series. The usually brief commentary does not fit into what we understand digressions, asides, or even background material to be and is worth discussion for two reasons. One is the nature of the commentary itself and its varying sensibility of cheekiness, humor, narcissism, obsession, self-indulgence, and preening know-it-allness. The second is what it suggests about the commentary's writer.

This issue of gratuitous commentary is not naturally a part of the debate over the use of footnotes in judicial opinions even though the gratuitous material often appears in footnotes. The fight over footnotes has looked mostly to whether citation to authority should appear in the text or in footnotes. Those opposing footnotes argue that the reader should not have to move his attention up and down, going from text to footnote and back to text, only to go down again to a footnote, on and on. The usual argument for judicial opinion footnotes is not just that they indicate the authority upon which the court is relying—a key idea in a system such as ours that is precedent-centric—but that footnotes also allow for judges to explain their thought processes. Here the idea is that the footnote explanation is not important enough to justify being made part of the text. But this second part can't be right. The judge's thought process is a ripe subject for the text itself, unless opinions are understood in the strictest sense as just delivering reasoning and results and a judge's thought process is somehow considered to be different from the reasoning process. In any event, however, gratuitous material of the sort I am describing would not even be the fit subject of a footnote. It's not part of a holding, and it is not a necessary explanation that does not fit neatly into the text, another reason for footnotes, according to the usual arguments. Nor does the information qualify as an aside—the playing out of an idea at the conclusion of which the writer acknowledges it as such and returns to the specific application of law to fact. Gratuitous material seems to be an orphan that judges cannot turn their backs on and instead insist on putting in the text or in footnotes, proper fit be damned.

Gratuitous commentary is by far the best place to find the personality of the writer. It is personality on display, personality featured. What other conclusion can be drawn, for example, from this footnote about a cue ball? The Ninth Circuit was reviewing the denial of a habeas corpus petition stemming from a conviction relating to a bar fight in which billiard balls were thrown. In a footnote, the court notes that at oral argument the lawyers for both sides had "indicated that cue balls were thrown." This slip prompts the court to state that it was "fairly confident that not everyone was throwing cue balls" because, even though the record does not detail it, only one pool table was involved. One table, one cue ball, the court both reasoned and had to point out. But why? The fact did not matter to the litigation and was not even a fact. It was just something said at oral argument. Any humor in the anomaly pointed out by the court is dwarfed by the smart aleckness of the footnote that we find in its final sentence: "[g]iven that there seems to have been only one pool table at the bar, there would have been a single cue ball." If the court wanted to point to humor, it would not have adopted a priggish tone.

Gratuitous commentary is not contemplated by opinion writing manuals, such as the Federal Judicial Center's *Judicial Writing Manual*, or by the commentary from both readers and writers of judicial opinions. The opinion manuals see structure as limited to an introduction, statement of issues, facts, discussion of legal principles, and a concluding paragraph. There is the usual discussion of what information should go into a footnote, but nothing about gratuitous material. Commentators take the same line.

Not all examples of gratuitous commentary have the tone of the cue ball footnote. Many have an eager tone, as in the writer's keenness to share something with the reader. There is, for example, the etymology set out in a footnote of the phrase "pig in a poke" in an Internet confidence game prosecution case. There are others: a footnote thumbnail sketch of Cazzie Russell's basketball career from the 1960s and 1970s in a criminal case in which a defendant had once been a teammate of Russell's; an opening paragraph with an evocative description of Buzzards Bay as a "beautiful jewel in the diadem of Massachusetts waters" and the history of its name in a National Environmental Policy Act case; an opinion-opening sketch of Jimmy Connors's tennis career in a case involving litigation between Connors and his lawyer, followed by a footnote paragraph recounting Connors's 1991 U.S. Open fourth round match at the age of 39; and a footnote describing Thomas Jefferson saying that he did not want his birthday celebrated in a case in which plaintiff had brought suit under the First and Fourth Amendments relating to events taking place at the Jefferson Memorial on what was the eve of Jefferson's 265th birthday.

What is not made clear in these opinions is why the information is being offered. There is a subject matter connection usually, but it is often tenuous and once-removed. We see this approach in other examples of information gratuitously included in an opinion. There is an extensive footnote description of the history of the Lego brand based on reference in transcript that a surveillance device looked like a Lego. There is a long description opening one opinion of how many days astronomers say there are in a year in a case interpreting what "one year" means for the purposes of 8 USC 1101(a)(43) (F); this even though the opinion then notes that, despite its precision, what astronomers report does not help answer the issue before the court. There is a detailed footnote explanation and history of the Quad Cities region prompted by reference in a drug case opinion to relocation of a defendant to Rock Island, Illinois. And there is a near full page (double columns) description of George Brett's major league baseball career, including a breathless description of the pine tar incident of 1983, that opens a trademark opinion involving a bat sold by a company George Brett owned with his brother Ken, another former major league player. As with my other examples of gratuitous commentary, there is no legitimate connection between the subject and analyses of the opinion and the gratuitous commentary to justify including it. The judge's justification each time seems to be that the case has touched, no matter how tenuously, on something he wants to tell us about, and that's enough reason for him.

The only remaining argument for including the gratuitous material also fails. This argument would be that we are applying the wrong footnote standard in rejecting the gratuitous commentary as footnote-worthy information. We should be looking to the uses other writers, such as historians, have put footnotes. There we would find a more expansive brand of information that perhaps has parallels to the gratuitous commentary of the judicial opinions. The problem here is that even if we think of footnotes in the way that historians have used them, the gratuitous material still does not qualify for inclusion. For someone such as Edward Gibbon in *The Rise and Fall of the Roman Empire*, the footnotes act as a subtext that allow Gibbon to communicate on two levels and to bridge the gap between his ancient subject matter and his contemporary audience. It is perhaps ironic that Gibbon's masterwork is read today primarily for its footnotes. If as James Joyce once boasted the text of his *Ulysses* would keep scholars busy for generations, Gibbon's footnotes are doing the same—though with much more reward for the effort spent sorting through their often dense and subtle meanings.

The urge to speak is never quite enough. There has to be a reason to speak. This is especially true for a genre of writing that has a specific purpose such as the judicial opinion. The genre's form can be shaped variously to accommodate more than just the need to declare a result, but it can't be reshaped to allow for the extraneous without diminishing that which needs to be in the opinion. There is, to be sure, much diversion, amusement, and, in the case of the astronomical year, much that we might actually be better off knowing. The same cannot be said for George Brett's career (though I was a fan throughout it) or the history of Legos.

The personalization of judicial opinions can go too far. The delivery of gratuitous information can be seen as an act of self-indulgence. Self-indulgence and the act of judging, to state the obvious, do not go together. Judges, like the rest of us, have role to a play in the profession. It's just that judges don't get to decide for themselves how many lines they will have in their speaking part.

ZEAL OR NO ZEAL

"Zealous representation" is perhaps one of the most often used phrases in the machinery of the law and in commentary about it—this even though the duty of representation it describes seems to be much misunderstood. The phrase has as a nice ring to it and it sounds right, with its aggressive stance. Lawyers like aggressive. But in truth zealous advocacy is not the actual standard that should be applied. Nor is zealous advocacy when properly understood what so many people think it is. In no small part, to make a big statement, to unravel the meaning and use of "zealous advocacy" is to get to the heart of real lawyering and what so many want to pass off as its appealing but empty substitute. Real lawyering doesn't have the aggressiveness, the sexiness, that "zealous advocacy" suggests.

The first of the two nineteenth-century figures most associated with zeal and a lawyer's ethical obligation, David Hoffman, puts ethics first and the client second. One of his *Resolutions in Regard to Professional Deportment* (1836) was, "I shall never permit zeal to carry me beyond the limits of sobriety and decorum." This view contrasts sharply with an earlier view famously stated in England by Lord Brougham in his defense of Queen Caroline against adultery changes filed by her husband the King. Brougham in 1820 asserted that a lawyer in his representation knew only one person, his client, and that he owes it to that client to save him (really her) by all expedient means. George Sharswood, the second major 19th-century American figure and, like Hoffman, also a law professor, split the baby and came out in his 1854 essay on professional ethics for "warm zeal." For him, the lawyer's duty called for "entire devotion to the interest of the client, warm zeal in the maintenance and defense of his rights, and the exertion of the utmost learning and ability." Sharswood had thought that Brougham had gotten a bit carried away and had been "led by the excitement of so great an occasion to say what cool reflection and sober reason certainly never can approve." Sharswood's influence was great enough that Alabama, in the first detailed ethical code in the nation, in 1887 followed Sharswood and endorsed the "warm zeal" approach. On the lawyer's duty to the client, the American Bar Association's first take on ethical codification, the 1908 Canons of Ethics, drew directly from the Alabama code and Sharswood in its Canon 15, using the "warm zeal" language. If there was any doubt as to the meaning of "warm zeal," Canon 15 condemned what Lord Braugham would have endorsed, that a lawyer is required "to do whatever may enable him to succeed in winning the client's cause." Zeal was back, though, when the ABA turned again to ethics codification with the 1969 Model Code of Professional Responsibility. Lawyers were to provide zealous representation. The "warm" component was gone, but it had been replaced to some extent by the phrase "within the bounds of the law," clearly indicating that an anything goes attitude was not being described, though the frequent references to zealous advocacy without the qualifier might have given the wrong impression. The ABA's last foray into the field has been the 1983 Model Rules of Professional Conduct and its Restatement-like approach. Oddly enough, given how frequently we find reference to zealous advocacy in the reports, the 1983 Model Rules all but ignored the phrase. It appears in the Preamble with qualifications that go beyond the "within the bounds of the law" qualification. Now we find that "as advocate, a lawyer zealously asserts the client's position under the rules of the adversary system." The rules themselves relating to advocacy do not mention zealous advocacy.

We know zealous advocacy when we see it, though it comes in variations and forms. For some it acts as a "get out of jail free" card to justify scorch-the-earth tactics or worse, as in misleading the court. This is the extreme position that Monroe Freedman takes in his argument that certain situations require (or at least allow) lawyers to breach their obligation to the court by lying to it or withholding information the lawyer would otherwise be required to give up, even if it came at the client's expense. In Freedman's world, it seems that nothing can ever come at the client's expense, even the professional life of the lawyer.

One approach to the general question of zeal or no zeal is to look to what the commentators from the 19th century meant when they used the word *zeal* in those first ethical codes. But even if we could get closer to what first *zeal* and then "warm zeal" might have meant at that time and place, we don't want to fall into the originalist trap of thinking that this is where the answer can be found. It would be too easy an answer to a thorny question. Looking elsewhere, there is always profit in looking to Shakespeare to understand our language. He used *zeal* thirty-three times and *zealous* six times, usually in the context of religious faith, god, or love. There is an element of excess associated with it, as when he pairs in *Love's Labour's Lost zeal* with *fury*, "[w]hat zeal, what fury hath inspired thee now." Those with zeal don't see quite straight. It is an excess that can be brought right, an excited electron brought under control, such as we find in *King John*, "[L]est zeal, now melted by the windy breath/ Of soft petitions, pity and remorse/ Cool and congeal again to what it was." Shakespeare's usage coincides with the way *zeal* has been used by the leading writers and thinkers of our culture. It has typically been associated with religious causes and is, in fact, most often paired with religion. There is the element of proselytizing, of passion that reaches beyond reason, which has defined the term. The zealot is a man on a mission, an important mission. Swift in *A Tale of a Tub* wrote that *zeal* is "the most significant word that hath been ever yet produced in any language."

A perhaps more useful approach for us would be to look to a contemporary definition. This is what legal profession ethicist Geoffrey Hazard does in his analysis. For him and co-treatise writer William Hodes, "a zealous person, according to the *Random House Dictionary of the English Language*, is 'ardently active, devoted, or diligent,' all qualities that most clients (as well as most observers of the legal scene) would agree are admirable in a lawyer—as are the synonyms listed: 'enthusiastic, eager, intense, passionate, and warm.'"

One writer who works within a state's bar discipline system has provided what we might call a profession-based definition. For Sylvia Stevens in her article "Whither Zeal? Defining Zealous Representation,'" *zeal* for lawyers has two components. The first is a sense of partisanship in which the lawyer wanting the client to win is combined with emotional energy and a sense of commitment to the job of representation. But balanced against this, the second part of the definition looks to the lawyer to maintain a sense of independence "which allows for dispassionate judgment to prevent losing sight of legal and ethical boundaries as well as the risks of contemplated action."

It might be better to look to the purpose to which *zeal* was being used by George Sharswood. His code of ethics built around *zeal* was designed to put some distance between the lawyer and the client. Those who argue that lawyers today do not have enough of the old fashioned zeal, that is, the unencumbered kind, bristle at the notion that lawyers need to keep some distance from the client, as set out in the second prong of Stevens's definition, to do the job properly. Opponents of zeal as it is currently understood champion commentators such as Monroe Freedman who want passionate zeal in which the lawyer sees the world through the client's point of view. This justifies misleading the court, for example.

Anita Bernstein, one of the fiercest zeal advocates, reveals in the casualness of a footnote what is for the bar perhaps the most important idea about zeal and the practice of law. The passion of zealous advocacy is good, she argues in her article "The Zeal Shortage." Then, after discussing the higher than average rate of depression that lawyers experience, she claims "that more zeal in the practice of law might induce more happiness among lawyers."

What would that happiness look like? I submit that it would have a certain terrifying quality to it if we interpret *zeal* in its ordinary sense of slightly losing your head in a cause. To be caught up in a constant state of zealousness would shockingly transform the lawyer's life, robbing him or her of that second prong of the current working definition of independence that allows for dispassionate judgment. To lose that would be to become the client, to adopt the cause completely as your own. That way mischief lies. After all, can we ever accept an interpretation of an ethical code that allows for lawyers to lie to or deceive a court? Rather than argue for, acknowledge, or even grudgingly accept the idea that lawyers have or can have interests that are different from their clients, we need to embrace this professional obligation to know where we end and the client begins. For our purposes, the Restatement on The Law Governing Lawyers (sec. 16, comment d) gets it right. "The term zealous representation should not be misunderstood to suggest that lawyers are legally required to function with a certain emotion or style of litigating, negotiating, or counseling. For legal purposes the term encompasses the duties of competence and diligence." In the choice between zeal or no zeal, we must choose no zeal.

Index